Irenaeus on the Christian Faith

D1553067

Irenaeus on the Christian Faith

A *Condensation of* Against Heresies

JAMES R. PAYTON JR.

PICKWICK *Publications* · Eugene, Oregon

IRENAEUS ON THE CHRISTIAN FAITH
A Condensation of *Against Heresies*

Pickwick Publications
An Imprint of Wipf and Stock Publishers
199 W. 8th Ave., Suite 3
Eugene, OR 97401

www.wipfandstock.com

ISBN 13: 978-1-60899-624-7

Cataloging-in-Publication data:

Payton, James R., Jr.
    Irenaeus on the Christian faith : a condensation of *Against Heresies* / James R.
Payton Jr.
    xx + 214 p. ; 23 cm. Includes bibliographical references and indexes.
    ISBN 13: 978-1-60899-624-7
    1. Irenaeus, Saint, Bishop of Lyon. 2. Christian life—History—Early church, ca.
60–300. 3. Theology, Doctrinal—History—Early church, ca. 60–300. I. Title.

BR1720 I7 P25 2011

Manufactured in the U.S.A.

For Chris Davis,
my deuterocanonical son

Contents

Preface / ix
Acknowledgments / xv
Abbreviations / xvii

Introduction / 1

BOOK 1   Exposing Heresy: The Views of the Gnostics / 27

BOOK 2   Exposing Heresy: Disunity among the Gnostics / 41

BOOK 3   The Christian Faith, as Drawn from the Apostles'
         Teachings / 55

BOOK 4   The Christian Faith, as Drawn from the Words Spoken
         by Christ / 85

BOOK 5   The Christian Faith, as Drawn from Further Teaching
         of Christ and the Apostles / 155

Bibliography / 195
Subject Index / 197
Scripture Index / 205

Preface

IRENAEUS OF LYONS (C. 130–202) was the greatest theologian to arise in the Church[1] since the time of the apostles. His *Against Heresies*[2] is a masterpiece of ancient Christian literature, written by one schooled by another who was trained by the apostle John; in this work, consequently, readers have access to the teaching of a spiritual grandson of the apostle John. This alone would make it enormously important, but even apart from that circumstance, *Against Heresies* is profoundly significant: it is the first major defense and presentation of the Christian faith. Undeniably, it is a classic work; like many other classics, though, it is more often praised than read.

This neglect is regrettable but understandable. For one thing, the work is a massive tome. Written by Irenaeus in five books, it was easily the longest and most elaborate work produced by any Christian author before the third century. In the only complete English version, *Against Heresies* runs to more than 250 pages of dense, double-columned print.[3]

Even so, many lengthy patristic works find numerous readers. A more significant reason this major work goes unread probably is the fact that it begins and for a long time continues with Irenaeus' painstaking description (book 1) and thorough refutation (book 2) of Gnostic teaching. In the English version, this treatment extends to nearly 100 pages,[4] mak-

---

1. In this volume, "Church" refers to the Church as a whole (which is, typically, Irenaeus' focus); "church(es)" refers to a local congregation(s).

2. The full title is *A Refutation and Subversion of What Is Falsely Called Knowledge* (alluding to the apostolic warning in 1 Tim 6:20); it is commonly known and cited, though, as *Against Heresies* (hereafter *AH*).

3. This English version appears in *ANF* 1:315–567.

4. *ANF* 1:315–413.

ing it about 40 percent of the entire work. Gnosticism had made much of ogdoads, decads, duodecads, and other number-fascinations; it concocted elaborate hierarchies for the universe; it assumed certain common pagan philosophical notions; and its various practitioners amalgamated these with elements of the Old Testament Scriptures, Christ's life and teachings, and apostolic writings to produce a bewildering variety of versions of ostensibly Christian teaching. Irenaeus had carefully researched the various Gnostic movements that claimed to be Christian, and he found it necessary to present those views in both their commonalities and in their far more considerable diversities, and then carefully to refute them. He did the job well, but unless one is a scholar of Gnosticism, the first two books of *Against Heresies* frankly make for thoroughly mind-numbing reading.

Irenaeus' laudable purpose was to help others in his day recognize that Gnosticism, in all its varieties, could not be accepted as Christian; to drive home that point required painstaking presentation of his opponents' views. Those who encountered Gnosticism as a living problem may well have found this thorough presentation stimulating and helpful, and it unquestionably had profound influence: within two generations of the publication of Irenaeus' tome, Gnosticism had virtually disappeared from Christian circles. To be sure, the entire credit for this cannot be accorded to *Against Heresies*; other Christian authors also opposed and wrote against Gnosticism. Even so, none of them offered anything approaching the depth and breadth of Irenaeus' treatment, and they relied on it for some of their own argument.

Separated from that experience by nearly two millennia, though, with Gnosticism nothing more than a possibly interesting ancient aberration, for a reader in the present day the first two books of *Against Heresies* are hardly riveting. Those who turn to Irenaeus' tome out of a desire to become familiar with another writing of one of the church fathers, or to find doctrinal or spiritual stimulation from classics of Christian writing, will almost certainly find the first major chunks of Irenaeus' presentation tedious.

That was certainly my experience. On two occasions I decided to read through *Against Heresies*, only to get bogged down in the elaborate presentation and assessment of Gnosticism and, finally, to give up. I had heard that Irenaeus offered keen insights into the Christian faith, so that reading *Against Heresies* would be valuable, but I could not force myself to plow through the entire work. Along the way in the first two books,

Irenaeus made passing, brief observations about Christian teaching, but since his focus was on exposing the fallacies of Gnosticism, these observations were concise and sporadic. No matter how much I found those all-too-brief segments stimulating, both times I eventually succumbed and put *Against Heresies* aside. It was only with my third attempt a few years later that I was able to muster the dogged determination to work through the whole of Irenaeus' magnum opus. After slogging through the first two books, I found reading the last three much more inviting and intriguing. In them Irenaeus spends most of his effort on setting forth what Christians believe, and I found this material stimulating, thought provoking, and edifying. *Against Heresies* offers a profound, rich presentation of the Christian faith. It is not only valuable as a historical record of what Christians thought and taught less than a century after the last of the apostles had died (John, c. 95); it is also valuable in its own right as a presentation of Christian teaching.

After I finished reading through *Against Heresies*, I recognized that it would be beneficial if it could be condensed, by drastically cutting back on the specific interaction with Gnosticism, while still offering what Irenaeus had to say about the Christian faith. This would allow more readers to be exposed to and explore Irenaeus' teaching than would be likely otherwise. More was needed than just condensation, though. The only available English version was produced in the mid-nineteenth century, in a much more prolix and complicated writing style than is the norm in the present. Beyond that, as the editor of the volume in which it appeared noted, the English version came in segments, from three different scholars[5]; indeed, I found the styles different enough to be jarring as I read through the whole work. So, a significant revision of the English version would also be necessary in such a condensation.

Not long after I had come to this assessment, I learned that an abridgment and new translation of *Against Heresies* had been published.[6] I eagerly bought the book and read through it. As I did so, though, I was deeply disappointed. In addition to significant problems in the introduction, the condensation still retained a considerable amount of the discussion of Gnosticism from books 1–2, and it excised far too much of Irenaeus' rich teaching on the Christian faith from books 3–5. I reviewed

---

5. These comments are found at *ANF* 1:310 n. 4.

6. This work is Grant, *Irenaeus of Lyons*.

the work,[7] urging that both Irenaeus and interested readers deserve better. In due course, I determined to try to offer it myself. This book is my attempt to live up to that determination.

I should explain how I have proceeded. My purpose throughout has been to make Irenaeus' presentation of the Christian faith accessible for readers. So, I have cut out most of the material in the first two books, keeping only a few brief segments on Gnosticism that seemed necessary to make sense of what Irenaeus teaches, but retained virtually all of what he presented of Christian teaching along the way in these two books. From books 3–5, which deal more expansively with the Christian faith, I excised Irenaeus' additional periodic engagements with Gnosticism, the pieces in which he belabors an argument (such as adding comments on additional Scripture references without appreciably furthering his point), and some of the various digressions Irenaeus occasionally takes. (Ancient authors did not have footnotes to handle such distractions.)

In the material that follows, I indicate where I have excised material. When the deletions were in a section (whether within or at the beginning or end of one), I have used ellipses to indicate them; the amount of material deleted varies, of course, among the sections. Where whole sections (occasionally, even chapters) were left out, this can be recognized by the gaps between the numbers at the end of the sections. (Readers should note that all the passages cited from *Against Heresies* in this preface and in the following introduction remain in the condensed version offered in this book.)

In that regard, I should explain how the respective sections are identified with these numbers. *Against Heresies* is comprised of five books; each book contains a number of chapters; each of the chapters is further subdivided into sections. In the material that follows, each section closes with its appropriate citation, enclosed in parentheses. Citations begin with the book number, followed by a colon; then the chapter number (or "pref" for the preface in the respective book), followed by a comma; and then the section number. Sometimes breaks in paragraphing have been introduced into sections, in order to clarify shifts in Irenaeus' focus or argument; readers may thus need to look a paragraph or two forward to find the identification for the particular section (which will appear, as noted, in parentheses at the end of each section).

---

7. Payton, "Condensing Irenaeus."

I have also extensively revised the English version, working through it five times. The first time, I worked through the English translation to simplify the grammatical constructions and the language used. In four subsequent efforts, I worked through my prior revisions to improve the result, with the goal of producing a faithful but contemporary idiomatic English rendering. In what follows, I trust that readers will find Irenaeus' presentation of the Christian faith in accessible, contemporary English.

One of the noteworthy characteristics of Irenaeus' great work is how thoroughly saturated it is with Scripture. Irenaeus relies on the Septuagint for his knowledge of the Hebrew Scriptures, which he cites extensively. While the New Testament canon had not yet been established, the various writings that later came to comprise it were already in wide circulation among Christian churches. Irenaeus was the first patristic author to treat these writings as Scripture, and he referred to almost all of them[8]; his use of and deference to them as apostolic offers some interesting perspectives for New Testament studies.[9] The editors of the only complete English edition identified some 1456 citations of or allusions to scriptural passages.[10] As I carefully worked through *Against Heresies*, I noted several mistakes in their identifications but also recognized scores of quotations and allusions they had overlooked. For most of these, Irenaeus—like other church fathers before and after him—did not regularly indicate the book or chapter in Scripture to which he was referring. (Since the chapters were not divided into verses until a bishop in the Middle Ages undertook that task, Irenaeus could not have offered such specific locations.) In what follows, I have indicated the scriptural passages cited or alluded to by identifying them within square brackets. I recognized scores of other fleeting allusions (two or three words) to passages in both the Hebrew Scriptures and the New Testament, but I did not identify them. While I may well have missed some further citations, I trust that the hundreds that are identified will help readers recognize and appreciate how deep and wide was

8. The only books eventually received in the NT canon that Irenaeus did not quote or allude to were Philemon and 3 John.

9. The way Irenaeus cites the books as written by apostles or their close associates challenges some critical scholarly views on apostolic authorship and dates of composition; it is especially noteworthy in that regard that Irenaeus clearly accepted the Pauline authorship of 1 and 2 Timothy and Titus (collectively called the Pastoral Letters).

10. This is found at *ANF* 1:598–602.

Irenaeus' familiarity with Scripture, as well as enable those interested in pursuing the question to consider how he uses Scripture.

Since this volume offers a contemporary English version of *Against Heresies*, I have also adopted a contemporary version of the Bible for Irenaeus' Scripture quotations: for this I used the New Revised Standard Version [NRSV] (which includes the Apocrypha/deuterocanonical books that were part of the Septuagint Irenaeus used and to which he referred). In three places, the point Irenaeus was making depended on the distinctive reading found in the Septuagint; these are identified accordingly with LXX after the biblical reference.[11] In one instance, the reading in the older Revised Standard Version [RSV] fits the form of Irenaeus' citation better and is so identified.[12] In another instance, a different reading of the punctuation in the NRSV allowed Irenaeus' point; I modified the punctuation accordingly, indicating this in a footnote.[13]

As a great champion of the faith, Irenaeus deserves better from the Church than she has given him, for he has not received the ongoing, continued interest to which he has just claim. This neglect may ironically arise from his success in attacking Gnosticism: with the further efforts by some others (who relied significantly on *Against Heresies* for their arguments), Gnosticism soon disappeared as a major problem. Because of this, the Church needed less and less to consult *Against Heresies* for information about the Gnostics—with which the first two books, lengthy treatments themselves, are concerned. To get to the last three books, where Irenaeus offers a rich, compelling, profound, and stimulating presentation of the Christian faith, readers have had to plow through the tedious treatment about the Gnostics. Over time, even the recollection that his positive presentation of Christianity in those last three books offered great benefit faded. Though revered as a masterpiece of the Church's literature, *Against Heresies* was too often left unread.

I hope that this condensation of Irenaeus' magnum opus will serve to revive interest in it and will enable many readers to profit from his presentation of the Christian faith. In that small way, may this book help many to recognize and acknowledge the great gift the Church received in Irenaeus.

11. These are citations of Gen 3:8 (at *AH* 5:17,1), Deut 10:16 (at 4:16,1), and Jer 17:9 (at 4:33,11).

12. This is the citation of Isa 2:3–4 (at *AH* 4:34,4).

13. This is found in the citation of Mark 1:1–2 (at *AH* 3:11,8n6).

Acknowledgments

I HAVE ACCUMULATED SEVERAL debts of gratitude along the way as I have pursued my interest in Irenaeus' *Against Heresies*. The first in order is to Edward Panosian, under whom I took a course on the History of Christian Doctrine as I embarked upon graduate studies. Under his direction and stimulating teaching, I finally found a way to tie together my love for history and my yearning to delve more deeply into the Christian faith. His comments on the importance of Irenaeus stuck with me over subsequent years of graduate study and eventually invited me to read the great second-century theologian's magnum opus.

I finally set out on this adventure after joining the faculty of Redeemer University College. The head librarian at the time, Daniel Savage, gave me the third copies of patristic works out of the library, which our institution had acquired from a Franciscan one that was closing its doors. None of these books was from Irenaeus, but as I began in earnest to read the church fathers, I soon enough turned to Irenaeus. Recognizing how much rich teaching and insight *Against Heresies* offered, but that it was encumbered with his extensive and intensive interaction with the Gnostics and weighed down by its sole, tediously complicated English version (a mid-nineteenth-century product, with all the florid verbiage and punctuation clutter common in that era), I applied to Redeemer University College for a grant to initiate the process of eliding the Gnostic materials and simplifying the English translation. I am grateful to my institution for that grant, for another used subsequently to carry the work forward, and for a one-term sabbatical in 2008 which allowed me to bring this project, among others, finally to completion. Further in that regard, I greatly appreciate the help afforded by my teaching assistant, Bethany Vanwyngaarden, who painstakingly worked through the penultimate version of my manuscript to check the accuracy of the citations from Scripture.

Some of my colleagues at Redeemer University College have shared my interest in Irenaeus over the years. For this, I express thanks to David Benner (now Distinguished Professor of Psychology at the Psychological Studies Institute, Atlanta), Al Wolters, Wayne Norman (now Professor of Psychology at Simpson University, Redding, California), Mark Bowald, and especially Jacob Ellens. I have also discussed this project with colleagues in patristics elsewhere and appreciate their encouragement and advice: these include David Rylaarsdam of Calvin Theological Seminary, Fr. John Behr of St. Vladimir's Orthodox Theological Seminary, Sr. Vera (Nonna Harrison) of St. Paul School of Theology, and Paul Blowers of Emmanuel School of Religion. I have benefited from their insights, but any remaining faults in this work are chargeable to me, not to them. Furthermore, I am grateful to the students in my upper-level church history courses who have read and commented appreciatively on earlier editions of this project, and who encouraged me to bring it to completion.

For compiling the Scripture and subject indexes, I am indebted to Judy Reveal, who always performs the task with joy, encouragement, and consummate expertise.

Finally, I need—as always—to express my deep gratitude to my wife, Sharon, and our four children, Chris (and Liza), Trevor (and Erin), Jessica, and Christopher. Their constant love and encouragement in the various projects I have pursued over the years stimulated me to continue; the joy of life with them invited me to set the projects aside. I am grateful for their understanding and love. All of our children are now grown and living on their own, but my family endured many times when I was distracted with this project. They knew somehow that it was important to me, and it somehow also therefore became important to them. They mean more to me than I can possibly express in mere words—an insight into life and love that comes, among others, from Irenaeus.

Abbreviations

GENERAL

AH   Irenaeus of Lyons, *Against Heresies*

ANF   *Ante-Nicene Fathers*, vol. 1: *The Apostolic Fathers,*
            Justin Martyr, Irenaeus, ed. Alexander Roberts and
            James Donaldson (Peabody, MA: Hendrickson, [1885]
            2004).

AposFrs   *The Apostolic Fathers: Greek Texts and English*
            Translations of Their Writings, ed. and rev. Michael W.
            Holmes, updated ed. (Grand Rapids: Baker, 1992).

CHE   *The Church History of Eusebius,* trans. Arthur
            Cushman McGiffert, in *Nicene and Post-Nicene*
            Fathers, 2nd. ser., 1:81–387 (Peabody, MA:
            Hendrickson, [1890] 2004).

GS   *The Gnostic Scriptures: A New Translation with*
            Annotations and Introductions, trans. Bentley Layton
            (Garden City, NY: Doubleday, 1987).

LXX   *Septuaginta: Id est Vetus Testamentum graece iuxta*
            LXX interpretes, ed. Alfred Rahlfs, 2 vols. (Stuttgart:
            Württembergische Bibelanstalt, 1935).

OTP   *The Old Testament Pseudepigrapha,* vol. 1: *Apocalyptic*
            Literature and Testaments, ed. James H. Charlesworth
            (New York: Doubleday, 1983).

OLD TESTAMENT

Dan	Daniel
Deut	Deuteronomy
Exod	Exodus
Ezek	Ezekiel
Gen	Genesis
Hab	Habakkuk
Hos	Hosea
Isa	Isaiah
Jer	Jeremiah
1 Kgs	1 Kings
Lev	Leviticus
Mal	Malachi
Mic	Micah
Num	Numbers
Prov	Proverbs
Ps	Psalms
1/2 Sam	1 Samuel
Zech	Zechariah

APOCRYPHAL/DEUTEROCANONICAL BOOKS

2 Esd	2 Esdras
Jdt	Judith
Wis	Wisdom of Solomon
Sir	Sirach
Sus	Susanna

NEW TESTAMENT

Col	Colossians
1 Cor	1 Corinthians
2 Cor	2 Corinthians
Eph	Ephesians
Gal	Galatians
Heb	Hebrews
Jas	James

1 Jn	1 John
2 Jn	2 John
Matt	Matthew
1 Pet	1 Peter
2 Pet	2 Peter
Phil	Philippians
Rev	Revelation
Rom	Romans
1 Thess	1 Thessalonians
2 Thess	2 Thessalonians
1 Tim	1 Timothy
2 Tim	2 Timothy

Introduction

I RENAEUS WAS A SIGNIFICANT figure in the history of the early Church. He received what he acknowledged to be his primary instruction in the Christian faith from someone who was himself trained by an apostle. Irenaeus insisted on the importance of remaining faithful to the Christian message as received from Jesus Christ and the apostles and passed on by succeeding generations of the Church through its leaders. With him, that message is at only one remove from the apostolic source; in *Against Heresies* he insisted that what he understood and presented as the Christian faith was the same message found everywhere throughout the Church in his day. Because of this, what Irenaeus presents in *Against Heresies* should be of keen interest to anyone interested in that message and its historical transmission. The rest of this introduction is intended to provide readers with information that will assist them in appreciating Irenaeus, his concerns in what he opposed and in what he proclaimed, and the significance of his magnum opus.

THE LIFE OF IRENAEUS

Irenaeus was born between AD 130 and 140 in Asia Minor. This seems certain from his declarations that he recalled sitting at the feet of Polycarp of Smyrna and receiving (along with others) extensive instruction in Christian teaching and practice.[1] Since Polycarp was martyred in 155, the tutelage to which Irenaeus refers had to have taken place before this date. With what Irenaeus says about how thoroughly and carefully he could recall Polycarp's teaching and example, it seems certain that the student must have been at least in his teenage years to have both the

---

1. He offers these comments at *AH* 3:3,4; they are also found in his "Letter to Florinus," preserved by Eusebius in *CHE* 5:20,5–8; Eusebius had already indicated that Irenaeus had been under Polycarp's tutelage (*CHE* 4:14,4).

capacity to understand and the ability to remember what was taught. Consequently, the judgment of scholars is that Irenaeus was born sometime in the fourth decade of the second century. The instruction he received from Polycarp also evidently was completed at some point before the latter's martyrdom, for Irenaeus gives no indication that his tutelage had come to an untimely or premature end.

Irenaeus passed from this life in the early third century (c. 202). It is possible that he died as a martyr: in the fourth century, Jerome urged that this had been the case. However, there are no earlier indications that Christians believed Irenaeus had endured martyrdom, so the claim is somewhat suspect. It is clear that the persecution under Emperor Septimius Severus was raging in the area of southern Gaul, where Irenaeus lived, so Jerome's statement may be accurate; however, the lack of an earlier supporting document or claim raises questions about it.

Sometime after his instruction under Polycarp, Irenaeus headed west. He spent some time in Rome, possibly studying with Justin Martyr (although this is uncertain). Eventually, he ended up in Lyons ("Lugdunum" in the Roman imperial designation) in southern Gaul. According to ancient records, a lively interchange of peoples and trade existed between Asia Minor and southern Gaul at the time, so it was not unusual for someone to take the path Irenaeus had followed. It may be that he was sent by Polycarp to assist the bishop of Lyons, Pothinus (whom Polycarp had earlier trained). Whether or not at Polycarp's bidding, Irenaeus soon was serving as a presbyter in Lyons.

In 177, Irenaeus undertook an embassy at the behest of his bishop and the congregation at Lyons and journeyed to Rome to confer with its bishop, Eleutherus, on problems then facing the churches in the west. By the time Irenaeus returned to Lyons, persecution had carried away many members of the Lyons church, including Bishop Pothinus. At some point, Irenaeus was elected bishop to succeed him.

Between 182 and 188, Irenaeus wrote his magnum opus, *A Refutation and Subversion of What Is Falsely Called Knowledge*,[2] which has come to be known by the shorter title *Against Heresies*.[3] Written in Greek, the

2. This title alludes to the warning in 1 Tim 6:20 (which Irenaeus unquestionably viewed as written by the apostle Paul).

3. The shorter title comes from Eusebius, who referred to Irenaeus' work thus several times (*CHE* 2:13,5; 3:18,2; 3:23,3; 4:11,1; 4:14,2; 4:21,9; 4:29,1). It can be questioned, from the way Eusebius writes, whether he intended this to be simply a description of the book's contents or a shorter title; whatever may have been Eusebius' intent, though, the

work was immediately recognized as valuable: early in the next century, it was circulating in Alexandria. At about the same time, in Carthage, Tertullian referred to it with appreciation. Rufinus, a notoriously flexible translator, soon rendered the work in Latin. In the sixth century an Armenian translation was made from the Greek, and in the ninth century the learned patriarch of Constantinople, Photius, indicated he had seen *Against Heresies* in a complete Greek text. At some point subsequently, though, the Greek text was lost, except for some citations found in other patristic literature. The complete text survives only in Latin.

Late in the second century, Irenaeus penned another treatise, *On the Apostolic Preaching*.[4] He also wrote some other works, which are no longer extant. In his *Ecclesiastical History*, written in the fourth century, Eusebius referred to and offered brief excerpts of some letters written by Irenaeus.[5]

In one of these, Irenaeus addressed Victor, who had succeeded Eleutherus as bishop of Rome. The Roman hierarch had adopted a rigid stance against the practice of some churches in Asia Minor whose commemoration of Christ's resurrection was determined by the date of the Jewish Passover. (This perspective came to be known as "Quartodeciman" [Latin for "fourteen"] since these churches celebrated Pascha [later referred to commonly as "Easter"] on Nisan 14, no matter which day of the week it fell on.) In Rome and most of the churches in the west, however, this celebration always fell on a Sunday, irrespective of the date for Passover. Unquestionably, Christ's resurrection was a major event in the Church, so agreement on when it should be celebrated was desirable. (In due course, the Quartodeciman practice fell out of favor among the churches generally, in favor of celebrations on Sunday.) In this correspondence, Irenaeus urged the pope to view the practice in Asia Minor with Christian charity, reminding him that prior leaders in Rome had not insisted on the absolute necessity of their practice being followed—citing to this effect an earlier visit of his mentor, Polycarp, to Anicetus, former bishop of Rome. While there, among other things, Polycarp had

shorter title has become the one commonly used to refer to Irenaeus' magnum opus. Eusebius cites Irenaeus' work by the full title only once (5:7,1).

4. Long thought to be lost, this work was discovered in 1904 in an Armenian translation at a monastic library in Erevan, Armenia. It is available in two English versions: Smith, *St. Irenaeus*; and Behr, *St. Irenaeus of Lyons*.

5. These include references to letters to Blastus and Florinus (*CHE* 5:20,1), with an excerpt from the latter (5:20,4), and to Victor, the bishop of Rome (5:24:14).

convinced the Roman bishop not to insist that the churches in Asia Minor conform to some specific western practices.[6] Irenaeus—whose name is derived from the Greek word for peace, *eirene*—played the peacemaker effectively in this regard, for Victor backed off his prior insistence.[7]

As we will see, though, Irenaeus was not ready to make peace at all costs. He was quite willing to oppose large swaths of those who claimed to be Christian but taught views he found in conflict with the apostolic message as passed down through the faithful teaching of the Church's leaders. In that situation, this otherwise peace-seeking man was a fearsome and thorough opponent.

OPPOSING GNOSTICISM

Throughout *Against Heresies* Irenaeus opposed Gnosticism. Only the first two books of his work deal directly with Gnosticism's problems and erroneous teaching, to be sure; the last three books focus on what Christians believe from the Scriptures as that had been taught and passed down since the time of the apostles. Even so, in these last three books, Gnosticism continues to remain in Irenaeus' purview; time and again comments directly challenge and asides obliquely critique elements of Gnostic teaching. As Irenaeus saw it, Christianity faced a serious threat from Gnosticism, and he wrote to oppose it and to provide readers with what they needed to recognize its problems and oppose it as well.[8]

What was this Gnosticism which Irenaeus resisted so strenuously? Since almost all of his direct interaction with and analysis of Gnosticism has been elided in this book, in favor of offering instead his positive teaching on the Christian faith, we need to offer some background on Gnosticism in general, and specifically as Irenaeus challenged it. This background will give readers enough information to appreciate what Irenaeus saw as Gnosticism's problems, to see how he opposed it, and to facilitate understanding of what remains of his interaction with Gnosticism in this condensation of *Against Heresies*.

It should be noted, first of all, that Gnosticism had not just burst on the scene in Irenaeus' time. Before the end of the first century AD,

6. Eusebius has preserved much of this letter in *CHE* 5:24,11–17.

7. At *CHE* 5:24,18, Eusebius made this point after reviewing Irenaeus' interaction with the Roman bishop.

8. This is clear in the statements in the prefaces to each book: see *AH* 1:pref,1–2; 2:pref,1–2; 3:pref; 4:pref,1–4; 5:pref.

an early form of Gnosticism had already arisen as a challenge for the Church: some of the apostle Paul's statements in his Letter to the Colossians may refer to early varieties of the movement,[9] but several in 1 John almost certainly do, and the more generally expressed warning in 2 John fits well with perceived dangers from Gnostic teachers.[10] Apostolic opposition did not manage to expel incipient Gnosticism from within Christianity, though: the movement continued, and the appeal to secret knowledge held a genuine attraction for many in the intellectual culture of the day.

Indeed, Gnostic movements were not restricted to Christian circles: they arose in several religions of the time. Gnosticism offered a way of tying together some elements of ancient intellectual culture with religious teaching, to produce a theosophy that could attire itself in several different religious dresses. But the Gnosticism to which Irenaeus responded was what had developed in Christian circles. By his time, a bewildering proliferation of Gnostic varieties had emerged, each claiming to present true Christianity. In each and all of them, Irenaeus argued, the Gnostics distanced themselves from what the apostles had taught and the Church had proclaimed.

A thoroughgoing assessment of and response to this burgeoning movement was necessary, Irenaeus adjudged, in order to expose its falsity and warn people against it. This is what he set out to offer in *Against Heresies*. An encounter in Rome may have been the final prod to push him to write it, though: there Irenaeus recognized someone from Smyrna who, like himself, had been instructed by Polycarp. To Irenaeus' consternation, he found that this person had turned from the apostolic teaching passed on by Polycarp to embrace Gnosticism.[11]

---

9. New Testament scholarship has discerned possible elements of early Gnostic teaching in what Paul warned against in Col 2:8-10, 18; if that is the case, then several other passages may also include responses to Gnostic teachings (e.g., Col 1:9-10, 16-17, 19-20, 22, 25-28). However, it may be that the errors against which the apostle wrote were not Gnostic in origin.

10. Several passages in 1 John speak directly to what seem, almost certainly, to be early Gnostic teachings: see 1 John 1:1; 2:18, 20-23, 26-27; 4:3, 6-7; 5:1, 20. Gnostic errors have been discerned as the probable background to the directives in 2 John 7-11. Irenaeus certainly viewed 1 John 4:1-3 and 2 John 7-8 in this fashion: see his argument at *AH* 3:16,8.

11. Eusebius mentioned this at *CHE* 5:20,4-5; Eusebius identifies this person as Florinus (who was not, however, mentioned by name in *AH*).

Until the discovery of a significant cache of Gnostic manuscripts in Nag Hammadi in 1945, most of what was known about ancient Gnosticism as it had related to Christianity was drawn from Irenaeus' *Against Heresies*, so scholars interested in Gnosticism had to rely, in the main, on what Irenaeus had written.[12] This very fact, though, indicates how successful Irenaeus' venture had been: his exposé and refutation of Gnosticism, a multiform movement that had proven attractive to many, was so thorough and devastating that the movement shortly disappeared within Christian circles. To be sure, *Against Heresies* was not the only anti-Gnostic treatise in the early Church: subsequently, Tertullian in North Africa, Clement and Origen in Alexandria, and Hippolytus in Rome all continued the attack. But all of them were considerably indebted to Irenaeus' magnum opus for the arguments they brought forward against Gnosticism. Irenaeus' *Against Heresies* was the first postapostolic, largest, and most imposing of these responses, and the lion's share of the credit for the exclusion of Gnosticism from Christian circles must be given to *Against Heresies*. So thoroughly did the Church come to reject and oppose Gnosticism that the movement died out in Christian circles, with its writings not resurfacing until the mid-twentieth-century discovery at Nag Hammadi.

THE GENERAL GNOSTIC PATTERN

Gnosticism as a general movement focused on the privileges and benefits of a specialized knowledge (Greek, *gnosis*) available only to a few. Typically, that knowledge fastened on the dualistic distinction of matter and spirit (or, in other contrasts, of visible and invisible, or flesh and spirit). The material realm was disparaged in favor of the immaterial realm; the "knower" ("Gnostic") was privileged and enabled to receive special insights into the operations of this immaterial realm, so that he or she not only now knew how it held together, but also knew how to negotiate the various steps through it to advance to oneness with the ultimate.

Gnosticism viewed humankind as made up of distinct categories of people.[13] The *carnal* or *fleshly* were satisfied with the material realm

12. Most of that treatment is excised in this book. Those who wish to see what Irenaeus presented about Gnosticism should consult the contemporary English translation of book 1 in Unger, *St. Irenaeus*; see also Nielsen, *Irenaeus of Lyons*.

13. Irenaeus recognizes that some Gnostics spoke of two such categories (*AH* 1:6,2),

and its blandishments, and would never arise from it to loftier realms; their future—if they had one—was only darkness. The *soulish* were also enmeshed in the material realm but did not find full satisfaction in it; if they gave themselves to nobler pursuits (which included seeking satisfaction in non-material pleasures), they might arise to a more privileged situation. The *spiritual* or *intellectual*—the "Gnostics"—were those who, although in this material world, were not of it: they had received special insights to enable them to turn fully toward the immaterial realm, and they would ultimately manage to totally escape matter and be absorbed into ultimate spirit. This third category included only a small portion of humankind.

Since the building blocks of all knowledge are numbers and letters, it is not surprising that Gnosticism discerned special significance in them, beyond their importance for counting and spelling. According to Gnostic predilections, some letters or numbers might carry special meaning, and certain combinations of them might serve for special purposes.[14] The recognition and deciphering of such significance would belong to the knowledge granted to the favored ones: it would enable them to infer relationships and figure out patterns in the way the universe had come to be that would be significant for their journey to the ultimate.

Related to this, Gnosticism had to account for the anomalous situation that the ultimate source (Greek, *arche*) and fullness (Greek, *pleroma*) of spirit or intellect could relate to the messy world of matter. The ingenious answer was that it did not: rather, a series of emanations (Greek, *aeons*) from that ultimate one were produced, each of which was still immaterial but was slightly less purely spirit or intellect. These Aeons joined in pairs and spawned further Aeons, who were yet further removed and who also joined others like them to produce additional Aeons; this process repeated itself a series of times. Different Gnostic systems posited various numbers of these Aeons, but eventually each system ended up with an artisan (Greek, *demiurge*) that brought matter into existence, thus producing the physical universe. This Demiurge was

---

but more common (at least, in Gnostic Christian circles) was a threefold distinction (with which he deals at 1:7,5); this latter approach is reflected in the comments above.

14. To appreciate this, however strange it may sound in the contemporary world, it is helpful to note that the ancient Pythagoreans discerned cosmic significance in certain numbers and engaged in a form of philosophical numbers-mysticism. So, the ancient intellectual world included a strong sense of a possible ultimate significance in letters and numbers as keys to unlock the mysteries of the cosmos.

so far distant from the Arche that the Demiurge did not even know the Arche or what it was like; nor did the Demiurge realize that what it was doing in producing the physical cosmos was an aberration.

For the special knowledge to come to the privileged "knowers," a teacher had to come from somewhere in the clusters of Aeons beyond the Demiurge to enlighten the privileged ones with whatever knowledge the system urged as necessary for the human to escape this realm of matter and return to the ultimate. This knowledge was unavailable to the masses of humanity; it was only for those worthy of such knowledge. It might include special words (combinations of letters) to allow them to move through the necessary steps on their intellectual journey; it might also entail special information framed around specific significant numbers declared to be important. These numbers might be pure or special in their own right—such as prime numbers or the first in a new range (e.g., 8 after the prime number 7, or 10 after the previous series of single integers); they might also be numbers that were significant to a culture or religion for other reasons (e.g., 12 or 40 in the history of Israel). These packages of numbers received their own recognizable designations: ogdoad (for 8), decad (for 10), duodecad (for 12), and so on.

Gnosticism thus allowed certain people who were (or thought themselves to be) intellectuals to claim special status for themselves in the universe. Because of this knowledge, they were denominated "perfect" or "complete" (Greek, *teleios*). It also allowed these people to draw on significant elements of the intellectual culture commonly embraced in antiquity as they embraced the teachings of various religions. Even so, we know less about how Gnosticism related to other religions than we do about its development within Christian circles.

GNOSTIC CHRISTIANITY

The general Gnostic pattern took root in Christian circles and produced a distinctive approach to the Scriptures and teaching of the Church. By Irenaeus' time, what contemporary scholars have denominated "Gnostic Christianity" included a wide variety of Gnostic systems, each claiming to be the genuine message of Christianity for the privileged spiritual or intellectual ones. Irenaeus opposed the general movement and its various manifestations alike. But why did he oppose Gnosticism? What were his criticisms of it?

Unquestionably, the discoveries at Nag Hammadi have opened up new vistas on Christian Gnosticism that move somewhat beyond the portrayal Irenaeus drew in *Against Heresies*. Even so, contemporary scholars recognize that Irenaeus had carefully sought out information about Gnosticism and presented it as it could be known in his day.[15] This is worth highlighting as we get ready to consider what Irenaeus set forth about Gnostic teaching.

It is important for readers to recognize that Irenaeus was not seeking to present an ostensibly objective, scholarly analysis of an interesting socio-religious phenomenon, as a twenty-first-century religion scholar might offer it. Rather, he was seeking to defend what he firmly believed to be the divinely revealed and ecclesiastically passed on understanding of the Christian faith, as received from the apostles, against what he considered to be an especially insidious threat to that faith. It is hardly surprising that he did not take great pains to give the various Gnostic teachers whose perspectives he described the benefit of the doubt. Even so, for those who keep abreast of political campaigning in the twenty-first century, for example, what should be remarkable is the care Irenaeus took to try to find out and to present responsibly and clearly what his opponents actually taught. Yes, Irenaeus pilloried, caricatured, mocked, and offered cutting asides about Gnostic teachings, but he also first read extensively in the works of several Gnostic leaders and their students, and interacted with some of them personally,[16] in order to learn what they were saying and how the successive generations of Gnostic teachers related to or differed from each other, and then set out to respond to them carefully.

This calls for a second comment. It should be kept in mind that Gnosticism as it had developed and been transmitted was secretive. Gnostic teachings were not proclaimed from the housetops; they were disseminated in closed meetings to a small coterie of "knowers"[17] who paid the requisite fees to receive this special knowledge.[18] Thus, accurate

---

15. In the general introduction to *GS*, and in the introductions to the various Gnostic documents translated in it, Layton shows appreciation for Irenaeus' portrayal of Gnosticism; similar respect is accorded to Irenaeus' presentation by Pagels, *Gnostic Gospels*.

16. See his comments at *AH* 1:pref,2.

17. Irenaeus points this out at *AH* 1:3,1.

18. See Irenaeus' comments, with sharp criticism for this practice, at *AH* 1:4,3.

knowledge of Gnosticism was difficult to obtain from outside the group: some would probably be available in distorted form from erstwhile devotees who became disenchanted with Gnostic teachings, but this would be suspect. Irenaeus diligently sought to avoid relying on hearsay: as he emphasizes, he sought out the written materials produced by these Gnostic teachers for their disciples and gave himself to peruse them diligently, as well as speaking with some Gnostic leaders in person.[19] This all indicates a determination to get the information from the genuine sources, as much as possible; that he at times relied on inferences he drew or on testimony from some who had turned away is hardly surprising or reprehensible. Unlike some of his successors, Irenaeus did not rush to assessment and judgment: he painstakingly laid out Gnosticism in its bewildering variety as he had come to know about it and responded to the movement in that variety. The first two books of *Against Heresies* are virtually entirely devoted to this; it would be difficult to find a similar ancient attempt to present one's opponents' views as carefully and responsibly as Irenaeus managed. (Indeed, when the secretiveness of Gnostic groups and their publications is taken into account, Irenaeus' endeavors to obtain a genuine grasp of what his opponents taught dwarfs similar attempts in much of the contemporary academic world.) That he presented some of it tendentiously is not a flaw restricted to Irenaeus or the second century; what is surprising is how thoroughly Irenaeus sought to understand his opponents and present their perspectives fully, given the secretive nature of most of the Gnostics' teachings.

So, what did Irenaeus present as Gnostic teaching, which he rejected and warned others to avoid? While Irenaeus recognized significant differences among the Gnostic Christian teachers and criticized them severely for that (on which more below), he pointed out several teachings they held in common. They all viewed the creation with disdain, since it was matter. This entailed the assessment that its creator was not good. However powerful that creator may have been, even if the Hebrew Scriptures call him "God," he played the role of the Demiurge; so, he was a lesser being than the true and ultimate God. As Irenaeus emphasized, the Gnostics said the creator was both a defect and the offspring of a

---

19. *AH* 1:pref,2; 3:11,9; 4:pref,2; cf. the comments at 1:16,3n4; 1:21,5n7; and 1:23,4n8.

defect[20]; indeed, some Gnostics adjudged him to be only an angel[21]; in either case, he was far inferior to the ultimate God. These two were opposed to each other: the God of the Old Testament (the Demiurge) favored a particular people (the Jews) and insisted on various physical, material ways of worshiping him; whereas the ultimate God eschewed material worship in favor of intellectual response via the right knowledge. With all this, the Gnostics affirm a multitude of gods, not the one God professed and worshiped in the Church.[22]

This all resulted in fracturing the oneness that, as Irenaeus had received and taught it, held together the way Christians interpreted the Old Testament and understood the work of Christ for salvation. Gnostic teachings divided the God of creation from the God of salvation, decisively removed the material realm from ultimate divine concern, and separated the savior from the promises and prophecies in the Old Testament Scriptures. For Gnostic Christianity, Christ came as the teacher or revealer of the hidden but necessary knowledge, which was unknown to the God of the Old Testament and was unanticipated in it. Christ did not come to fulfill the Old Testament's promises; indeed, he came to destroy the God of the Jews.[23] As revealer of the ultimate God, he himself was not and could not be directly involved in this material world. So, the Word of God did not become incarnate, and Christ took nothing from Mary (through whom he passed as water does through a pipe).[24] To be sure, since matter cannot be saved, the Christ could not have had a genuine body: he only seemed to have one.[25] Some allowed that a human being named Jesus was born of Mary, and that he was later adopted by the immaterial Christ, who descended on Jesus at his baptism but left him before his crucifixion. The one called the savior did not suffer: indeed, he could not, since he belonged to the immaterial realm.[26]

20. *AH* 1:16,3; 2:1,1; 2:19,9; 4:33,3.

21. Irenaeus points this out as Saturninus' teaching at *AH* 1:24,1–2.

22. Irenaeus disparages Gnostic teaching for "insanely fabricating a multitude of gods" (*AH* 4:34,5; see his comments also at 3:16,8); as against that, he vigorously affirms the oneness of God (from a plethora of possibilities, see his explicit assertions at 3:9,1; 3:11,1; 3:11,7; 3:12,11).

23. *AH* 1:24,2.

24. See the assertions at *AH* 1:6,1; 1:7,2; 1:9,2–3; 3:11,3.

25. *AH* 1:24,2; 2:22,4; 5:1,2.

26. *AH* 1:7,2; 1:26,1; 3:11,3; 3:16,8.

There was no need for this savior to suffer in a body, in any event, since nothing material can partake of salvation.[27] He came to bring salvation via knowledge for the spirit or intellect; this salvation had nothing directly to do with the body or the creation.

In the face of this commonality, Irenaeus emphasizes that the Gnostic leaders differed significantly in teachings that were certainly not inconsequential. He interacts with the specific teachings of a wide number of Gnostic teachers and their disciples, all of whom he styles heretics: Valentinus, Ptolemy, Saturninus, Basilides, Carpocrates, and Cerinthus.[28] Irenaeus shows the similarity of much of Marcion's teaching with what Gnostic leaders urged,[29] while recognizing that Marcion held distinct views on a number of issues. Like others, Irenaeus traced all these heretics back to Simon Magus[30] as the one who spawned all subsequent heretics.[31]

For Irenaeus, the disagreement among them was especially telling as an argument that they were not presenting the truth from God: he returned to this point time and again.[32] He urged that "there are as many schemes of redemption among these heretics as there are teachers among them," and that "they differ so widely among themselves about doctrine and tradition." Irenaeus observed that they each "want to be teachers on their own, and to branch off from the particular heresy in which they have been involved. . . . They insist upon teaching something new." All this indicates that they have not followed the tradition passed down from the apostles, as received from God through Christ; rather, in Irenaeus' assessment, "the very fathers of these fables differ among themselves, as if they were inspired by different spirits of error."[33] Irenaeus denied that such diversity could subsist, either with the Gnostics' claim

27. *AH* 1:6,1–2; 1:24,5; 1:27,3; 4:pref,4; 5:2,2–3; 5:6,2.

28. Irenaeus deals with Valentinus at *AH* 1:pref,2; 2:pref,1; 3:pref; 3:3,4; 3:4,3; 3:11,9; 4:pref,2; 4:33,3; 5:26,2; with Ptolemy at 1:pref,2; with Saturninus at 1:24,1–2; with Basilides at 1:24,4; with Carpocrates at 1:25,1; and with Cerinthus at 1:26,1; 3:3,4.

29. Irenaeus treats Marcion at *AH* 1:27,2–3; 3:3,4; 3:4,3; 4:13,1; 4:33,2; 5:26,2.

30. Acts 8:9–24 presents the story of Simon Magus; subsequently he achieved the status he sought, for his exotic religious teachings and lifestyle brought him notoriety and a following in Rome; see Eusebius' presentation at *CHE* 2:1,10–12; 2:13,1–5 (where he cites both Justin Martyr and Irenaeus); and at 2:14,1–2:15,1.

31. See Irenaeus' comments on Simon Magus at *AH* 1:23,4; 1:27,4; 3:pref; 4:33,3.

32. In addition to the citations which follow above, see *AH* 4:35,4; 5:20,1; 5:20,2.

33. These quotations come, respectively, from *AH* 1:21,1; 1:21,5; 1:28,1; 1:9,5.

to be presenting what Christ taught, or with passing on the apostolic tradition.[34] Indeed, Irenaeus categorically rejected the Gnostic assertion that their teaching had been secretly divulged by the savior to the apostles and disseminated surreptitiously afterwards to worthy hearers.[35] He repudiated the way they dealt with the Old Testament Scriptures, the Gospels, and the apostles' writings.[36]

IRENAEUS' PRESENTATION OF CHRISTIANITY

So, where could one find Christ's teaching, sound exposition of Scripture, and the apostolic tradition? For Irenaeus, that question was simply answered: the teaching of Christ had been carefully passed on in the Church, which expounded the Scriptures faithfully and passed on the apostolic tradition publicly, openly, and without diversity.[37]

Unity and Coherence

Throughout his presentation of the Christian faith in *Against Heresies*, Irenaeus stressed oneness. One God is both creator and redeemer. That one God also gave the Old Testament Scriptures to prepare the way for the savior he would send. The coming savior was the Word through whom those revelations were granted and who offered anticipations of his future advent in various ways. When the savior came, he fulfilled the Old Testament expectations and promises. The savior was the same Word, who became incarnate in order to be the savior of humanity and all creation. He accomplished salvation by a recapitulation of all things.[38]

---

34. Basilides claimed that he received his teaching from one named Glaucias, who had received it from the apostle Peter (*GS* 417); the disciples of Valentinus vigorously asserted the apostolic provenance of Valentinus' teaching, claiming the apostle Paul as their source (*GS* 303): see the bold assertion in "Ptolemy's Letter to Flora" (*GS* 308–15), where the author speaks of "the apostolic tradition, which . . . we have received by succession" (33.7.9 [*GS* 314]).

35. He presented this claim at *AH* 1:25,5.

36. Irenaeus devotes a substantial portion of books 1 and 2 of *AH* to exposing the fallacies of Gnostic interpretations of the Hebrew Scriptures, the Gospels, and the apostles' writings; much of this material has been elided for this volume. Even so, in his presentation of the Christian faith as it appears below in this condensed version of *AH*, Gnostic error is often in the background of Irenaeus' exposition, so readers will have abundant opportunity to see his assessment of Gnostic exegesis.

37. *AH* 1:10,1–2; 3:pref; 4:35,4.

38. The reader of this volume will have ample opportunity to observe these emphases in Irenaeus' teaching.

Irenaeus set this forth, first of all, by expounding Old Testament Scripture, the Gospels, and the apostles' writings: he does this extensively.[39] This was his first line of attack against Gnostic teaching. But recognizing that they claimed apostolic tradition for their views, he also deftly handled the question of apostolic tradition.

This tradition taught that there was only one God, who created all things, formed humankind, and promised them deliverance after they fell into sin.[40] The creation itself is good; indeed, the salvation achieved in Christ reclaims the entirety of creation, not just the immaterial realm.[41] This savior is the Son of God, who came to fulfill the promises and prophecies of the Hebrew Scriptures; to do this, that Word genuinely became incarnate.[42] In his body he suffered, died, and rose again from the dead. He empowered his disciples to become his heralds, and they trustworthily handed on what he had taught them. The apostles carefully instructed those who would follow them as leaders within the Church, to assure a faithful transmission of the apostolic message.[43]

Irenaeus repeatedly and insistently urged an "apostolic succession" of faithful communication of the tradition by the Church's leaders.[44] He declared that the leaders of the Church—the presbyters and the bishops—had carefully handed on that teaching since the time of the apostles.[45] He urged that this could readily be seen by the fact that, wherever one went in the entire inhabited earth, all the churches founded by the

---

39. This condensation of *AH* includes more than 760 citations of the OT and NT. Some of these are only passing allusions, showing how readily Irenaeus' thought touched on scriptural data; some are extended quotations; and some offer careful analysis and exegesis. Together, these indicate how extensively Irenaeus relied on Scripture for what he presented.

40. *AH* 2:1,1; 2:2,4–5; 2:3,2; 2:30,9; 3:9,1; 3:11,1.

41. *AH* 3:5,3; 3:10,2–3; 3:11,1; 3:18,2; 4:9,3; 4:17,6; 4:20,4; 5:18,3; the abundant fruitfulness of creation which Irenaeus asserts will come to pass in the eschaton (see *AH* 5:33,3; 5:34,2; 5:36,1; 5:36,3) is a result of the salvation of the entire creation.

42. *AH* 1:22,1; 2:9,1; 3:9,1; 3:11,1; 5:18,3.

43. *AH* 2:20,3; 3:pref; 3:1,1; 3:4,1; 3:5,2; 3:17,2; 3:24,1.

44. See *AH* 1:10,2; 2:9,1; 3:pref; 3:1,1; 3:2,2; 3:3,1–4; 3:4,1–2; 3:5,1; 4:26,2; 4:26,5; 4:32,1; 4:33,8; 5:pref; 5:20,1.

45. Irenaeus credits this to the presbyters at *AH* 3:2,2; 4:32,1; to the bishops at 3:3,2; 4:33,8; to both at 4:26,2. (Like most other Church leaders in the first two centuries [with the exception of Ignatius of Antioch], Irenaeus used the two terms almost interchangeably; the distinction in role and responsibility had not yet become the firm practice of the entire Church.)

apostles held to the same faith. Each of those churches could list their leaders in succession, from the apostles down to that day.[46] While some of those leaders were more gifted in eloquence or insight than others, their teaching was consistent: the Church believed the same faith, everywhere.[47] That proclamation was summarized in "the rule of truth," received and confessed at one's baptism.[48] This "rule of truth" served to guide the Church in the proper interpretation of Scripture[49] and to summarize what Christians believed.[50] Irenaeus offered a written rendition of that rule.[51]

Irenaeus presented a thoughtful perspective on the Gospels and the apostles' letters when he urged that these were the apostolic tradition *in written form*—that is, what would in due course be called the New Testament was *tradition written down*.[52] For Irenaeus, Scripture was not in competition or conflict with tradition: they were two sides of the same coin. Faithful adherence to and communication of the apostolic tradition, also in its written form, had marked the Church throughout the world[53]; indeed, among the peoples who were illiterate but had become Christians, the apostolic tradition was known only in the oral form in which it had been handed down within the Church since the time of the apostles; commitment to this tradition was sufficient to ensure rejection of Gnostic teaching.[54]

He went on to argue that the apostolic tradition came first and has been passed on reliably in the intervening generations, whereas Gnostic teaching developed later, as a distortion or corruption of the truth which had historically preceded it.[55] This comports with the related allega-

---

46. See Irenaeus' extended argument to this effect at *AH* 3:3,1–4.

47. Irenaeus makes this point repeatedly, with slight variations: see *AH* 1:10,3; 3:12,7; 3:24,1; 4:35,4; 5:20,1.

48. *AH* 1:9,4; the rule of truth would eventually find a fixed form, with some modifications, in the Apostles' Creed and, as elaborated in light of the early christological controversies, in the Niceno-Constantinopolitan Creed.

49. *AH* 2:27,1–2.

50. *AH* 2:28,1.

51. This appears at *AH* 1:10,1; see also a condensed version at 3:4,2.

52. See Irenaeus' argument to this effect in *AH* 3:1,1; cf. 3:5,1.

53. *AH* 1:20,2.

54. Irenaeus asserts this was true of the people among whom he labored in Lyons (*AH* 3:4,2).

55. See *AH* 3:3,3; 3:4,3; 3:21,3; 5:14,4; 5:20,1; note also the way he uses this argument about historical originality to urge Christians to humility at 2:28,2.

tion that the Gnostics had forged some writings, passing them off as if written by apostles,[56] something Irenaeus declares the Church has not done.[57] He urged that the Gospels written by Matthew, Mark, Luke, and John faithfully presented the apostolic tradition about Jesus Christ and were sufficient for the Church's needs, without any falsified gospels being added to them.[58]

For Irenaeus, the abstract philosophizing about immaterial privilege offered by the Gnostics was not what Christianity taught or offered. Instead, the Christian faith was firmly rooted in history, in this material creation.[59] The Word of God had fully entered into it, becoming incarnate; he had come to fulfill the promises made long ago by a merciful creator, the God whom he called Father. The savior's birth, life, death, and resurrection had taken place in history, in this creation.[60] His salvation would restore humanity and all creation, to enable them to become what God had intended.[61] The savior had empowered his disciples to be his heralds and granted them a full knowledge of his message,[62] which they proclaimed and passed on to designated followers who would succeed them as leaders in the Church. These successors had themselves faithfully passed on that apostolic tradition down through the generations since then.[63] The Christian faith was found, not in the secret coteries of

---

56. See the assertions at *AH* 1:20,1; 4:33,8; Irenaeus also specifically refers (at 3:11,9) to "The Gospel of Truth," produced by Valentinus' followers, which is among the Gnostic writings discovered at Nag Hammadi in 1945; for a translation, see *GS* 253–64.

57. *AH* 4:33,8. This is a striking claim in the face of much critical New Testament scholarship, which asserts that several works which are part of the NT canon are pseudonymous; it should be recalled here that Irenaeus unhesitatingly accepts the Pauline authorship of the letters historically accredited to him, including the Pastoral Letters; Irenaeus also accepts Petrine authorship for 2 Peter and Johannine authorship for the Gospel of John, the Apocalypse, and 1 and 2 John. (Whether Irenaeus was aware of 3 John or thought it apostolic is unknown, since he did not refer to or cite it in any of his extant works.)

58. See his argument at *AH* 3:1,1; 3:11,9; Irenaeus argues vigorously (if not quite convincingly) that there could only be four gospels at 3:11,8 (a section that offers, in other regards, some stimulating information about each of the four NT gospels).

59. *AH* 3:24,1.

60. *AH* 3:23,3; 3:18,7.

61. *AH* 3:18,1; 3:19,1.

62. *AH* 3:pref; 3:12,5.

63. *AH* 3:12,13.

Gnostic assemblies, but in the Church—in any and every church, for it had received and passed on the apostolic tradition.

According to Irenaeus, the Church took her stand on the Scriptures properly expounded and on the apostolic tradition faithfully handed down. While the Gnostics' claimed they handled Scripture rightly and passed on a special tradition, Irenaeus argued that they submitted neither to Scripture nor to apostolic tradition. When pressed to compare their Gnostic teachings with what the Church taught in these regards, Irenaeus urged that the Gnostics refused to subject their teaching either to Scripture or to apostolic tradition, claimed to be superior to the apostles in their teaching, and rejected even the idea that there could be a "rule of truth."[64]

Irenaeus' assertions on all the points above could be examined further, with many stimulating possibilities for further insights into his rich teaching. To do so, though, would carry this introduction far beyond its purpose. Even so, two closely related points need to be explored somewhat further, to point out some striking emphases of Irenaeus in his presentation of the Christian faith.

One Lord, One Faith, One History

As over against Gnostic teaching that there were numerous gods,[65] Irenaeus vigorously asserted that there is only one God. The one who created both the visible and the invisible realms had formed humanity and had promised them deliverance after they fell into sin. That same God had structured his dealings with humankind to offer anticipations of the coming savior and had spoken to prepare his way. The Hebrew Scriptures' anticipations and prophecies were alike fulfilled in Jesus Christ.[66] That one savior had communicated the truth to his disciples, who then passed it on faithfully to others, who themselves handed it on to yet others. All this "took place," in the strictest sense: Christ came, not to bring hidden knowledge, but to reclaim creation—in space and time. The Church stood, in identifiable places, in her continuity, as witness to what God had done in Christ and how he had accomplished and would

---

64. *AH* 3:2,1–2; 3:12,6.
65. *AH* 3:16,8; 4:34,5.
66. *AH* 3:12,3; 3:24,1.

continue to achieve his purposes. The truth was not multiple, but one, a faith shared by the entire Church.

This oneness of truth reflected the oneness of God. The multiple, dissimilar systems of Gnostic thought already demonstrated that the Gnostics did not teach the truth. By contrast, no matter where one traveled in the world, what he or she would find in the teaching of any and every church founded by one of the apostles was precisely what could be found in all the others. The truth had been declared and passed on; the apostolic tradition had been transmitted; the faith had been preserved: it could be found in the Church, and only in the Church. This led Irenaeus to make a bold, even audacious claim, to which we will return below. But before turning to it, we should pause to consider another main element of Irenaeus' teaching—a special application of this emphasis on one Lord, one faith, one history.

Recapitulation

In *Against Heresies*, Irenaeus presents salvation as recapitulation in Jesus Christ. Irenaeus' approach assumes and builds on the contrast the apostle Paul had articulated, in Romans 5 and 1 Corinthians 15, between Adam and Christ as the first Adam and the last Adam. In Irenaeus' teaching, the Son of God became human so as to begin humanity anew: Christ achieved salvation for humankind and for the cosmos by taking on the task originally given to Adam, living up to it faithfully and defeating the enemies that, since the primordial fall, had held humanity in bondage. As can be seen in Justin Martyr and Melito of Sardis,[67] the teaching of the early Church reveled in unpacking this divine economy of salvation beyond the explicit utterances of the apostle; Irenaeus proved to be the leading spokesman in that endeavor.

Irenaeus interprets the entirety of the savior's work in this fashion: "When he became incarnate and was made human, he began anew the long line of human beings and, to state it briefly, furnished us with salvation. Consequently, what we had lost in Adam—namely, the image and likeness of God—we recovered in Christ Jesus." This was deliberate on God's part: "God recapitulated in himself the ancient formation of man, so that he might kill sin, deprive death of its power, and give life again

---

67. Justin Martyr expanded on this apostolic approach somewhat (see his *Dialogue with Trypho* 100 [*ANF* 1:249], and Melito of Sardis gave it extensive consideration throughout his *On Pascha*.

to humankind."[68] This was why the savior had to be formed with the same physical body as Adam had,[69] which would enable the last Adam to suffer pain and death in the place of fallen humanity, in order to bring them to eternal life with God.[70]

According to Irenaeus, this recapitulation in Jesus Christ embraced everything that had previously transpired in the history of God's merciful dealing with humanity[71]: the shedding of the savior's blood served as the recapitulation of the blood of the righteous shed in previous ages, and the temptation of the last Adam was a recapitulation of the original temptation of the first Adam.[72] As Irenaeus unpacked the elements of this recapitulation, he drew specific contrasts between Eve, the disobedient virgin through whom sin entered the world, and Mary, the obedient virgin through whom the savior entered it, and between the tree that led to death and the tree that led to life.[73] At other times, Irenaeus' view was expansive as he presented this recapitulation in Jesus Christ, embracing the whole of the history of salvation from the primeval paradise to the new heavens and new earth.[74] He urges that the savior recapitulated everything in himself: in so doing, he granted "a second creation through his passion."[75] The whole of salvation, in all its breadth and depth, comes via the recapitulation accomplished in Jesus Christ.

SIGNIFICANCE OF *AGAINST HERESIES*

Much more could be said, even by way of introduction, to Irenaeus' magnum opus. But rather than pursue such inquiries, we turn to reflect on the significance of the work. Among many things that could be considered, we comment on three.

---

68. These citations are, respectively, from *AH* 3:18,1; 3:18,7.
69. *AH* 3:21,10; 5:1,2; 5:14,2.
70. *AH* 3:22,1; 4:22,1; 5:1,3.
71. *AH* 3:23,1; 3:24,1.
72. *AH* 5:14,1; 5:21,1-3.
73. *AH* 3:22,4; 5:16,3.
74. For this, see the presentation at *AH* 5:19,1.
75. *AH* 5:18,3; 5:23,2.

First in a Long Line

We have already noted that *Against Heresies* offered an extended presentation of the Christian faith, the first of a long line of such works which has continued to the present. Some scholars have spoken of *Against Heresies* as the Church's first systematic theology, but that misses Irenaeus' focus: the work's concern is not for a systematic presentation, whether built on philosophical or logical categories. (Indeed, Irenaeus was suspicious of any approach that relied too readily on human logical structures.) Rather, Irenaeus' concern was to defend and set forth the basics of the Christian faith passed down from Christ and the apostles in the Church. Against what he denounced as the aberrant perspectives of a wide range of Gnostic teachers, Irenaeus worked from the bases of the rule of truth he so highly prized as a condensation of the apostolic tradition; from it he urged the oneness of God, the goodness of creation, the unity of Scripture, and the fulfillment of both Scripture and humanity's original purpose in Jesus Christ, in whom all things have been recapitulated and found salvation. Even so, Irenaeus' determination to defend and expound the Christian faith would lead to many other such presentations over the ensuing centuries, including many that could be styled systematic theologies.

An Audacious but Unanswered Claim

In addition, we have noted that *Against Heresies* served as the major assault on Gnosticism. Other authors in the next generations articulated their own positions against Gnostic teaching, but each of them drew significantly upon the arguments Irenaeus had offered. In that regard, it is worth noting that, in the midst of all the arguments Irenaeus puts forth, he makes an utterly audacious claim—one that, if exposed as a falsehood, would have been sufficient to scuttle the whole ship he was piloting. Irenaeus deliberately and consciously argued that, wherever one might go in any of the churches founded by an apostle, one would find precisely the same teaching offered by the respective churches' leaders. He urged:

> While scattered throughout the whole world, the Church has received this message and this faith and still—as if living in only one house—carefully preserves it. She believes these points of doctrine as if she had only one soul, and one and the same heart.

She proclaims them, teaches them, and hands them down harmoniously, as if she had only one mouth. Although the languages
of the world are dissimilar, yet the meaning of the tradition has
remained one and the same.[76]

He credited this to the faithful transmission of the apostolic
tradition, from the apostolic founder to the appointed successors,
who had continued the pattern down to his day. Recognizing that the
various leaders differed in eloquence and exegetical insight, Irenaeus
nevertheless urged that they all so abode by the rule of truth, which
enshrined the apostolic tradition, that no one would be able to find
any leader in any such church who taught in conflict with or other
than the rule of truth.[77]

Irenaeus was not naïve in this claim. He knew from personal
experience that some who had been accepted as teachers in various
churches—including some of these Gnostics—had shown they were
unfaithful,[78] so it was not just a question of someone engaging in teaching within a church. He dealt with that problem explicitly, immediately
after exhorting his readers to follow the teaching of the presbyters in the
church, who "have received the certain gift of truth."[79] He warned against
those "whom many believe to be presbyters," but whose teaching and
lifestyles do not square with Christ's teaching and apostolic tradition.
Instead, those who seek the truth must "turn away from all such people"
and "hold fast to those who hold the doctrine of the apostles."[80] These
were the true presbyters, whose teaching stayed within and led people
to the truth.

Clearly, Irenaeus intended all this as a startling contrast to the
Gnostic teachers, who differed so significantly from each other in what
they presented. However, if one moves beyond the shock factor to
consider the import of the claim, Irenaeus' statement leaves his whole
argument fatally exposed: it would only require one Gnostic leader

76. *AH* 1:10,2; to the same effect, see 3:24,1.

77. See his argument at *AH* 1:10,3; also, at 5:20,1.

78. Irenaeus wrote letters to two such presbyters, Blastus and Florinus (referred to
in *CHE* 5:20,1). He also knew that Valentinus, the fountainhead of much Gnostic teaching, had served as a teacher in the church in Rome for some time before his views were
exposed as suspect.

79. *AH* 4:26,2.

80. *AH* 4:26,3–5.

(or anyone else who wanted to examine the issue) to find and expose a single example of such a dissonance within these apostolically founded churches to undermine the entirety of Irenaeus' argument. This seems a dangerous tactic for the bishop of Lyons to adopt: after all, his opponents prided themselves on their knowledge, and Irenaeus acknowledged that they were well versed in the analytical and logical tools of Aristotle,[81] so they had the intellectual wherewithal to recognize such a weakness in his argument. Since Gnosticism was a phenomenon widespread throughout the ancient world, the leaders and adherents of the movement had plenty of opportunity to test Irenaeus' claim and discover any example of its fraudulence. Further, given the fact that Gnosticism was shortly struggling for its very existence within Christian circles, largely because of the argument put forward in *Against Heresies*, it is striking that there is no evidence whatsoever that any Gnostic Christian rose to Irenaeus' challenge and offered even one such example.

The claim by Irenaeus was audacious, indeed—unless it was true. The fact that it was not challenged or disproved is telling. That leads to a consideration of another way in which *Against Heresies* is significant— now, not with a view to the ancient Christian world, but to the scholarly one of the twentieth and twenty-first centuries.

Irenaeus and "Normative" Christianity

Over the last few generations, scholarship on ancient Christianity has strongly emphasized the diversity found within Christianity in the first three centuries of the Church. Undoubtedly, this has been a helpful corrective for an idealized presentation of the ancient Church, which is more suited to an introductory catechetical presentation on the Christian faith than to a careful scholarly consideration of what could actually be found within Christianity in that early era. The repudiation of what has come to be called "normative" Christianity (or "proto-orthodoxy") as the true pattern, in favor of a more freewheeling, swirling variety of early Christianities, out of which one of the variants eventually attained dominance (under the assistance of Constantine), has become a widely held perspective within contemporary scholarship.[82] Irenaeus' magnum opus

81. Irenaeus asserts that the Gnostics were facile in "that hairsplitting and subtle mode of handling questions learned from Aristotle" (*AH* 2:14,5).

82. A handy recent summary of this scholarly assessment, offered at a popular level, is Ehrman, *Lost Christianities*.

raises some serious questions, though, about this scholarly assessment and how well it actually has read the relevant information.

For one thing, neither Irenaeus nor any other early church father claimed that there were no rivals in teaching or practice; indeed, scholars today must depend, in large part, on the proto-orthodox church fathers for much of the information they have on these rival groups. Irenaeus mentions several of them in *Against Heresies*—Marcionites, Gnostics, and Ebionites,[83] among others. The question is not whether these groups existed; they certainly did, and Irenaeus and the early church fathers give information about them. The question is also not whether these rival groups claimed to present the truth about Jesus Christ and Christianity; why else would they have existed, but to live by their teaching? Rather, the question is whether the claims of these rival groups stood the test of actually presenting that truth. The suspicion of "normative" Christianity rules that question out of consideration, in favor of an open-ended perspective that any such claim must be honored as valid.

However, this contemporary perspective does not square, either with the claims of these rival groups or of the proto-orthodox. All these groups claimed that God had acted in Jesus Christ (in some fashion) to bring salvation; equally, all claimed that God had intervened to assure a right presentation of the message about that salvation, as well as its preservation in the generations since the apostles. While contemporary scholarly predilections may not commonly move within these constraints, those ancient convictions gave the perimeters within which the argument could be conducted. The search was for the genuine article: the apostolic tradition that presented the truth about the savior and salvation.

In that regard, the utterly audacious claim of Irenaeus deserves to be given more consideration among scholars than it has received to this point. Further, the fact that it stood unanswered, given what was at stake for his opponents, is surely more telling about the actual situation in ancient Christianity than many otherwise scholarly arguments in the present day. If nothing else, this shows the significance of Irenaeus' *Against Heresies* and argues that it deserves a more careful reading than it so often has received, even from scholars of ancient Christianity.

83. In addition to the material presented on these groups in books 1 and 2, see *AH* 4:33,2–4.

STRUCTURE OF *AGAINST HERESIES*

Last, but certainly not least, we turn to consider the structure of Irenaeus' magnum opus. This seems straightforward enough, since in the prefaces to its five books Irenaeus indicates what he intends to treat in that book or subsequent ones (often commenting also on what he has already dealt with in previous ones). He states that book 1 will set forth the Gnostics' views and their differences from each other; book 2 will present the Gnostics' diversities and criticize their various perspectives; book 3 will consider the evidence of Scripture, which supports the teaching of the Church, drawing from the teaching of the apostles; book 4 will focus on the words spoken by Jesus Christ; and book 5 will draw from further teaching of the savior and of the apostles.[84] The challenge for readers in these descriptions is that what Irenaeus actually offers in each book goes considerably beyond or wanders quite a way from what he indicates in these statements.

Beyond this, within the respective books, Irenaeus' argument can be puzzling for contemporary readers. Irenaeus often deals with a question but does not quite complete the entire argument before moving on to another question. Later (in a different chapter, or even in a later book) he sometimes returns to an earlier argument and carries it further or in another direction. This pattern can repeat more than once in the five books. This can be frustrating for those looking for straight lines and definitive conclusions.

This all has led more than one scholar to question the logic of Irenaeus' tome. Other scholars have defended Irenaeus in this regard.[85] Something further deserves to be noted on this problem.

Too much should not be made of Irenaeus' suspicion of Aristotle's dialectic: to be sure, he condemns it as a major shaper of Gnostic thought,[86] but that hardly necessitates the conclusion that Irenaeus throws all organization of thought to the winds. Irenaeus certainly does not present his arguments in the straight lines of Aristotle's logic, but that does not mean his argument has no structure. Further, as noted above, he is

---

84. For Irenaeus' indications about the content of book 1, see *AH* 1:pref,2; 2:pref,1; 3:pref; for book 2, see *AH* 2:pref,2; 3:pref; for book 3, see *AH* 3:pref; 4:pref,3; for book 4, see *AH* 4:pref,1; and for book 5, see *AH* 5:pref.

85. On this scholarly disagreement, see the discussion in Osborn, *Irenaeus of Lyons*.

86. See *AH* 2:14,5.

not concerned to produce a systematized version of Christian teaching. Again, too much should not be made of this. He has no desire to be disorganized in his presentation: after all, he was defending the Christian faith from what he considered a serious perversion, so he recognized the need to offer a solid presentation.

In this regard, it may be helpful to keep in mind that Irenaeus saw himself as the spiritual grandson of the apostle John.[87] If a reader is familiar with the apostle's pattern of thought in 1 John, the frustration with Irenaeus' presentation may at least be lessened. The apostle deals with several questions in this letter in circular fashion, treating an issue nearly to a conclusion but then turning to something else. Later the original issue comes again to the fore and receives further or other comment. It is striking that a similar pattern appears in Polycarp's sole surviving writing, his letter to the Philippians.[88] Polycarp addresses various issues and then, before bringing the arguments to conclusions, comments on something else—only to return later to the earlier issues, with further comments or conclusions.[89]

It may be that this is a pattern of argument marking this spiritual line: the apostle John, Polycarp, and then Irenaeus seem to follow a similar way of presenting their respective cases. This is only a suggestion of a possible line of investigation in this regard: much more remains to be done to explore this similarity, articulate what held their lines of argument together, and assess how contemporaries in the ancient world would respond to it. But the very success of *Against Heresies* in commanding attention among the leaders of the Church, in attracting translators in the early centuries of the Church, and in shaping argument against the Gnostics indicates that the ancient world had less difficulty with this pattern of argument than recent scholars have had.

In the face of this, it is still possible to sketch out, in broad strokes, the way Irenaeus structured his work. The actual treatment in *Against Heresies* follows the general pattern indicated by the author in the respective prefaces to the five books. After dealing extensively with Gnosticism

---

87. See *AH* 3:3,4.

88. See *AposFrs* 207–21.

89. Polycarp calls his readers to prepare for the coming judgment (2), warns against loving money (4), gives directives regarding offices and roles within the church (4–6), returns to preparations for the judgment (8–10), and then critiques a presbyter who has turned aside for money (11).

in books 1 and 2, Irenaeus gives in books 3–5 an expansive presentation of the Christian faith. Beyond what is explicitly indicated in the prefaces, in the latter three books Irenaeus offers extensive citation of and argument from the Old Testament, the Gospels, and the apostles' writings. In the whole, he presents a thorough exposition of Christian teaching, rooted in the rule of truth. To get a complete treatment of any question, though, the reader needs to read all three of these books, alert to recurring themes and issues. Those who do are in for a treat: Irenaeus offers a rich, stimulating presentation of the Christian faith.

OOK 1 | *Exposing Heresy*
The Views of the Gnostics

SOME PEOPLE HAVE BEEN setting the truth aside in favor of myths and endless genealogies which, as the apostle says, "promote specula-tions rather than the divine training that is known by faith" [1 Tim 1:4]. Through their subtly concocted arguments they seduce the minds of the inexperienced and take them captive. They deal unfaithfully with the oracles of God and show that they are bad interpreters of the good word of revelation. They overthrow the faith of many by drawing them away, under a pretense of superior knowledge, from him who founded and adorned the universe, as if they had something more exalted to proclaim than the God who made heaven and earth and everything in them. . . . (1:pref,1)

Error is never set forth in its naked deformity, lest, being thus ex-posed, it should immediately be detected for what it is. It is craftily decked out in attractive dress, so that, by its outward form, it might appear to the inexperienced—ridiculous as the expression may seem—truer than truth itself. . . . What inexperienced person can readily detect the pres-ence of brass when it has been mixed with silver? . . . The language of these deceivers resembles ours, but what they mean with it is very differ-ent. I have read through several works of Valentinus' disciples and have interacted personally with some of them, and so have become familiar with their teachings. . . . I intend to set forth as well as I can, briefly and clearly, the opinions of these purveyors of heresy. (I am referring espe-cially to the disciples of Ptolemy, whose followers constitute an offshoot of Valentinus.) I will also try, as much as my moderate abilities allow, to provide what is necessary to overthrow them, by showing how absurd and inconsistent with the truth their statements are. . . . (1:pref,2)

. . . They claim that their views[1] are great, wonderful, and hitherto unspeakable mysteries, which they have been called to develop. That is, in fact, precisely what they do when they find anything in the Scriptures which they can adopt and accommodate to their baseless speculations. (1:1,3)

. . . They tell us that their special knowledge has not been openly divulged, because all are not capable of receiving it. Rather, it has been mystically revealed by the savior through parables to those qualified to understand it. . . . (1:3,1)

In the account which they all give of their "Pleroma" ["fullness"] and of the formation of the universe, they try to adapt the good words of revelation to their own evil inventions. They not only attempt, by perverse interpretations and deceitful expositions, to wring supposed proofs for their views from the writings of the evangelists and the apostles; they deal the same way with the law and the prophets, which contain many parables and allegories that can be taken in various ways, depending on the kind of exegesis used to interpret them. With great craftiness, others of these false teachers try to force various parts of Scripture to agree with the figments of their own imaginations. In this way they lead away captive from the truth those who do not retain a steadfast faith in one God, the Father Almighty, and in one Lord Jesus Christ, the Son of God. (1:3,6)

. . . These false teachers have good reason not to feel inclined to teach these things in public to everyone, but only to those who are able to pay a high price for an acquaintance with these supposedly profound mysteries. For these doctrines bear no resemblance to those of which our Lord said, "You received without payment; give without payment" [Matt 10:8]. . . . (1:4,3)

. . . These heretics deny that the savior actually took anything material to himself [in the incarnation], since—according to them—matter is incapable of salvation. Further, they hold that the consummation of all things will take place when all that is spiritual has been formed and perfected by knowledge ["gnosis"]—by which they mean spiritual people who have attained to the perfect knowledge of God and have

---

1. In the intervening paragraphs, Irenaeus has summarized Gnostic teaching on the thirty names and major groups of the Aeons, seen as the spiritual meaning behind the thirty years the savior lived before beginning his public ministry.

been initiated into their mysteries. These teachers claim that they and their followers are these "spiritual" people. (1:6,1)

According to these false teachers, "animal" people are instructed in animal things. "Animal" people are those who are established in their works and faith, but who do not have complete knowledge. They say that we who are members of the Church are these persons. These false teachers maintain that good works are necessary for us, because otherwise it would be impossible for us to be saved.

But as for themselves, they hold that they will surely be saved, not by their conduct, but because they are "spiritual." For just as it is impossible that matter should partake of salvation . . . so also it is impossible that those who are spiritual—by which they mean themselves—should ever come under the power of corruption, no matter what kind of activities they indulge in. For just as gold, even if it is dropped into filth, does not lose its beauty since filth cannot damage gold, so they claim that they cannot suffer loss or damage to their "spirituality," no matter what they do. (1:6,2)

Consequently, it is not surprising that the "most perfect" among them addict themselves without fear to all those kinds of things forbidden in Scripture, which declares that "those who do such things will not inherit the kingdom of God" [Gal 5:21]. . . . (1:6,3)

Although they engage in many abominations and impieties, they disparage us as utterly contemptible and ignorant since from fear of God we guard against sinning even in thought or word. All the while, they exalt themselves highly, claiming they are already perfect and are the elect. . . . (1:6,4)

Some of them also maintain that . . . Christ passed through Mary as water flows through a tube . . . , and that the savior never suffered: that would have been impossible, since he was incomprehensible and invisible. So, they teach that the Spirit of Christ, who had been placed within him, was taken away when he was brought before Pilate. . . . (1:7,2)

These heretics teach that there are three kinds of people—material, animal, and spiritual—represented by Cain, Abel, and Seth. These three natures are not found in a single person; the terms refer to various kinds of people. "Material" people will certainly endure ultimate corruption. If "animal" people live well, they will eventually experience rest in an intermediate place, but if they live badly, they also will be destroyed. They teach that the "spiritual" people ... will ultimately be made perfect and be given as brides to the angels of the savior.... (1:7,5)

This system of theirs is something which the prophets did not proclaim, the Lord did not teach, and the apostles did not pass on. Nevertheless, these false teachers boast that they have a more perfect knowledge than all of them. These heretics gather their views from other sources than the Scriptures. To use a common proverb, they try to "weave ropes out of sand" when they attempt to present their peculiar notions as the meaning of the parables of the Lord, the sayings of the prophets, and the words of the apostles. They do this in order that their scheme may not seem altogether without support. But to do so, they have to disregard the order and the connections within the Scriptures, and as far as they are able, they dismember and destroy the truth. By moving passages from one place to another and inventing new meanings for them, they have adapted the oracles of the Lord to their notions and so have deceitfully deluded many people. They act like those who, when a beautiful mosaic of a king has been made by some skillful artist out of precious jewels, then dismantle that likeness and rearrange the gems into the form of a dog or a fox (and even that poorly done!). ... Similarly, these heretics patch together old wives' tales and then, by grossly misinterpreting the words, expressions, and parables which they find, they make the oracles of God fit what they have concocted.... (1:8,1)

In this way, these people deceive themselves, abusing the Scriptures to force them to support their own system of ideas.... (1:9,1)

The fallacy of their views is manifest. John, proclaiming one God, the Almighty, and one Jesus Christ, the only-begotten, by whom all things were made, declares that this was the Son of God, the only-begotten [John 1:18], the maker of all things [John 1:3], the true light who enlightens every person [John 1:4], the creator of the world [John. 1:10], the one who came to his own [John 1:11], the one who became flesh and dwelled among us [John 1:14]. But these people pervert these statements by their supposed exposition, to maintain that another "only-begotten" was produced, whom they style the "Arche" ["beginning"]. They also proclaim that there was another savior, and another Logos, the son of the only-begotten, and another Christ who was produced to reestablish the "Pleroma" ["fullness"]. In this way, twisting all the expressions which have been cited and misusing terms found in them, these false teachers have claimed them for their own system. The result is that, according to these heretics, in all these terms John makes no mention of the Lord Jesus Christ. . . .

But the apostle said nothing about their speculative fancies; he spoke about our Lord Jesus Christ, whom he confesses to be the Word of God, as he makes clear. For summing up the statements he had previously made about the Word, he declared, "And the Word became flesh and lived among us" [John 1:14]. But according to the hypothesis of these false teachers, the Word did not become flesh at all. . . . (1:9,2)

Learn then, you foolish people, that the Jesus who lived among us and suffered for us is himself the Word of God. . . . If the Word of the Father who descended is the same one who also ascended [Eph 4:10]—namely, the only-begotten Son of the only God, who, according to the good pleasure of the Father, became flesh for the sake of humankind—then the apostle certainly is not speaking about someone or something else, but about our Lord Jesus Christ. According to these heretics, though, the Word did not originally become flesh. They maintain that the savior assumed an animal body, formed in a unique manner by an indescribable providence, so that it would be visible and palpable. But what God formed out of the dust at the beginning for Adam was flesh—and that is what John declared the Word of God became. . . . (1:9,3)

. . . One who holds steadfastly in his heart to the rule of truth,[2] which he received at baptism, will undoubtedly recognize the names, expressions, and parables taken from the Scriptures by these heretics, but he will not tolerate the blasphemous way they use them. Although he will recognize the gems, he will definitely not accept a fox's likeness instead of the king's. . . . (1:9,4)

But we should offer a finishing stroke to this exposition, so that anyone who follows out the farcical teaching of these heretics to the end will be able to give an argument which will overthrow it. So, we will point out, first of all, the ways the very fathers of these fables differ among themselves, as if they were inspired by different spirits of error. This fact itself forms an a priori proof that the truth proclaimed by the Church is

---

2. The "rule of truth" (or "rule of faith," the designation Irenaeus uses in *On the Apostolic Preaching*) is a basic element in Irenaeus' teaching. By it he refers to the "standard of sound teaching" (2 Tim 1:13) which he understood the Church had followed to assure faithful adherence to apostolic proclamation. He gives a rendition of it at 1:10,1, and another version at 3:4,2.

sure, and that the theories of these false teachers are only a flimsy tissue of falsehoods. (1:9,5)

The Church dispersed throughout the whole world to the ends of the earth has received from the apostles and their disciples this faith: We believe in one God, the Father Almighty, maker of heaven and earth and sea and all that is in them; and in one Christ Jesus, the Son of God, who became incarnate for our salvation; and in the Holy Spirit, who proclaimed through the prophets the works of God, and the advents, and the birth from a virgin, and the passion, and the resurrection from the dead, and the ascension into heaven in the flesh of the beloved Christ Jesus, our Lord, and his future manifestation from heaven in the glory of the Father "to gather up all things in him" [Eph 1:10], and to resurrect the entire human race, so that to Christ Jesus, our Lord and God and savior and king, according to the will of the invisible Father, "every knee should bend, in heaven and on earth and under the earth, and every tongue should confess" [Phil 2:10–11] him, and that he should execute just judgment on all. At that time he will send the "spiritual forces of evil" [Eph 6:12] (the angels who rebelled and became apostate), along with the ungodly, unrighteous, wicked, and profane among humanity, into everlasting fire; but in the exercise of his grace, he will grant eternal life to the righteous and holy (those who have kept his commandments and persevered in his love, some from the beginning of their lives, but others from their repentance) and will surround them with everlasting glory. (1:10,1)

While scattered throughout the whole world, the Church has received this message and this faith and still—as if living in only one house—carefully preserves it. She believes these points of doctrine as if she had only one soul, and one and the same heart. She proclaims them, teaches them, and hands them down harmoniously, as if she had only one mouth. Although the languages of the world are dissimilar, yet the meaning of the tradition has remained one and the same, for the churches planted in Germany do not believe or hand down anything different than those in Spain or in Gaul or in the East or in Egypt or in Libya or in the central regions of the world.[3] Just as the sun created by God is one and the same throughout the whole world, so also the

---

3. By this designation, Irenaeus referred to Palestine. He may have used this designation because the lands at the eastern end of the Mediterranean Sea were geographically "central" to the known world of his day; since those lands had been the locus of God's redemptive work for humanity over the centuries, culminating in Jesus Christ, though, Irenaeus' use of the designation may carry more than just geographical import.

preaching of the truth shines everywhere and enlightens all those who are willing to come to a knowledge of the truth. No leader in any of the congregations, however highly gifted in eloquence, teaches doctrines different from these (for no one is greater than the master); nor, on the other hand, does even one who is deficient in expression injure the tradition. The faith always remains one and the same: the one who is able to expound it at great length does not add anything to it, and the one who can say only a little does not thereby diminish it. (1:10,2)

It does not follow that, since people are endowed with greater or lesser degrees of intelligence, they end up changing the subject matter of the faith itself, such that someone conceives of some other God than the one who is the framer, maker, and preserver of this universe (as if he were not sufficient for them), or another Christ, or another only-begotten. It only means that one may more fully than another bring out the meaning of what has been spoken in parables and accommodate it to the general scheme of the faith; and set forth with greater clarity what God has done for human salvation; and show that God manifested longsuffering in regard to the apostasy of the angels who transgressed, as well as toward the disobedience of humanity; and set forth why it is that one and the same God made some things temporal but others eternal, some heavenly and others earthly; and understand why God, although invisible, showed himself to the various prophets in different ways [Heb 1:1]; and indicate why more than one covenant was given to humankind, and teach what the special character of each of these covenants was; and search out why "God has imprisoned all in disobedience so that he may be merciful to all" [Rom 11:32]; and gratefully describe why the Word of God became flesh and suffered; and relate why the advent of the Son of God took place in these last times (that is, in the end, rather than in the beginning, of the world); and unfold what the Scriptures teach about the end of all things and the things to come; and not be silent about how God has made the Gentiles, whose salvation was despaired of, fellow heirs and of the same body and partakers with the saints [Eph 2:19]; and discourse how it is that "this perishable body must put on imperishability, and this mortal body must put on immortality" [1 Cor 15:53]; and proclaim what God means when he says, "Those who were not my people I will call 'my people,' and her who was not beloved I will call 'beloved'" [Rom 9:25; cf. Hos 2:7]; and in what sense he declares that "the children of the desolate woman are more numerous than the children of the one who is married" [Gal 4:27; cf. Isa 54:1]. For in reference to these points, and others like them, the apostle exclaims: "O the depth of the riches and wisdom and knowledge of God! How unsearchable are his judgments and how inscrutable his ways!" [Rom 11:33]. . . . The catholic Church possesses one and the same faith throughout the whole world. . . . (1:10,3)

When you have read through all this,[4] you can enjoy a hearty laugh at the preposterous folly of these heretics! But people who promulgate such a religion, playing with letters and numbers perversely and, without any ultimate benefit, dividing and rearranging the greatness of the genuinely unspeakable power and works of God which are so striking, deserve to be mourned. All those who turn away from the Church and give heed to such old wives' fables as these are truly self-condemned [1 Tim 4:7; Titus 3:11]. These are the people about whom Paul commands us, "after a first and second admonition, have nothing more to do with" [Titus 3:10]. John, the disciple of the Lord, has intensified their condemnation when he tells us not even to bid them welcome if they come to us, since, he says, "to welcome is to participate in the evil deeds of such a person" [2 John 11]—and that with good reason, for the Lord says, "there is no peace for the wicked" [Isa 48:22]. Beyond even the usual limits of wickedness are these heretics who dare to claim that the maker of heaven and earth, the only God Almighty, besides whom there is no God, was the product of a defect, which itself sprang from another defect—so that, according to them, he was the product of the third defect. . . . When sick people fall into delirium, the more they laugh and believe they are well, and do everything as if they were healthy or even in superior health, the sicker they show themselves to be. Similarly, while these people claim that they excel others in wisdom, their ravings show that they are fools. . . . (1:16,3)

While they affirm a wide variety of nonsense about the creation,[5] each of them generates something new every day, according to his ability. Indeed, no one is deemed perfect among them who does not develop further prodigious fables! . . . (1:18,1)

---

4. In chs. 11–15 Irenaeus has rehearsed the views of a number of heretical teachers, including Valentinus, Secundus, Ptolemy, Colorbasus, Marcus, and their various followers.

5. In the intervening paragraphs, Irenaeus pointed out the Gnostics' focus on the "four elements" (earth, water, fire, and air) argued about in ancient philosophy, reliance on the zodiac, and their fixation on numerology.

Beyond all this, they appeal to an incredible number of apocryphal and spurious writings[6] which they themselves have forged, to bewilder the minds of foolish people and those who do not know the Scriptures of truth.... (1:20,1)

The "tradition" they hold about redemption focuses on the invisible and so is incomprehensible.... However, it is impossible to describe their teaching on this simply and in one piece, since each of them hands it down as he sees fit. Consequently, there are as many schemes of redemption among these heretics as there are teachers among them. When we turn to refuting them, we will show in its proper place that these men have been instigated by Satan to deny that baptism which is regeneration to God [Titus 3:5] and thus to renounce the whole Christian faith. (1:21,1)

... Since they differ so widely among themselves about doctrine and tradition,[7] and since those of them who are recognized as most up-to-date daily endeavor to invent some new opinion and to declare something no one else has ever thought of previously, it is difficult to describe all their opinions. (1:21,5)

The rule of truth which we hold is this: there is one God Almighty, who made all things by his Word, and fashioned and formed everything that exists out of nothing. This is what Scripture teaches: "By the Word of the Lord the heavens were made, and all their host by the breath of his mouth" [Ps 33:6], and "All things came into being through him, and without him not one thing came into being" [John 1:3]. No exception or exclusion is allowed here: the Father made all things by him, whether

---

6. By these terms, Irenaeus is pointing to the numerous books produced by various Gnostics, usually purporting to have come from one or another of the apostles. Many of these books have been lost over the centuries: with Gnostic teaching being repudiated by the Church, most of these books were destroyed, and there was little reason to keep or copy them. However, in 1945 at Nag Hammadi, a cache of Gnostic books was found. While some of these were known (at least by name) to scholars of the NT and of early Christianity, some others were not. Irenaeus subsumed them all—including, probably, others not found at Nag Hammadi—in this category of "apocryphal [i.e., "hidden"] and spurious writings." (It should be noted that, like most of the Church fathers, Irenaeus used the Septuagint of the Old Testament, which included several books that were ultimately not accepted into the Hebrew canon. As can be seen below, Irenaeus quoted and alluded to these books—commonly denominated "Apocrypha" in Protestant circles—as Scripture. It is certain that he is not using the term here to refer to those books.)

7. In the intervening sections, Irenaeus has laid out the particulars of the various Gnostic teachers' views on the question.

visible or invisible, objects known by the senses or by intelligence, temporal or everlasting. He did not make the everlasting things with the assistance of angels. . . . God needed no help creating: by his Word and Spirit he makes and disposes and governs all things, and commands all things into existence; he is the one who formed the world; he is the one who fashioned humankind—he is the one who is the God of Abraham and Isaac and Jacob. These is no other God above him, nor any "initial principle," nor "power," nor "pleroma": he is the Father of our Lord Jesus Christ, as we will show. Diligently holding this rule of truth, we will easily demonstrate, despite the great variety and multitude of their opinions, that these heretics have deviated from the truth. . . .

Reluctant as they may be to do so, these false teachers will one day rise again in the flesh, to confess the power of him who raises them from the dead. Because of their unbelief, though, they will not be numbered among the righteous. (1:22,1)

. . . These heretics are called Simonians, after Simon Magus,[8] the author of these impious doctrines. From them "what is falsely called knowledge" [1 Tim 6:20] received its beginning, as one may learn from their own claims. . . . (1:23,4)

. . . Saturninus set forth a father who was unknown to all, but who made angels, archangels, powers, and potentates. The world and everything in it were made by a special group of seven angels. Humanity too was the workmanship of angels. It was a shining image bursting forth below from the presence of the supreme power. When the angels could not keep it under control, because it kept soaring upwards again, they said to each other, "Let us make humankind in our image, according to our likeness" [Gen 1:26]. Accordingly, humanity was formed but was not yet able to stand erect, because the angels could not convey that ability. . . . (1:24,1)

Saturninus has also laid it down as truth that the savior had no birth, body, or shape, and that he only seemed to be a visible man. Further, Saturninus maintained that the God of the Jews was one of the angels. . . . Christ came to destroy the God of the Jews, but to save those who believe in him (that is, those who possess the spark of his life). This heretic was the first to affirm that two kinds of people were formed by the angels,

8. In the intervening sections, Irenaeus presented the views and influence of Simon Magus of Samaria, whom Christian teachers in antiquity commonly viewed as the originator of heresies (cf. Irenaeus' comments to that effect below: 1:27,4; 3:pref).

one wicked and the other good. Since the demons assist the wicked, the savior came to destroy evil people and the demons, but to save the good. He also declares that marriage and procreation are from Satan. Many of those who belong to his school also abstain from meat and impress many people with such abstinence [1 Tim 4:3].... (1:24,2)

According to Basilides, the angels who dwell in the lowest heaven—the one visible to us—formed everything in the world and apportioned it and the nations on it among themselves. The head angel is the one thought to be the God of the Jews, but since he tried to make all the other nations subject to his own people, the Jews, all the other angels resisted and opposed him. As a consequence, all the other nations hated his nation. But the father without birth and without name, perceiving that they would be destroyed, sent his own first-begotten "Nous" ["mind"], who is called Christ, to grant to all who believe in him deliverance from the power of those angels who made the world. Toward this end, he appeared on earth as a man to the nations of these powers and worked miracles, but he did not himself suffer death. Simon of Cyrene was compelled to bear the cross in his place, but Simon was transfigured by him, so that Simon was thought to be Jesus. So, through ignorance and error, Simon was crucified, while Jesus took on the appearance of Simon and, standing nearby, laughed at them. (Since he was an incorporeal power, and the Nous of the unborn father, he could transfigure himself as he pleased.) Then he ascended to him who had sent him, deriding the ones who had intended to crucify him, for they could not lay hold on him, since he was invisible to all.

The ones who know these things have been freed from the principalities who formed the world. The result of this teaching is that it is not necessary to confess him who was crucified, but rather one who came in the appearance of a man, and was thought to be crucified, and was called Jesus.... If anyone, therefore, he [Basilides] declares, confesses the crucified, that person is still a slave, under the power of the angels who created our bodies; but the one who denies him has been freed from these beings and has come to know the ways of the unborn father. (1:24,4)

According to the heretics, only the soul will be saved, since the body is by nature subject to corruption.... (1:24,5)

Another heretic, Carpocrates, and his followers maintain that the world and the things in it were created by angels greatly inferior to the unbegotten Father. They also hold that Jesus was the son of Joseph and was just like other men—with only this difference, that, since his soul was steadfast and pure, he perfectly remembered those things which he had witnessed within the sphere of the unbegotten God. Because of this, a power descended upon him from the Father, so that through it he could escape from the creators of the world.... (1:25,1)

...Some of them have come to such a pitch of pride that they declare they are similar to Jesus. Others of them claim they are superior to his disciples, Peter and Paul and the other apostles—whom they consider equal to Jesus!... (1:25,2)

...Satan has sent forth these false teachers to dishonor the Church. When people hear what the heretics teach, they imagine that we all are like them, and so they turn away their ears from the preaching of what is truth. Or, seeing the things these false teachers practice, people speak evil of us all, even though we have no fellowship with these heretics in doctrine, morals, or daily conduct. They lead a licentious life and abuse the name of Christ as a way of concealing their wicked deeds and doctrine. For all this, "their condemnation is deserved" [Rom 3:8]: they will certainly receive fitting retribution from God. (1:25,3)

Their madness is so unbridled that they claim to have power over all that is irreligious and impious, and so are at liberty to engage in such acts. They teach that the distinction between evil and good is nothing more than human opinion. Indeed, some teach that it is necessary for souls, by transmigration from body to body, to experience every kind of life and action.... (1:25,4)

...In their writings we read ... that Jesus privately taught mysteries to his disciples and apostles, and that they asked and received permission to hand down the things thus taught them to others who would be found worthy and believing.... (1:25,5)

...Another heretic, Cerinthus, taught that Jesus was not born of a virgin, but was the son of Joseph and Mary according to the ordinary course of human generation. Even so, Jesus was more righteous, prudent, and wise than other people. After his baptism Christ descended upon him in the form of a dove from the Supreme Ruler. Then Jesus began to proclaim the unknown Father and to perform miracles. But later Christ departed from Jesus, and then Jesus suffered and rose again—while Christ remained impassible, since he was a spiritual being. (1:26,1)

Marcion of Pontus ... advanced the most daring blasphemy against the one who is proclaimed as God by the law and the prophets, declaring that he is the author of evil, delights in war, is inconstant, and even is contrary to himself.... Besides this, he mutilates the Gospel of Luke, removing all that is written in it about the generation of the Lord and deleting many passages in the teaching of the Lord in which he clearly confesses that the maker of this universe is his Father.

Marcion likewise persuaded his disciples that he himself was worthier to be believed than the apostles who have handed down the gospel to us, although Marcion only provided them with a fragment of the gospel. He similarly dismembered the letters of Paul, removing all the passages in which the apostle clearly spoke of the God who made the world as the Father of our Lord Jesus Christ, as well as those passages from the prophets which the apostle quotes to show that they announced beforehand the coming of the Lord. (1:27,2)

He teaches that salvation will only be attained by those souls who have learned his doctrine. The body, though, since it was taken from the earth, cannot share in salvation.... (1:27,3)

This man is the only one who has dared openly to mutilate the Scriptures.... But all those who corrupt the truth in any way and damage the preaching of the Church are the disciples and successors of Simon Magus of Samaria.... To be sure, they put forth the name of Christ Jesus as a lure, but in various ways they introduce the blasphemies of Simon. In this way they destroy multitudes.... (1:27,4)

Many heretical branches have already developed out of those heretics we have described. This happens because many of them—we might even say all—want to be teachers on their own, and to branch off from the particular heresy in which they have been involved.... They insist upon teaching something new.... (1:28,1)

 . . . We should pity those who, embracing these miserable and baseless fables, have reached such a pitch of arrogance that they count themselves superior to everyone else because of this knowledge—or, as it should rather be called, ignorance. They have now been fully exposed; to set forth their teachings is enough to win a victory over them. (1:31,3)

 . . . Not many words will be needed to overturn their system of doctrine, now that it has been made manifest to all.... (1:31,4)

BOOK 2 | *Exposing Heresy*
Disunity among the Gnostics

IN THE FIRST BOOK exposing "what is falsely called knowledge" [1 Tim 6:20], I laid out the whole false system, in its various contradictory forms, fabricated by the school of Valentinus. I also set forth the tenets of their predecessors, showing that they not only differed among themselves, but had long ago swerved from the truth itself. . . . Further, I carefully pointed out passages which they garble from the Scriptures, so as to adapt them to their own fictions. As well, I methodically laid out their audacious attempts to establish what they regard as truth by way of numbers and by the letters of the alphabet. . . . (2:pref,1)

In this book, my thorough examination will bring forward all that is necessary to destroy their whole system. This will offer an exposure and subversion of their views, as the title of this work promises. . . . (2:pref,2)

It is fitting to begin with the first and most important point—God the creator, who made heaven and earth and everything in them, but whom these heretics blasphemously dismiss as the result of a defect. There is nothing either above or after him; he was not moved to create by another: he did so freely. He is the only God, the only Lord, the only creator, the only Father, who alone contains all things and who called everything into existence. (2:1,1)

The way the heretics argue may seem plausible or even convincing to those who do not know God, and who liken him to needy human beings or to those who cannot accomplish anything by themselves without help, but who have to use various aids to produce whatever they intend. But it will not be regarded as at all probable by those who know that God needs nothing, and that he created and made all things by his Word. He did not need the help of angels or any other power inferior to himself to produce the things which were made. . . . He himself, by himself alone, in a way we can neither describe nor understand, having predestined all things, formed them as he chose, bestowing harmony on all things, assigning them their particular place and the beginning of their creation. . . . He formed all things that were made by his Word that never wearies. (2:2,4)

It is unique to God that, in his preeminence, he needs no tools to create the things which he summons into existence. His own Word is both suitable and sufficient to create all things, as John, the disciple of the Lord, declares: "All things came into being through him, and without him not one thing came into being" [John 1:3]. Clearly, our world must be included among the "all things." It too was made by his Word: Scripture tells us in the book of Genesis that he made all things connected with our world by his Word. David also expresses the same truth: "For he spoke, and it came to be; he commanded, and it stood firm" [Ps 33:9].

Whom, therefore, shall we believe as to the creation of the world: these heretics who, as we have shown, prate so foolishly and inconsistently on the subject, or the disciples of the Lord, and Moses, who was both a faithful servant of God and a prophet? He began the narration of the formation of the world in these words: "In the beginning God created the heavens and the earth" [Gen 1:1]. . . . (2:2,5)

Let the heretics stop teaching that the world was made by another. As soon as God formed a conception in his mind, what he had thus conceived was done. It was not that one being mentally formed the idea but that another actually produced the things which had been conceived in his mind. . . . (2:3,2)

. . . But if, as some say, their Father permitted these things[1] without approving of them, then he gave permission because of some necessity— for he must either have been able to prevent it or not. If he could not hinder it, though, then he is weak and powerless; but if he could but did not, then he is a seducer, a hypocrite, and a slave to necessity, since he does not approve of what happens but still allows it as if he did. . . . (2:5,3)

However, it is not appropriate to say that the one who is God over all, who is free and independent, was a slave to necessity, or that anything takes place with his permission but against his will. In that case, neces-

---

1. In the intervening paragraphs, Irenaeus has described how the Gnostics accounted for the variety of defects they alleged were found in creation.

sity would be greater and more majestic than God, since whatever has the most power is superior. . . . It would have been much better, more consistent, and more God-like to cut off the principle of this kind of necessity at the beginning, than afterwards, as if moved by repentance, to try to overcome the results of necessity once they had reached such a development. . . . (2:5,4)

. . . His being is invisible and mighty; all people have a profound mental intuition and perception of his sovereign and omnipotent greatness. Therefore, although "no one knows the Father except the Son; and no one knows the Son except the Father, and anyone to whom the Son chooses to reveal him" [cf. Matt 11:27], yet all know this fact at least, since reason, implanted in their minds, moves them and reveals to them that there is one God, the Lord of all. (2:6,1)

All things have been placed under the control of him who is called the Most High and the Almighty. By calling on him, even before the incarnation of our Lord, people were saved from wicked spirits, from all kinds of demons, and from every sort of apostate power. . . .

By way of comparison, those who live under the empire of the Romans, even if they have never seen the emperor but are far separated from him by land and sea, know very well, as they experience his rule, who it is that possesses the principal power in the state. . . . (2:6,2)

That God is the creator of the world is accepted even by people who otherwise speak against him, since they still acknowledge him as creator. . . . All the Scriptures proclaim this, and the Lord teaches us only about this Father who is in heaven, as I will demonstrate subsequently. For the present, though, the proof derived from those who allege doctrines opposite to ours is sufficient of itself; indeed, all people consent to this truth. For their part, the ancients preserved this conviction carefully from the tradition of the first-formed man, for they celebrated the praises of one God, the maker of heaven and earth. Later on, others also were reminded of this fact by the prophets of God, while the heathen learned it from creation itself, which reveals him who formed it: the work thus made gives intimations of the one who made it, and the world shows forth the one who ordered it. The universal Church, moreover, throughout the whole world, has received this tradition from the apostles. (2:9,1)

It deserves to be believed and accepted that the substance of created things came from the power and will of him who is God over all. It also squares with reason, and it may well be said about such a belief

that "what is impossible for mortals is possible for God" [Luke 18:27].
... (2:10,4)

But the heretics do not believe that he who is God over all formed by his Word, in his own place and as he himself pleased, the various and diverse works we find in the creation. He is the one who formed all things, like a wise architect and a powerful monarch. But they believe that angels, or some power other than God (who was ignorant of him) formed this universe.... They are like the dog of Aesop that dropped the bread when it tried to seize its shadow, thus losing the real food. It is easy to prove from the words of the Lord that he acknowledges one Father and creator of the world and fashioner of humanity, the one who was proclaimed by the law and the prophets, while he knows no other—and that this one is really God over all. Further, he teaches that the adoption of children (which is eternal life) comes from this same Father, and that it takes place through himself, since he confers it on all the righteous. (2:11,1)

But these heretics delight in attacking us. These triflers assail us with points which really do not tell at all against us, bringing up a host of fables and supercilious questions. In reply, I think it fair to raise the questions that follow about their own doctrines, to show their improbability and put an end to their audacity. After this, I will examine the Lord's teachings, to take from these heretics the means of attacking us. Since they will be unable to reply reasonably to the questions that will be raised, I hope that they may see that their plan of argument is destroyed—so that, either returning to the truth and humbling themselves and ceasing from their multifarious fantasies, they may propitiate God for the blasphemies they have uttered against him and thus find salvation; or that, if they still persevere in that proud system which has taken possession of their minds, they may at least find it necessary to change the kind of argument they use against us. (2:11,2)

... If they had understood the Scriptures and been taught the truth, they would have known beyond doubt that God is not as people are, and that his thoughts are not like ours [Isa 55:8]. The Father of all is at a vast distance from those affections and passions which operate among us. He is a simple, uncompounded being, without separate parts, and entirely like and equal to himself: he is wholly understanding, wholly spirit, wholly thought, wholly intelligence, wholly reason, wholly hearing, wholly seeing, wholly light, and the whole source of all that is good—

as those who are religious and pious are accustomed to say about God. (2:13,3)

However, he is above all these properties, and therefore indescribable. For he who comprehends all things may well and properly be called "understanding," but he is not therefore like human understanding; and he may most properly be termed "light," but he is nothing like the light with which we are acquainted. And so, in every other regard, the Father of all is not at all like us in our human weakness. We speak of him in these ways because of our love for him, but his greatness far surpasses our thoughts and words about him. . . . (2:13,4)

. . . Just as the person does not err who declares that God is all vision and all hearing (for in the way he sees he also hears, and in the way he hears he also sees), so also the one who affirms that he is all intelligence and all word, and that, in whatever respect he is intelligence, in that also he is word, and that this Nous ["mind"] is his Logos, will still have only an inadequate conception of the Father of all. But that person will have far more appropriate thoughts about God than will those who transfer what is true about how people produce words to the utterance of the eternal Word of God, assigning a beginning and sequence of production to him as they would for their own words. In what respect will the Word of God—who is God himself, since he is the Word—differ from a human word, if he is captured by the same order and produced in the same way? (2:13,8)

. . . In heaping together with a kind of plausibility all the human feelings, mental exercises, and intentions involved when we speak and attributing them to God, they declare crude falsehoods about God. But when they ascribe the things that happen with human beings and whatever they recognize themselves as experiencing to the divine reason, they seem to those who are ignorant of God to make statements which seem suitable enough. . . . (2:13,10)

The account which the ancient comic poets give as to the origin of all things is much more like the truth—and more pleasing! . . . Indeed, these heretics transplant into their own system the things comedians loudly declaim everywhere in the theaters, teaching them by the same arguments but changing the names. (2:14,1)

Not only are they guilty of plagiarism, since they bring forward the ideas found among the comic poets as if they themselves had dreamed them up; they also jumble together the things which have been said by all those who were ignorant of God and who are termed philosophers.[2] Sewing together, as it were, a motley garment out of a pile of miserable rags, the heretics, by their subtle manner of expression, have furnished themselves with a cloak which, again, is really not their own. It is true that they introduce a new kind of doctrine, which they try to substitute for the old; however, in reality it is both old and threadbare, since these opinions have been sewed together out of ancient teachings which reek of ignorance and irreligion.... (2:14,2)

... These heretics also try to transfer to faith that hairsplitting and subtle mode of handling questions learned from Aristotle. (2:14,5)

The account which we give of creation is harmonious with the regular order of the world. Our scheme fits with what has actually been made, but theirs necessarily collapses into the greatest confusion.... (2:15,3)

How much safer and better a course it is to confess at once what is true: that this God, the creator who formed the world, is the only God, that there is no other God besides him, and that he himself planned and made all things.... (2:16,3)

... Let me now examine the rest of their scheme. Because of their madness, I will be inquiring about things which do not even exist. It is necessary to do this, though, since the treatment of this subject has been entrusted to me, since I desire everyone to come to the knowledge of the truth, and since you yourself have asked me to provide you with full and complete means for overturning the views of these false teachers. (2:17,1)

Enough has been said[3] to show that their system is weak and untenable, utterly fanciful. As a common proverb says, "It is not necessary to drink the entire ocean to learn that its water is salty".... (2:19,8)

... They can be charged, then, not only with impiety against the creator, since they say he was the product of a defect, but also against Christ and the Holy Spirit, since these heretics affirm that they were produced by that defect. In the same way, they urge that the savior was

2. In the following sections (2:14,2–6), Irenaeus interacts with the perspectives of many of the leading philosophers of antiquity, arguing that the Gnostics had borrowed and modified some of their views. In this treatment, Irenaeus deals with the views of Thales of Miletus, Anaximander, Anaxagoras, Democritus, Epicurus, Plato, Aristotle, Empedocles, the Stoics, the Cynics, and the Pythagoreans.

3. In the intervening paragraphs, Irenaeus has engaged in an extended discussion of various facets of Gnostic teaching.

spawned after the formation of that defect. Who will put up with the rest of their vain talk, which they subtly try to accommodate to the Lord's parables, by which they have plunged both themselves and those who believe them into the deepest abysses of impiety? (2:19,9)

. . . Our Lord Jesus Christ underwent a genuine passion, not just the appearance of one. Even so, he was in no danger of being destroyed; instead, by his own power he established fallen humanity and called it anew to incorruption. . . . The Lord suffered so that he might bring those who have wandered from the Father back to knowledge and communion with him. . . . Having suffered, the Lord granted us salvation, bestowing on us the knowledge of the Father. . . . By his passion our Lord also destroyed death, dispersed error, put an end to corruption, and destroyed ignorance, while he manifested life, revealed truth, and granted the gift of incorruption. . . . (2:20,3)

. . . "The year of the Lord's favor" [Isa 61:2; Luke 4:19] is this present time, in which those who believe him are called by him and accepted by God—that is, the whole time from his advent to the consummation, during which he acquires for himself those who are saved by his mercy. . . . (2:22,2)

. . . He did not appear as one thing while being something else, as those heretics teach who say he only seemed to be human: he manifested himself for what he was. As a master, he possessed the age of a master. He did not despise or evade any human condition. He did not set aside in his own case the order he had appointed for the human race; rather, he sanctified every stage of human development by participating in it himself. For he came to save all in himself, all those who are born again to God through him—infants,[4] toddlers, young children, youths, and the mature. He passed through every stage, becoming an infant for infants, thus sanctifying infants; a child for children, thus sanctifying those of this age, and serving them as an example of piety, righteousness, and submission; a young person for young people, serving as an example to youths and thus sanctifying them for the Lord; so also he was a mature person for the mature. In this way, he was a perfect master for all, not

4. In speaking here of "infants" being "born again," Irenaeus seems to allude to infant baptism; cf. his presentation of baptism as "the power of regeneration into God" [i.e., being "born again" into God] at 3:17,1. If this assessment is valid, this passage is one of the earliest references in the history of the Church to the practice and acceptance of paedobaptism.

merely in setting forth the truth, but also in being mature, sanctifying at the same time those who are mature, as well, and becoming an example for them also. Then, finally, he came on to death itself, so that he would be "the first-born from the dead, so that he might come to have first place in everything" [Col 1:18], the author of life [Acts 3:15], existing before all and going before all. (2:22,4)

The right way to approach knowledge is not to try to rise above God in your thoughts: he cannot be surpassed. Do not try to find one greater than the creator; that would be futile. The one who made you cannot be contained within limits. Even if you could measure the cosmos and traverse the entire creation, and carefully examined it in all its depth and height and length, you would still not be able to come up with one superior to the Father. You will never be able to comprehend him. . . . (2:25,4)

It is better and more beneficial to be classed with the simple and illiterate, but to be near God in love, than to imagine yourself learned and insightful but be numbered with those who blaspheme him, conjuring up a superior god to be the father. This is why Paul declared, "Knowledge puffs up, but love builds up" [1 Cor 8:1]. By this he did not disparage genuine knowledge of God, for then he would have been condemning himself. But he knew that some people, inflated with their pseudo-knowledge, fall away from the love of God, imagining themselves to be perfect. . . .

It is better to have no knowledge whatever of even one reason why a single thing in creation has been made, but to believe in God and continue in his love, than it would be to be puffed up through knowledge of the kind offered by the heretics and so fall away from that love which gives life to humanity. It is better to search after no other knowledge than that of Jesus Christ the Son of God, who was crucified for us, than to fall into impiety by subtle questions and hair-splitting expressions. (2:26,1)

A healthy mind, one which does not expose its possessor to danger and is devoted to piety and the love of truth, eagerly meditates on those things which God has placed within the power of humankind and has subjected to our knowledge. It will advance in them, learning them easily by daily study. These things are open to our observation and are clearly, unambiguously set forth in the sacred Scriptures.

That is why the parables should not be adapted to fit with ambiguous statements. If one keeps this caution in mind, the one who interprets the parables will avoid danger, and they will receive the same interpretation by all. In this way, the whole body of truth holds together harmoniously, without conflict. But if one uses ambiguous notions to interpret the parables, such as anyone might invent for himself on his whims, then no one will possess the rule of truth any longer. The number of persons offering interpretations will equal the diverse systems of supposed truth, all mutually opposed, presenting contradictions, as one finds with the philosophers. (2:27,1)

In this approach, people would always be seeking but never finding the truth [2 Tim 3:7], because they have turned away from the way to discover it. . . . Indeed, the entire Scriptures, the prophets, and the gospels can be clearly, unambiguously, and harmoniously understood by all, even if all do not believe them. . . . (2:27,2)

Since parables can be interpreted in many ways, everyone who loves truth will recognize that for these heretics to assert that God is to be searched out from the parables, while these false teachers disregard what is certain, undoubted, and true, is the folly of those who thrust themselves into danger and act like those destitute of reason. . . . (2:27,3)

So, having the truth itself as our rule and the testimony concerning God set clearly before us, we should not cast away the firm and true knowledge of God by scurrying after a multitude of contradictory responses to questions. It is much more appropriate that we guide our inquiries to investigate the mystery and administration of the living God, and so increase in love for him who has done and still does such great things for us. . . . (2:28,1)

If, though, we cannot find solutions for all the questions raised in Scripture, we should not seek for some other God than the one who is: that would be the greatest impiety. We should leave things like that to God, who created us, with the assurance that the Scriptures are perfect, since they were spoken by the Word of God and his Spirit. We are much inferior to them, since we came along much later than the Word of God and his Spirit, and so we are unable to attain full understanding of his mysteries. It should be no surprise that this is the case for us with spiritual and heavenly things, which can only be made known to us by revelation, when even those things which lie at our very feet—I mean those that belong to this world, which we handle and see and are around us—surpass our knowledge [2 Esd 4:10–11]. Even these we must leave in God's hands. He is superior to everything. . . . (2:28,2)

If, therefore, even with respect to creation, there are some things only God knows, while others come within the range of our knowledge, why should we complain if, in regard to those things which we investigate in the Scriptures (which are thoroughly spiritual), we are able by the grace of God to explain only some of them, while we must leave the rest in the hands of God—and that not only in the present world but also in that which is to come—so that God will forever teach and human beings will forever learn the things God teaches? The apostle declared in this regard that, when other things have passed away, then "faith, hope, and love abide" [1 Cor 13:13]. *Faith*, which focuses on our master, stands firm, assuring us that there is only one true God. It calls us genuinely to *love* him for ever, since he alone is our Father. It encourages us always to *hope* confidently that we will always receive more and more from God and learn from him, since he is good and has boundless riches, an unending kingdom, and inexhaustible instruction.

If, then, following the advice I have given, we leave some questions in the hands of God, we will keep our faith from injury and will continue without danger. Moreover, we will find all Scripture, which has been given to us by God, to be entirely consistent. Then the parables will harmonize with the passages which are perfectly plain, and the statements which are clear in meaning will help explain the parables, and in all the various utterances of Scripture we will hear one harmonious melody, praising in hymns the God who created all things.

So, for instance, if any one asks, "What was God doing before he made the world?," we reply that the answer to such a question lies hidden with God himself. The Scriptures teach us that this world was formed complete by God, receiving its beginning in time, but no Scripture tells us what God was doing prior to creation. The answer to that question belongs to God alone. No one should dream up foolish, rash, and blasphemous questions. . . . (2:28,3)

. . . Similarly, if anyone asks, "How was the Son produced by the Father?," we reply that no one understands that production, or generation, or calling, or revelation, or whatever term may be used to describe his generation: it is utterly indescribable. . . . While the heretics acknowledge him to be indescribable and unnameable, they nevertheless set about to describe how he was first produced and formed—as if they themselves had assisted at his birth! . . . (2:28,6)

. . . We have learned from the Scriptures that God holds the supremacy over all things. But Scripture has not revealed to us the way he produced it. . . . In the same way, we must leave unanswered the question why, since all things were made by God, some of his creatures sinned and revolted from a state of submission to God. . . . Since we know only in part [1 Cor 13:12], we must leave all sorts of questions in the hands of him who gives us grace by measure. . . . (2:28,7)

. . . If those who supposedly are perfect cannot even understand what is in their hands, at their feet, before their eyes, and around them on earth (like the number of hairs on their head), why should we believe what they teach about spiritual and super-celestial matters which they superciliously claim are above God?. . . (2:28,9)

. . . Who can even count all the things made by God's power and governed by his wisdom? Who can fathom the greatness of the God who made them? (2:30,3)

. . . From the authoritative Scriptures we prove that all things, visible and invisible, were made by one God. These heretics are not more trustworthy than the Scriptures! Nor should we give up the declarations of the Lord, Moses, and the rest of the prophets, who have proclaimed the truth, and give credit to the heretics instead, for they utter nothing that makes any sense but only rant about untenable opinions. . . . (2:30,6)

. . . There is one only God, the creator—who is above every principality and power and dominion and virtue. He is Father, he is God, the founder, the maker, the creator who made those things by himself (that is, through his Word and his Wisdom)—heaven and earth, the seas, and everything in them. He is just; he is good; he it was who formed humanity, who planted paradise, who made the world, who sent the flood, who saved Noah. He is the God of Abraham, Isaac, and Jacob, the God of the living [Mark 12:26, 27]. He it is whom the law proclaims, whom the prophets preach, whom Christ reveals, whom the apostles make known to us, and in whom the Church believes. He is the Father of our Lord Jesus Christ. Through his Word, who is his Son, he is revealed and manifested to all to whom he is revealed—for only those know him to whom the Son has revealed him. But the Son, eternally co-existing with the Father from of old, indeed, from the beginning, always reveals the Father to angels, archangels, powers, virtues, and all those to whom he wills that God should be revealed. (2:30,9)

... The heretics cannot raise the dead, as the Lord raised them, and as the apostles did by prayer, and as has been frequently done in the brotherhood because of some necessity. At times, the entire church in a particular locality has entreated for this extraordinary gift by much fasting and prayer, and the spirit of the dead person has returned, in answer to the prayer of the saints. But the heretics do not even believe this can be done. . . . (2:31,2)

If, however, they maintain that the Lord, too, only appeared to perform miraculous works, we will direct them to the prophets' writings, and prove from them that such miraculous things were predicted about him, that they unquestionably took place, and that he is the only Son of God. So also, those who genuinely are his disciples receive grace from him to perform miracles in his name for the welfare of others—all according to the gift which each has received from him [cf. Rom 12:6–8; 1 Cor 12:7, 10]. Some exorcize demons, and many who have thus been cleansed from evil spirits come to believe in Christ and join the Church. Others have foreknowledge of things to come: they see visions and utter prophecies. Still others heal the sick by laying their hands upon them, and they are made well. Moreover, as I have said, even the dead have been raised, and have remained among us for many years.[5]

What else should I say? It is not possible to number all the gifts which the Church, throughout the whole world, has received from God, in the name of Jesus Christ (who was crucified under Pontius Pilate), and which she exercises day by day for the benefit of the nations, without practicing deception toward anyone, and not taking any reward from them for these miracles. As she has received freely from God, she also freely ministers to others [Matt 10:8]. (2:32,4)

The Church does nothing by angelic invocations or incantations or any evil art. Her practice is to direct her prayers in a pure, sincere, and honest spirit to the Lord who made all things, calling on the name of our Lord Jesus Christ. That is the way the Church works miracles for humanity's advantage. She does not mislead them, for even now the name of our Lord Jesus Christ grants benefits to human beings and thoroughly and effectively cures, anywhere, all who believe in him. . . . From this, it can

---

5. Irenaeus here vigorously claims that the charismatic gifts were still found in the Church in his day. He clearly did not embrace the idea, later averred by some theologians, that these gifts were limited to the apostolic age and had ceased with the death of the last apostle.

readily be seen that, when he was made man, he had fellowship with his creation and did everything through the power of God, according to the will of the Father of all—as the prophets had foretold. (2:32,5)

...Each of us receives body and soul by the skillful working of God, for God is not so poor or destitute in resources that he cannot confer its own proper soul on each individual body, just as he gives it also its own special character. Therefore, when the number is completed—the number which he predetermined in his own counsel—all those who have been enrolled for eternal life will rise again, having their own bodies and their own souls and spirits, in which they had pleased God. On the other hand, those who deserve punishment will go away into it, they too having their own souls and their own bodies, in which they remained distant from the grace of God.... (2:33,5)

...God alone, who is Lord of all, is without beginning and without end, being truly and forever the same, and always remaining the same unchangeable being. But all things that proceed from him, everything that has been made and is made, has its own beginning. Consequently, they are inferior to him who formed them, since they are not unbegotten.... (2:34,2)

...Life does not arise from us, or from our own nature; it is granted by the grace of God. Therefore the one who takes care of the life received and gives thanks to him who imparted it will also receive everlasting life. But the one who rejects it and shows himself ungrateful toward his maker, since he has been created and has not recognized him who bestowed life, deprives himself of ongoing existence.... (2:34,3)

...This is why the prophetic word says about the first-formed, "The man became a living being" [Gen 2:7], teaching us that by participating in life the soul became alive. We must distinguish between the soul and the life it possesses. When God gives life, souls which did not previously exist receive life, which will endure from that time onwards, since God wills that they should exist and continue to do so.... (2:34,4)

The remainder of those who are falsely termed Gnostics, who maintain that the prophets uttered their prophecies under the inspiration of various gods, are easily overthrown by the fact that all the prophets proclaimed one God and Lord, the true maker of heaven and earth and everything in them. Further, the prophets announced the advent of his Son, as I shall demonstrate from the Scriptures themselves in the books which follow. (2:35,2)

The preaching of the apostles, the authoritative teaching of the Lord, the announcements of the prophets, the utterances dictated by the apostles, and the ministration of the law, all praise one and the same Being, the God and Father of all, and not many diverse beings or one deriving his substance from different gods or powers. They declare that all things—the visible and the invisible and everything that has been made—were made by one and the same Father. He adapted his works to the natures and potencies of the materials he used, but he did not rely on the help of angels or powers. He alone, God the Father, made them all.... (2:35,4)

BOOK 3 | *The Christian Faith, as Drawn from the Apostles' Teachings*

DEAR FRIEND, YOU ASKED me to expose the Valentinian teachings (which their devotees imagine to be concealed), show their disagreements, and compose a treatise refuting them. I have endeavored to present both their doctrine (which springs from Simon Magus, the father of all heretics) and the succession of their teachers, and to present arguments against them. To expose these heretics is enough to convict them; to help with that, I have sent you two books so far. The first comprises the opinions of all these heretics and shows what they practice and how they live; the second casts down and overthrows their perverse teachings simply by laying them bare and open to view.

In this third book, I will bring forward proofs from the Scriptures to supply more of what you request. Above and beyond what you counted on, you will receive the means of combating and defeating those who, in whatever way, are propagating falsehood. . . . All this will enable you to defend the only true and life-giving faith, which the Church has received from the apostles and imparted to her children. The Lord of all gave his apostles the power of the gospel, and we have come to know the truth through them. That truth is the teaching of the Son of God, who declared: "Whoever listens to you listens to me, and whoever rejects you rejects me, and whoever rejects me rejects the one who sent me" [Luke 10:16]. (3:pref)

We have learned the plan of our salvation from no one else than the ones through whom the gospel has come down to us. At first, they proclaimed it in public, but later on, in accordance with God's will, they handed it down to us in the Scriptures,[1] to be the ground and pillar of our faith [1 Tim 3:15]. It is unlawful to assert that they preached before they possessed "complete knowledge" ["gnosis"], as the heretics dare to say, who boast that they have improved on the apostles. After our Lord rose from the dead, the apostles received power from on high [Luke 24:49] when the Holy Spirit came down upon them [Acts 1:8], were filled with all his gifts, and thus received complete knowledge. They departed to the ends of the earth, preaching the glad tidings of the good things sent from God to us, and proclaiming the peace of heaven toward humankind [Luke 2:14]. They all equally and individually possessed the gospel of God. Matthew produced a written gospel for the Hebrews in their own language, while Peter and Paul were preaching at Rome, laying the foundations of the church there. After their departure, Mark, the disciple and interpreter of Peter, handed down to us in writing what Peter had preached. Luke also, the companion of Paul, recorded in a book the gospel Paul preached. Afterwards, John, the disciple of the Lord, who had leaned upon his breast [John 13:23], also published a gospel while he was living at Ephesus in Asia. (3:1,1)

These have all declared to us that there is one God, the creator of heaven and earth, announced by the law and the prophets, and one Christ the Son of God. If anyone does not agree to these truths, that person despises the companions of the Lord. Even more, that person despises Christ himself the Lord. Beyond even that, such a person also despises the Father and so stands self-condemned, resisting and opposing his own salvation—as is the case with all heretics. (3:1,2)

However, when these heretics are shown from the Scriptures to be in error, they respond by disparaging these same Scriptures, as if they were not correct, do not have authority, and are ambiguous. These false teachers urge that the truth cannot be extracted from them by anyone who is ignorant of tradition: they allege that the truth was not handed on by written documents, but orally. They claim that this is what Paul meant when he declared, "among the mature we do speak wisdom, though it is not a wisdom of this age" [1 Cor 2:6]. And this "wisdom" which each of them sets forth turns out to be the ideas he has dreamed up! . . . (3:2,1)

---

1. Irenaeus' formulation offers insight into how Christians viewed the relationship of Scripture and tradition in the late second century: he speaks of written Scripture as part of tradition (Greek, *paradosis*—that which is "handed down").

When we refer them to the tradition which originated from the apostles, which has been preserved through the succession of presbyters in the Churches, they object to tradition, claiming to be wiser—not merely than the presbyters, but even than the apostles—because they have discovered the unadulterated truth.... So it comes down to this, that these people will not yield, either to Scripture or to tradition. (3:2,2)

This is how the adversaries with whom we have to deal act: like slippery serpents, they try to escape at all points. Consequently, they need to be opposed at all points, so that possibly, by cutting off their retreat, we may succeed in turning them back to the truth. While it is not an easy thing for a soul under the influence of error to repent, yet, on the other hand, it is not altogether impossible to escape from error when the truth is brought alongside it. (3:2,3)

Everyone who wants to see the truth can behold the tradition of the apostles in any church anywhere in the world. We can list all those whom the apostles instituted as bishops in the churches, and the succession from them down to our own times. None of them taught or knew of anything like what these heretics rave about. If the apostles had known "hidden mysteries" which they were going to impart to "the perfect" apart and privately from the rest, the apostles would undoubtedly have delivered them to those to whom they were committing the churches. After all, they wanted these men whom they were leaving behind as their successors, to whom they were committing the leading role in governing the Church, to be perfect and blameless in all things.... (3:3,1)

However, it would be tedious to list the successions of all the churches in a volume like this. Even so, we can answer the heretics and their adherents by ... pointing to that tradition derived from the apostles which is found in the very great, very ancient, and universally known church founded and organized at Rome by the two most glorious apostles, Peter and Paul. The faith they preached to humanity has come down to our time through the successions of bishops. It is necessary for every church to agree with this church because of its significance: many faithful have traveled to Rome from all places and found there the apostolic tradition which has been preserved everywhere else also. (3:3,2)

Having founded and built up the church in Rome, the blessed apostles committed the office of bishop there into the hands of Linus. Paul mentions this Linus in his letters to Timothy [2 Tim 4:21]. Anacletus succeeded him; and next, in the third place from the apostles, Clement received the bishopric. He had seen the blessed apostles and conversed with them, so he might be said to have the preaching of the apostles still echoing in his ears and their traditions before his eyes. He was not alone in this: many were still alive who had been taught by the apostles. In Clement's time, a serious conflict arose in the church at Corinth; the church in Rome sent a vigorous letter to the Corinthians,[2] exhorting them to peace and renewing their faith by declaring again the tradition which it had recently received from the apostles. That apostolic tradition proclaims that there is one God Almighty, the maker of heaven and earth, the creator of humankind, who sent the flood, who called Abraham, who led the people from the land of Egypt, who spoke with Moses and gave the law, who sent the prophets, and who has prepared fire for the devil and his angels. Whoever wants to may learn from this letter that the Father of our Lord Jesus Christ was preached by the churches; that person can then understand the apostolic tradition of the Church, since this letter is older than these heretics who are now propagating falsehood and who conjure into existence another god besides the creator and maker of all things. After Clement came Evaristus; Alexander followed Evaristus. Then, sixth from the apostles, Sixtus was appointed; after him, Telephorus, who was gloriously martyred; then Hyginus; after him, Pius; then after him, Anicetus. Soter having succeeded Anicetus, Eleutherus—in the twelfth place from the apostles—now has the inheritance of the episcopate.[3] In this order and via this succession, the ecclesiastical tradition from the apostles, the preaching of the genuine truth, has come down to us. This is most abundant proof that there is one and the same life-giving faith, which has been handed down and faithfully preserved in the Church from the apostles until now. (3:3,3)

Further, Polycarp was instructed by apostles and conversed with many who had seen Christ; the apostles in Asia appointed him bishop of the church in Smyrna. I saw him in my early youth, for he lived a long time. As a very old man, he endured a glorious and noble martyrdom and departed this life.[4] He had always taught what he had learned

2. Formerly known as "1 Clement," this document is now commonly referred to as "The Letter of the Romans to the Corinthians," written c. 95 CE; it is available in *AposFrs* 28–101.

3. Since Eleutherus served as bishop of Rome from 174 to 189, this helps date the composition of (at least the first three books of) *AH*.

4. Irenaeus is referring to what is reported in "The Martyrdom of Polycarp," available in *AposFrs* 226–45.

from the apostles—which is what the Church has handed down, and which alone is true. All the Asiatic churches testify to these things, as do those who have succeeded Polycarp down to the present time. They are leaders of much greater significance and are more steadfast witnesses of truth than Valentinus, Marcion, and the rest of the heretics. Indeed, Polycarp came to Rome in the time of Anicetus and turned many people away from these heretics to the Church of God. He declared that he had received only one truth from the apostles—the one handed down by the Church.

Some also heard from him that when John, the disciple of the Lord, went to the baths at Ephesus but discovered that Cerinthus was there, he rushed out of the bathhouse without bathing, exclaiming, "Let us flee, in case the bathhouse falls down, because Cerinthus, the enemy of the truth, is inside it." On another occasion, Marcion met Polycarp and asked, "Do you know who I am?" Polycarp responded, "I know who you are: you are the first-born of Satan!" These stories reveal the determination of the apostles and those who had learned from them not even to interact with those who corrupt the truth. This squares with what Paul instructs, "After a first and second admonition, have nothing more to do with anyone who causes divisions, since you know that such a person is perverted and sinful, being self-condemned" [Titus 3:10].

There is also a very powerful letter of Polycarp written to the Philippians,[5] from which those who are eager to learn about salvation can get to know the character of his faith and the preaching of the truth. Furthermore, the church in Ephesus, founded by Paul, among whom John remained until the times of Trajan, is a faithful witness of the tradition of the apostles. (3:3,4)

Since we have such proofs, we do not need to seek from others the truth which is easy to get from the Church: the apostles, like a rich man depositing his wealth in a bank, placed everything related to the truth in her hands, so that whoever wants to can draw the water of life out of her [Rev 22:17]. She is the door to life; all others are thieves and robbers [John 10:7–8]. Consequently, we should turn away from the heretics and be sure to turn to the Church, so that we may lay hold of the tradition of the truth. . . .

---

5. Irenaeus refers to "The Letter of Polycarp to the Philippians," available in *AposFrs* 206–21.

What would we do if the apostles had not left us writings? Would it not be necessary, in that case, to follow the course of the tradition which they handed down to those to whom they committed the churches? (3:4,1)

This is what the numerous barbarian nations who believe in Christ do. Salvation has been written in their hearts by the Spirit, without paper or ink, but they carefully preserve the ancient tradition—believing in one God, the creator of heaven and earth, and everything in them, through Christ Jesus, the Son of God; who, because of his surpassing love towards his creation, condescended to be born of the virgin, thus uniting humanity in himself to God; having suffered under Pontius Pilate, and rising again, and having been received up in splendor, he will come again in glory as the savior of those who are saved and the judge of those who are judged, and will send into eternal fire those who pervert the truth and despise his Father and his advent.

As regards our language, those who have believed this faith without recourse to written documents are barbarians, but as regards doctrine, manner, and tenor of life, they are very wise indeed because of faith: they please God, living their lives in all righteousness, chastity, and wisdom. If anyone were to preach to them in their own language what the heretics have dreamed up, they would immediately stop their ears and run as far away as possible, unwilling even to listen to such blasphemy. Rooted in the ancient tradition of the apostles, they do not accept any of the instruction offered in the elegant diction of these teachers, among whom neither Church nor doctrine has ever taken root. (3:4,2)

Before Valentinus, none embraced his views; no one held notions like Marcion's before him; indeed, none of these perversely-minded heretics had a forerunner for his particular teaching.... All of them brought forward their apostasy much later, after the Church had already long been in existence. (3:4,3)

Since then the tradition from the apostles exists and is preserved in the Church, let us turn to the Scriptural proof furnished by the apostles who wrote the gospel, in which they recorded the doctrine about God, pointing out that our Lord Jesus Christ is the truth [John 14:6], and that no lie is found in him. . . . Since they were disciples of the truth, the apostles would not stoop to falsehood, for a lie has no fellowship with the truth, just as darkness has none with light [2 Cor 6:14]; one drives the other out.... (3:5,1)

... The apostles, who were commissioned to find those who were wandering, to be sight for those who could not see and medicine for the sick, did not just offer them their own ideas: they presented the truth that had been revealed to them.... They learned this approach from the Lord himself, who used to teach his disciples, healing those who were suffering and restraining sinners from sin. He did not tell them what would fit with the ideas they already held or would square with the views of those who asked him questions; without hypocrisy or respect of person, he proclaimed the doctrine that leads to salvation. (3:5,2)

This is clear from the words of the Lord, who genuinely revealed to the circumcision the Son of God, who had been foretold as Christ by their prophets. He presented himself as the one who had restored liberty to humankind and granted them incorruption as an inheritance. As well, the apostles taught the Gentiles to turn aside from their wood and stone idols, which they imagined to be gods, and to worship the true God, who had created and made the entire human family, and who nourished, increased, strengthened, and preserved their lives by his creation [Acts 14:15, 17]. The apostles taught them to trust in his Son Jesus Christ, who redeemed us from apostasy with his own blood so that we could become a holy people [1 Pet 2:9]. They further declared that he will descend from heaven in his Father's power and judge all, and will abundantly bestow the good things of God on those who will have kept his commandments. He who appeared in these last times, the chief cornerstone, has gathered into one and united those who were far off and those who were near [Eph 2:17]—that is, the circumcision and the uncircumcision—enlarging Japheth, and placing him in the dwelling of Shem [Gen 9:27]. (3:5,3)

Neither the Lord, nor the Holy Spirit, nor the apostles would ever have called him God who was not God definitely and absolutely, unless he was truly God; nor would they have called anyone Lord except God the Father, who rules over all, and his Son, who has received dominion from his Father over all creation, as this passage has it: "The LORD says to my lord, 'Sit at my right hand until I make your enemies your footstool'" [Ps 110:1]. Here the Scripture presents the Father addressing the Son: he gave him the inheritance of the nations and subjected all his enemies to him. Since the Father is truly Lord and the Son truly Lord, the Holy Spirit has fitly designated them by the title of Lord.... (3:6,1)

No other is named as God or is called Lord except the one who is God and Lord of all, who also said to Moses, "I AM WHO I AM. Thus you shall say to the Israelites, 'I AM has sent me to you'" [Exod 3:14]; and his Son Jesus Christ our Lord, who makes those who believe in his name the children of God [John 1:12]. Further, the Son spoke to Moses and said, "I have come down to deliver them" [Exod 3:8], for he was the one who descended and ascended for the salvation of humanity [Eph 4:9,10]. God has been declared through the Son, who is in the Father and has the Father—the one who is—in himself. So, the Father bears witness to the Son, and the Son announces the Father. Isaiah also says, "You are my witnesses, says the LORD, and my servant whom I have chosen, so that you may know and believe me and understand that I am he" [Isa 43:10]. (3:6,2)

Therefore I also call upon you, LORD God of Abraham, Isaac, Jacob, and of Israel, the Father of our Lord Jesus Christ, who, in the abundance of your mercy have had favor towards us, that we may know you who made heaven and earth, who rules over all, who are the only and the true God, above whom there is no other God. By our Lord Jesus Christ, pour out the governing power of the Holy Spirit; grant to every reader of this book to know you, that you alone are God, to be strengthened in you, and to avoid every heretical, godless, and unfaithful teaching. (3:6,4)

. . . Nothing created can ever be compared to the Word of God by whom all things were made, who is our Lord Jesus Christ. (3:8,2)

John declared that all things—whether angels, archangels, thrones, or dominions—were both established and created by the one who is God over all, through his Word. When he had spoken of the Word of God as having been in the Father, he added, "All things came into being through him, and without him not one thing came into being" [John 1:3]. David also, when he had enumerated his praises, specifically included all that I have mentioned, both the heavens and all the powers in them: "He commanded and they were created; he spoke, and it came to be" [Pss 148:5; 33:9]. Whom did he thus command? The Word, no doubt: "By the word of the LORD, the heavens were made, and all their host by the breath of his mouth" [Ps. 33:6]. But David indicates that God himself made all things freely, just as he pleased: "Our God is in the heavens; he does whatever he pleases" [Ps 115:3]. The things established are distinct from the one who established them, and what has been made from the one who made it. He himself is uncreated, without beginning or end, and needs nothing. He is sufficient for himself, but he gives being to everything else. The things he made received their beginnings; whatever has a beginning, though, is also liable to dissolution, so it always needs the care of him who made all things. . . . (3:8,3)

It has already been demonstrated and will still further be clearly shown that neither the prophets, nor the apostles, nor the Lord Christ himself acknowledged any other Lord or God except the God and Lord supreme; that the prophets and the apostles confessed the Father and the Son, but called no other "God" and confessed no other as Lord; and that the Lord himself handed down to his disciples that the Father is the only God and Lord, that he alone is God and ruler of all. It is incumbent on us to follow their witness on this, if we are truly their disciples. . . . So, there is one and the same God, the Father of our Lord, who promised through the prophets that he would send his forerunner. He made his salvation (that is, his Word) visible to all flesh, by the Word himself becoming incarnate, so that in all things their king might become manifest. . . . (3:9,1)

. . . There is one and the same God, who was proclaimed by the prophets and announced by the gospel; and his Son, who was of the fruit of David's body (that is, of the virgin of the house of David) and was called Immanuel. Balaam prophesied about his star: "A star shall come out of Jacob, and a scepter shall rise out of Israel" [Num 24:17]. Matthew says that the Magi, coming from the east, declared, "We observed his star at its rising and have come to pay him homage" [Matt 2:2]; and that, having been led by the star to the house of Jacob to Immanuel, they showed who it was they worshiped by the gifts they offered. . . . (3:9,2)

Then, speaking of his baptism, Matthew said, "The heavens were opened to him and he saw the Spirit of God descending like a dove and alighting on him. And a voice from heaven said, 'This is my Son, the Beloved, with whom I am well pleased'" [Matt 3:16–17]. "Christ" did not descend on Jesus then, for Christ was not one and Jesus another. The Word of God—who is the savior of all, and the ruler of heaven and earth (Jesus, as I have already pointed out), who took flesh to himself and was anointed by the Spirit from the Father—was made Jesus Christ. As Isaiah said, "A shoot shall come out from the stump of Jesse, and a branch shall grow out of his roots. The spirit of the LORD shall rest on him, the spirit of wisdom and understanding, the spirit of counsel and might, the spirit of knowledge and the fear of the LORD. His delight shall be in the fear of the LORD. He shall not judge by what his eyes see, or decide by what his ears hear; but with righteousness he shall judge the poor, and decide with equity for the meek of the earth" [Isa 11:1–4]. Further, pointing out ahead of time that and why he would be anointed, Isaiah declared, "The Spirit of the Lord God is upon me, because the LORD has anointed me; he has sent me to bring good news to the oppressed, to bind up the brokenhearted, to proclaim liberty to the captives, and release to the prisoners; to proclaim the year of the LORD's favor, and the day of vengeance of our God; to comfort all who mourn" [Isa 61:1]. (3:9,3)

Speaking in reference to the angel, Luke said that Gabriel was sent by God and said to the virgin, "Do not be afraid, Mary, for you have found favor with God" [Luke 1:30]. Concerning the Lord, he said, "He will be great, and will be called the Son of the Most High, and the Lord God will give to him the throne of his ancestor David. He will reign over the house of Jacob forever, and of his kingdom there will be no end" [Luke 1:32–33]. Who else is there who can reign over the house of Jacob forever, except Jesus Christ our Lord, the Son of the Most High God, who promised by the law and the prophets that he would make his salvation known to all flesh?

He became the Son of man for this purpose, that humans also might become the children of God. . . . With his incarnation everything entered a new phase. The Word arranged his coming in the flesh in a unique way, so that he might win back to God that human nature which had departed from God. . . . (3:10,2)

. . . The angels' exclamation, "Glory to God in the highest heaven, and on earth peace" [Luke 2:14], glorified him who is the creator of the highest (that is, of super-celestial beings) and the maker of everything on earth, who has sent the blessing of his salvation from heaven to his own handiwork (that is, to human beings). . . . (3:10,3)

. . . John, the disciple of the Lord, desiring to put an end to all false teaching and to establish the rule of truth in the Church, taught that there is one almighty God who made all things, both visible and invisible, by his Word—showing at the same time that by the Word, through whom God made the creation, he also bestowed salvation on that humanity which was created. That is why John began his teaching in the gospel by declaring, "In the beginning was the Word, and the Word was with God, and the Word was God. He was in the beginning with God. All things came into being through him, and without him not one thing came into being. What has come into being in him was life, and the life was the light of all people. The light shines in the darkness, and the darkness did not overcome it" [John 1:1–5]. He says, "all things," which includes this creation of ours. (3:11,1)

. . . But none of the heretics believe that the Word of God became flesh. If anyone carefully examines all their systems, that person will find that all of them teach that the Word of God did not become incarnate. . . . Some teach that "Christ" seemed to be human, but that he was not really born and did not become flesh. Some others hold that he did not assume a human form at all, but that, like a dove, he descended upon that Jesus who was born from Mary. But the Lord's disciple exposed them all as false witnesses when he said, "The Word became flesh and lived among us" [John 1:14]. (3:11,3)

These are the first principles of the gospel—that there is one God, the maker of this universe, who was proclaimed by the prophets and who through Moses brought in the law, which proclaims the Father of our Lord Jesus Christ and acknowledges no other God or Father except him. . . . (3:11,7)

It is not possible for the gospels to be either more or fewer in number than they are. Since there are four zones of the world in which we live, and four principal winds, and since the Church has spread throughout the whole world, and since the "pillar and bulwark" [1 Tim 3:15] of the Church is the gospel and the Spirit of life, it is fitting that she has four pillars, breathing out immortality in all directions and giving new life to humankind. From this it is evident that the Word, the artificer of all, who sits enthroned upon the cherubim [Ps 80:1; cf. Exod 25:17–22] and contains all things, who was manifested to humanity, has given us the gospel under four viewpoints, which are nonetheless bound together by one Spirit. . . . As the Scripture says, "The first living creature [was] like a lion," symbolizing his ability to achieve his purposes, leadership, and royal power; "the second living creature like an ox," signifying his sacrificial and sacerdotal order; but "the third living creature with a face like a human face," a significant description of his advent as a human being; "and the fourth living creature like a flying eagle" [Rev 4:7], pointing out the gift of the Spirit hovering with his wings over the Church.

The gospels we have comport with these descriptions. John tells of his original, effectual, and glorious generation from the Father, declaring: "In the beginning was the Word, and the Word was with God, and the

Word was God" [John 1:1]; also, "All things came into being through him, and without him not one thing came into being" [John 1:3]. This is also why his gospel is full of confidence, for that is who he was. Luke focuses on his priestly character: he begins his gospel with Zechariah the priest offering sacrifice to God—for now the fatted calf is ready, which will be sacrificed in order to bring the younger son home [cf. Luke 15:11–32]. For his part, Matthew declares his generation as a man, beginning his gospel with "An account of the genealogy of Jesus the Christ, the son of David, the son of Abraham" [Matt 1:1], and "Now the birth of Jesus the Christ took place in this way" [Matt 1:18]. His is the gospel of his humanity. . . . Mark, on the other hand, begins with the prophetical spirit coming down from on high to people: "The beginning of the good news of Jesus Christ, the Son of God, as it is written in the prophet Isaiah" [Mark 1:1–2[6]]. . . . That is why he offers a condensed, running narrative, for that is characteristic of the prophets.

The Word of God himself used to speak with the patriarchs before Moses' time, in ways suited to his divinity and glory, but for those under the law he set up the priestly and liturgical service. Afterwards, when he became human for us, he poured out the gift of the heavenly Spirit over all the earth, protecting us with his wings. The way the Son of God took was the pattern for the living creatures, and the respective living creatures manifested the character of each gospel.

The living creatures are four in number, as are the gospels. This is the way the Lord arranged things. There were four principal covenants given to the human race: one, before the flood, was with Adam; the second, after the flood, came under Noah; the third was the giving of the law through Moses; and the fourth renews human beings and repristinates all things in itself through the gospel, raising and carrying human beings on its wings into the heavenly kingdom. (3:11,8)

. . . The followers of Valentinus are utterly reckless. They put forth their own fantasies, boasting that they possess more gospels than there really are. Indeed, they have arrived at such a pitch of audacity as to entitle the writing they have recently compiled "The Gospel of Truth,"[7] although it does not agree with the gospels of the apostles in anything. The result is that they really have no gospel which is not full of blas-

6. The punctuation of the NRSV has here been adjusted to accommodate Irenaeus' point.

7. This was the title of a Gnostic gospel; it is available in *GS* 253–64.

phemy. For if what they have published is the gospel of *truth*, but it is utterly unlike those handed down to us from the apostles, then some may decide that what has been handed down from the apostles can no longer be reckoned the true gospel. But I have proved by numerous arguments that the apostolic gospels alone are true and reliable, and that their number can be neither increased nor decreased. Since God "made all things by measure" [Wis 11:20] to work together, it was fitting that the emphases of the gospels should also be well arranged, in harmony with each other. . . . (3:11,9)

. . . The apostles preached faith in him to the Jews who did not believe on the Son of God. From the prophets, the apostles declared that the Christ whom God had promised to send he had sent in Jesus, the one whom they crucified and God raised up [Acts 2:36]. (3:12,2)

. . . Peter, along with John, preached to them this straightforward message of good news, that the promise which God had made to the fathers had been fulfilled in Jesus. They certainly did not proclaim some other god; they preached the Son of God, who was made human and suffered. In this way they led Israel into knowledge, preaching the resurrection of the dead through Jesus [Acts 4:2], showing that God had fulfilled whatever the prophets had proclaimed about the suffering of Christ. (3:12,3)

. . . These are the voices of the Church from which every church had its origin. These are the founding voices of the great city composed of the citizens of the new covenant. These are the voices of the apostles. These are voices of the disciples of the Lord, the truly "perfect," who, after the Lord had ascended into heaven, were perfected by the Spirit and called upon the God who made heaven and earth and the sea— as was announced by the prophets—and Jesus Christ his Son, whom God anointed. They knew no other [God]. . . . "With great power," it was added, "the apostles gave their testimony to the resurrection of the Lord Jesus" [Acts 4:33], saying to them, "The God of our ancestors raised up Jesus, whom you had killed by hanging him on a tree. God exalted him at his right hand as Leader and Savior that he might give repentance to Israel and forgiveness of sins. And we are witnesses to these things, and so is the Holy Spirit whom God has given to those who obey him" [Acts 5:30–32]. "And every day," it is said, "in the temple and at home they did not cease to teach and proclaim Jesus as the Christ" [Acts 5:42], the

Son of God. This was the knowledge of salvation, by which those who acknowledge his Son's advent became "complete" in God's sight. (3:12,5)

... According to what the heretics teach, nobody can have the rule of truth. Anyone who has received their instruction will remember that their teachers adjusted what they said to the way each person thought, depending on his capabilities. But the advent of the Lord would have been superfluous and without purpose, if he came intending to accept and maintain whatever ideas about God people had grown up with. It was a much more difficult challenge to preach that the one whom the Jews had seen as a man, and had fastened to the cross, was Christ the Son of God, their eternal king.... The apostles did not speak to the Gentiles in conformity with their notions, but told them with boldness that their gods were not gods, but the idols of demons [1 Cor 10:19–20; cf. Ps 96:5]. ... Thus they pushed aside what were no gods and turned their hearers to the one who alone is God, the true Father. (3:12,6)

We can understand what the apostles used to proclaim, the nature of their preaching, and their idea about God from the words which Peter spoke in Caesarea to Cornelius the centurion and the Gentiles who were with him.... Peter saw the vision in which the voice from heaven said to him, "What God has made clean, you must not call profane" [Acts 10:15]. This happened to teach him that the God who in the law had distinguished between clean and unclean had purified the Gentiles through the blood of his Son, the very one whom Cornelius worshiped....

The apostles preached the Son of God about whom people were ignorant, and his coming to those who had already been instructed about God.... It is clear from Peter's words that he proclaimed to them the God whom they already knew, but he also testified to them that Jesus Christ was the Son of God, the judge of the living and the dead. He commanded them to be baptized into him for the remission of sins. He also witnessed that Jesus was himself the Son of God, who, having been anointed with the Holy Spirit, is called Jesus Christ.... Throughout the world, the entire Church, firmly rooted in the apostles' teaching, perseveres in the very same conviction about God and his Son. (3:12,7)

... This is the mystery which Paul says was made known to him by revelation [Eph 3:3], that he who suffered under Pontius Pilate is Lord of all, king, God, and judge, and that he has received power from him who is the God of all, because he "became obedient to the point of death— even death on a cross" [Phil 2:8].... (3:12,9)

Those who so wish may consult the very words and acts of the apostles and can see for themselves that the whole range of the doctrine of the apostles proclaimed one and the same God, who led Abraham from his homeland and promised him an inheritance; in due course, this same God gave him the covenant of circumcision. Later, this same God called out of Egypt his descendants, who had been outwardly preserved by circumcision, which he had given as a sign so that they might not be like the Egyptians. The apostles preached that he was the maker of all things, the Father of our Lord Jesus Christ, and the God of glory. This God is one, with no other above him. . . . The Mosaic law and the grace of the new covenant, each fitted appropriately for their respective times, were granted by one and the same God for the benefit of humanity. (3:12,11)

Some people of perverse mind have repudiated the Mosaic legislation because they adjudge it different from and opposed to the teaching of the gospel, but they have not carefully examined why each covenant is different. . . . In what remains in this work[8] I will deal with the reasons for the difference between the covenants, on the one hand, and, on the other, show their unity and harmony. (3:12,12)

Both the apostles and their disciples taught as the Church preaches. . . . The apostles preached to the Jews that the Jesus whom they had crucified was the Son of God, the judge of the living and the dead, and that he received from his Father an eternal kingdom in Israel. To the Greeks they preached one God, who made everything, and Jesus Christ his Son. (3:12,13)

Luke tells us, not in boasting but as one bound by the truth, that he was closely associated with Paul as his fellow laborer in the Gospel (3:14,1). . . . Through Luke we have become acquainted with many important parts of the gospel—for instance, the generation of John, the history of Zechariah, the coming of the angel to Mary, the exclamation of Elizabeth, the descent of the angels to the shepherds, the message they brought, the testimony of Anna and of Simeon about Christ, and that at twelve years of age he was left behind at Jerusalem, as well as the baptism of John, how old the Lord was when he was baptized, and that this occurred in the fifteenth year of Tiberius Caesar. . . . Besides all these, he records what Christ said to his disciples after the resurrection, and that they recognized him in the breaking of the bread. (3:14,3)

8. Irenaeus refers here to this third book of *AH*.

... The heretics wander from the truth, because their teaching departs from the one who is the true God. They do not believe that his only-begotten Word—who is always present with the human race, who was united to and mingled with his own creation, according to the Father's pleasure, and became flesh—is himself Jesus Christ our Lord, who suffered for us and rose again on our behalf, and who will come again in his Father's glory to resurrect all who have lived, to show his salvation, and to judge with consummate justice everything he has made. ... In every respect, he is human, the formation of God: he took humanity into himself, the invisible becoming visible, the incomprehensible being made comprehensible, the impassible becoming capable of suffering, and the Word being made human, thus summing up all things in himself. So, just as in super-celestial, spiritual, and invisible things, the Word of God is supreme, so also in things visible and corporeal he possesses the supremacy. He has taken to himself the pre-eminence and has constituted himself head of the Church, in order to draw all things to himself at the proper time [Col 1:15–20]. (3:16,6)

With him nothing is incomplete or at the wrong time, as with the Father nothing is incongruous. The Father foreknew all these things, and the Son accomplished them at the proper time, in the proper order. ... As Paul says, "When the fulness of time had come, God sent his Son" [Gal 4:4]. Our Lord accomplished all that had been foreknown by the Father in the appointed and fitting order, season, and hour. ... He accomplishes the overarching and all-embracing will of his Father, for he himself is the savior of those who are saved and the Lord of those who are under authority. He is the God of everything that has been made, the only-begotten of the Father, the Christ who was announced, and the Word of God who became incarnate when the fulness of time had come—when the Son of God had to become the son of man. (3:16,7)

Consequently, no one can be accepted as a Christian who, pretending to great insight, teaches that Jesus was one, but Christ was another, and the only-begotten still another (from whom again is the Word), and that the savior is yet another—who these disciples of error claim were produced by those who, in a degenerate state, were made Aeons. Outwardly, such people seem to be sheep: in what they publicly say, they sound like us, for they use many of the same words we do. But inwardly they are wolves. Their doctrine is homicidal: it conjures up a number of gods, multiplies Fathers, and demeans (and divides!) the Son of God in many ways. These are the ones against whom the Lord warned us ahead of time, and his disciple, in his letter, commands us to avoid them: "Many deceivers have gone out into the world, those who do not confess that Jesus Christ has come in the flesh; any such person is the deceiver and the antichrist! Be on your guard, so that you do not lose what we have worked for" [2 John 7–8]. He also says, "Many false prophets have gone out into the world. By this you know the Spirit of God: every spirit that confesses that Jesus Christ has come in the flesh is from God, and every spirit that does not confess Jesus is not from God. And this is the spirit of the antichrist" [1 John 4:1–3]. (3:16,8)

...Giving to the disciples the power of regeneration into God, Christ said to them, "Go therefore and make disciples of all nations, baptizing them in the name of the Father and of the Son and of the Holy Spirit" [Matt 28:19]. God had promised that in the last times he would pour the Spirit upon servants and handmaids, so that they would prophesy [Joel 2:28]. That is why the Spirit descended on the Son of God made the son of man: by fellowship with him, the Spirit became accustomed to living in the human race, resting upon human beings, and dwelling in the handiwork of God, in order to accomplish the will of the Father in them and renew them from their old habits into the newness of Christ. (3:17,1)

David asked for this Spirit: "Sustain in me a willing spirit" [Ps 51:12]. As Luke says, after the Lord's ascension, the Spirit descended upon the disciples on the day of Pentecost, giving them power to admit all nations into life and to open the new covenant to them. This is why the disciples praised God with one accord in all languages [Acts 2:4–6,11]: the Spirit thus brought distant tribes to unity and offered to the Father the first-fruits of all nations. This is also why the Lord promised to send the helper [John 16:7] who would join us to God. . . . As dry earth does not produce unless it receives moisture, so we, like dry trees, could never have brought forth fruit unto life without the rain he freely poured out from above. Our bodies have been united through the washing which leads to incorruption, but our souls have been united by the Spirit. . . . The Lord, receiving the Spirit as a gift from his Father, grants it to those who partake of him, sending the Holy Spirit upon all the earth. (3:17,2)

The Spirit descended at the appointed time, and the Son of God, the only-begotten, who is also the Word of the Father, came in the fulness of time, becoming incarnate for the sake of humankind. He became fully human while remaining one and the same, as the Lord himself testifies, the apostles confess, and the prophets announce.... (3:17,4)

Since it has now been clearly demonstrated that the Word, who existed in the beginning with God, by whom all things were made [John 1:1, 3], who was also always present with humanity, was in these last days, at the time appointed by the Father, united to his own workmanship, since he became a human being subject to suffering, it follows that every objection is set aside of those who say, "If our Lord was born at that time, then Christ had no previous existence." I have already shown that the Son of God did not then begin to exist, since he was with the Father from the beginning. When he became incarnate and was made human, he began anew the long line of human beings and, to state it briefly, furnished us with salvation. Consequently, what we had lost in Adam—namely, the image and likeness of God—we recovered in Christ Jesus. (3:18,1)

It was impossible that those who had once for all been conquered, and who had been destroyed through disobedience, could reform themselves and grasp the prize of victory. It was impossible that those who had fallen under the power of sin could attain salvation. So the Son accomplished both these things. As the Word of God he descended from the Father, became incarnate, humbled himself, even to death [Phil 2:8], and fulfilled the plan of our salvation. Paul does not hesitate to exhort us to believe this when he urges, "Who will ascend into heaven? (that is, to bring Christ down) or who will descend into the abyss? (that is, to bring Christ up from the dead)" [Rom 10:6–7]. Then he continues, "If you confess with your lips that Jesus is Lord and believe in your heart that God raised him from the dead, you will be saved" [Rom 10:9]. He tells us why the Son of God did these things: "For to this end Christ died and lived again, so that he might be Lord of both the dead and the living" [Rom 14:9]. Further, writing to the Corinthians, he declares, "But we proclaim Christ crucified" [1 Cor 1:23], and he adds, "The cup of blessing that we bless, is it not a sharing in the blood of Christ?" [1 Cor 10:16]. (3:18,2)

But who is it, then, that has had fellowship with us in the matter of food? ... He is the one preached by Paul: "I handed on to you as of first importance what I in turn had received: that Christ died for our sins in accordance with the Scriptures, and that he was buried, and that he was raised on the third day in accordance with the Scriptures"

[1 Cor 15:3–4]. It is clear that Paul knew no other Christ except the one who suffered and was buried and rose again, who also had been, and of whom he speaks as, human. For after remarking, "Now if Christ is proclaimed as raised" [1 Cor 15:12], he continues, offering the reason for his incarnation: "for since death came through a human being, the resurrection of the dead has also come through a human being" [1 Cor 15:21].

Every time he refers to the passion of our Lord, to his human nature, or to his subjection to death, he uses the name of Christ: "Do not let what you eat cause the ruin of one for whom Christ died" [Rom 14:15]; and again, "But now in Christ Jesus you who once were far off have been brought near by the blood of Christ" [Eph 2:13]; and again, "Christ redeemed us from the curse of the law by becoming a curse for us—for it is written, 'Cursed is everyone who hangs on a tree'" [Gal 3:13; cf. Deut 21:23]; and again, "So by your knowledge those weak believers for whom Christ died are destroyed" [1 Cor 8:11]. This clearly shows that a Christ who could not suffer did not descend upon Jesus, but that he himself, because he was Jesus Christ, suffered for us. He who lay in the tomb and rose again, who descended and ascended, was the Son of God who had been made the son of man, as the name itself indicates.

The title "Christ" implies the one who anoints, the one who is anointed, and the anointing itself with which he is anointed. It is the Father who anoints, but the Son is anointed by the Spirit, who is the anointing, as the Word declares through Isaiah, "The Spirit of the Lord God is upon me, because the Lord has anointed me" [Isa 61:1]: this points out the anointing Father, the anointed Son, and the anointing which is the Spirit. (3:18,3)

. . . As man contending for humanity, the Lord fought and conquered. Through obedience he completely did away with disobedience: he bound the strong man [Matt 12:29], set the weak free, and granted salvation to his own handiwork by destroying sin. He is a most holy and merciful Lord, and he loves humanity. (3:18,6)

He caused human nature to cleave to and become one with God. On the one hand, unless a human being had overcome the enemy of humanity, the enemy would not have been justly defeated. On the other hand, unless it had been God who had freely given salvation, we could never have possessed it securely. Unless humanity had been joined to God, humanity could never have become a partaker of incorruptibility. So, it was incumbent upon the mediator between God and men [1 Tim 2:5], via his relationship to both, to bring them to friendship and peace, and so to present humankind to God, while revealing God to humankind. . . .

This is also why he passed through every stage of life, restoring all of them to communion with God. . . . It behooved him who was to destroy sin and redeem humankind under the power of death to be made human, for humanity had been drawn by sin into bondage and was held by death, so that sin should be destroyed by man, and humankind should be delivered from death. For as by the disobedience of the one man who was originally molded from virgin soil, many were made sinners and forfeited life, so it was necessary that, by the obedience of one man, who was originally born from a virgin, many should be justified [Rom 5:19] and receive salvation. . . . What he appeared to be he also was: God recapitulated in himself the ancient formation of man, so that he might kill sin, deprive death of its power, and give life again to humankind. His works are sure. (3:18,7)

. . . Since the heretics refuse to know him who from the virgin is Immanuel, they are deprived of his gift, which is eternal life [Rom 6:23]. Since they do not receive the incorruptible Word, they remain in mortal flesh and are debtors to death, for they do not obtain the antidote of life. . . . Those who despise the incarnation of the Word of God rob human nature of its exaltation unto God and show themselves ungrateful to the Word of God, who became flesh for them. This was why the Word of God was made human, and he who was the Son of God became the son of man—that human beings, taken into the Word and receiving adoption, might become the children of God.

By no other means could we have attained incorruptibility and immortality, unless we had been united to incorruptibility and immortality. How could we be joined to incorruptibility and immortality unless incorruptibility and immortality had first become what we are, so that the corruptible might be swallowed up by incorruptibility, and the mortal by immortality [1 Cor 15:53], so that we might receive adoption as children [Gal 4:5]? (3:19,1)

. . . Even those who have attained only a small portion of the truth understand that he is utterly unique, for he is God and Lord and king eternal and the incarnate Word—as proclaimed by all the prophets, the apostles, and by the Spirit himself. The Scriptures would not have declared these things about him if he had only been a human being like others. But the divine Scriptures testify that, beyond all others, he who had a pre-eminent birth from the Most High Father also experienced a pre-eminent birth from the virgin [Isa 7:14]. They also declare that he was a man without beauty who would experience suffering [Isa 53:2–3]; that he sat upon the foal of a donkey [Matt 21:5; Zech 9:9]; that he received sour wine to drink [Matt 27:48; Ps 69:21]; that he was despised among the people [Isa 53:3]; that he humbled himself even to death [Phil 2:8]; and that he is the holy Lord, the Wonderful Counselor, the beautiful in appearance, and the Mighty God [Isa 9:6], the one coming on the clouds as the judge of all [Dan 7:13]. (3:19,2)

As he became human to experience temptation, so also he was the Word who is glorified. The Word remained quiescent, so that he could be tempted, dishonored, crucified, and suffer death, but the human nature was borne along by the divine nature when it conquered, endured, performed acts of kindness, rose again, and was received up into heaven. The Son of God, our Lord, being the Word of the Father was also the son of man, since he was born according to his human nature from a human being, Mary. The Lord himself gave us a sign of this, which no one asked for in the depth below or in the height above [Isa 7:11]: no one expected that a virgin could conceive, or that it was possible for one who remained a virgin to bring forth a son, so that what was thus born should be "God with us" [Isa 7:14]. He thus descended to the earth below, seeking the sheep which had perished (that is, his own peculiar handiwork), and ascended to the height above, offering and commending to his Father that human nature which had been found. In himself he became the first-fruits of the resurrection of humankind, so that, just as the head rose from the dead, so also the remaining parts of the body—that is, everyone who receives eternal life—may arise when the time of that judgment which came because of disobedience has arrived. . . . (3:19,3)

God showed himself long-suffering when humanity failed him, since God foresaw the victory which the Word would achieve for him. When strength was made perfect in weakness [2 Cor 12:9], it showed the kindness and transcendent power of God. In his patience, God allowed Jonah to be swallowed by the whale. His purpose was not that Jonah would be consumed and perish, but that, having been vomited up, he might be subject to God and glorify him more who had granted him such an unanticipated deliverance, and so might bring the Ninevites to a lasting repentance. This would result in their being converted to the Lord, who would deliver them from death, since they would be struck with awe by the portent which had been wrought in Jonah's case, as the Scripture says that the king of Nineveh proclaimed: "All shall turn from their evil ways and from the violence that is in their hands. Who knows? God may relent and change his mind: he may turn from his fierce anger, so that we do not perish" [Jonah 3:8–9].

In the same way, from the beginning, God permitted humanity to be swallowed up by the great whale, who was the author of transgression, but not so that humankind should perish altogether when so engulfed. God arranged and prepared the plan of salvation, which was accomplished by the Word through the sign of Jonah for those like Jonah who submit to the Lord and confess themselves to be his servants, saying, "I worship the LORD, the God of heaven, who made the sea and the dry land" [Jonah 1:9]. Thus, humankind would receive an unexpected salvation from God, rise from the dead, glorify God, and repeat the word uttered in prophecy by Jonah: "I called to the LORD out of my distress, and he answered me; out of the belly of Sheol I cried, and you heard my voice" [Jonah 2:2]. For this, humankind would forever glorify God and give thanks without ceasing for that salvation which he has bestowed, "so that no one might boast in the presence of God" [1 Cor 1:29]. . . . (3:20,1)

This was God's purpose: that humanity, enduring all things and acquiring the knowledge of death, and then attaining the resurrection from the dead and learning by experience who is the source of his deliverance, might always live in a state of gratitude to the Lord for the gift of incorruptibility. Thus, humankind should come to love God more, for the one to whom more is forgiven, loves more [Luke 7:41–43]. Human beings should recognize how weak and mortal they are; they should thus come to understand that God is immortal and so powerful that he can confer immortality on what is mortal and eternity on what is temporal. Then they should also appreciate the other attributes of God and think of him in accordance with his divine greatness. . . . The Word of God lived among us and became the son of man, so that he might accustom humankind to receive God, and God to dwell in humanity, as the Father intended. (3:20,2)

Consequently, the Lord himself, who is Immanuel from the virgin [Isa 7:14], is the sign of our salvation: the Lord himself saved them, because they could not be saved by their own efforts. Therefore, when Paul emphasizes human infirmity, he says, "I know that nothing good dwells within me" [Rom 7:18], showing that the "good" of our salvation is not from us, but from God. He also declares, "Wretched man that I am! Who will rescue me from this body of death?" [Rom 7:24]. Then he introduces the deliverer: "Thanks be to God through Jesus Christ our Lord!" [Rom 7:25]. Isaiah makes the same point when he says, "Strengthen the weak hands, and make firm the feeble knees. Say to those who are of a fearful heart, 'Be strong, do not fear! Here is your God. He will come with vengeance, with terrible recompense. He will come and save you'" [Isa 35:3–4]. Here we see that we must be saved, not by ourselves, but by the help of God. (3:20,3)

So God became human, and the Lord himself saved us, giving us the sign of the virgin. This should not be understood as some now presume to expound the Scripture: "Behold, *a young woman*"—not "*a virgin*"—"shall conceive, and bear a son" [Isa 7:14], as Theodotion the Ephesian, Aquila of Pontus, and some Jewish proselytes have translated the verse. . . . This prediction was uttered before the people were deported to Babylon, before the Medes and Persians came to power. It was translated into Greek by the Jews themselves as "*a virgin*"[9] long before our Lord's advent. . . . (3:21,1)

Before the Romans developed their empire, while the Macedonians still held Asia, Ptolemy the son of Lagus, eager to adorn the library which he had founded in Alexandria with a collection of the valuable writings of all sorts of people, requested that the people of Jerusalem translate their Scriptures into the Greek language.[10] At that time, they were still subject to the Macedonians, and so they sent to Ptolemy seventy of their elders, who were thoroughly skilled in the Scriptures and in both languages, to fulfill his desire. However, he wanted to test them individually, since he was concerned that they might consult with each other and conceal the truth in the Scriptures by their translation, so he separated them from each other and commanded them all to produce the identical translation. He did this with respect to all the books. When they had completed

9. Here Irenaeus embarks on a defence of the Greek translation of Isa 7:14 as found in the Septuagint (LXX). The Hebrew word *almah* means "young woman," without indication whether she was a virgin or not; the LXX translated the Hebrew term with the Greek *parthenos*, which means "virgin."

10. Irenaeus is summarizing the relevant sections of "The Letter of Aristeas," which recounts the story; it is available in *OTP* 12–34.

their work and assembled before him, each of them compared his translation with that of all the others. God was glorified and the Scriptures were acknowledged as truly divine, for all of them read out a common translation, which each had prepared, in the identical words and the very same names, from beginning to end—so that even the Gentiles present perceived that the Hebrew Scriptures had been translated into Greek by the inspiration of God.... (3:21,2)

The Scriptures were translated with such fidelity by the grace of God. He has prepared and shaped our faith in his Son from them and has preserved the unadulterated Scriptures for us in Egypt—where the house of Jacob flourished long ago after fleeing from the famine in Canaan [Gen 46:5–7], and where our Lord also was preserved when he fled from Herod's persecution [Matt 2:13–15]. Since this translation of the Scriptures was made before our Lord's descent to earth and was produced before the Christians appeared (for our Lord was born about the forty-first year of the reign of Augustus, but Ptolemy, in whose time the Scriptures were translated, was much earlier), these men who would now try to translate the term differently are clearly shown to be impudent and presumptuous, especially when we refute them out of these Scriptures and push them toward a belief in the advent of the Son of God. Our faith is steadfast, unfeigned, and the only true one, clearly proven from these Scriptures, which were translated in the way I have related. The preaching of the Church is without interpolation: the apostles, who are more ancient than all the heretics, agree with the translation (as "a virgin"), and it harmonizes with the tradition of the apostles.... (3:21,3)

The one and only Spirit of God, who proclaimed the advent of the Lord, gave by these elders a proper translation of what had been truly prophesied. Through the apostles he announced that the fullness of time had come, that the kingdom of heaven had drawn near, and that he was dwelling within those who believe on him who was born Immanuel of the virgin.... (3:21,4)

... In this promise, Scripture excluded all male influence.... It stressed "the fruit of the womb," to declare that he would be from a virgin, as Elizabeth testified when filled with the Holy Spirit, saying to Mary, "Blessed are you among women, and blessed is the fruit of your womb" [Luke 1:42].... Those who alter the passage of Isaiah to say, "Behold, a young woman will conceive," will thus end up presenting him as Joseph's son.... (3:21,5)

. . . But when he said, "The Lord himself will give you a sign," he spoke about something unanticipated in regard to his conception, something which could be accomplished only by God the Lord of all. . . . What would have been remarkable, or what would have been the "sign," in a young woman conceiving by a man and having a child? That happens all the time. But since an unexpected salvation was to be provided through the work of God, so also was an unexpected birth from a virgin. God gave the sign and accomplished it without male involvement. (3:21,6)

Because of this, Daniel, foreseeing his advent, said that a stone, cut out without hands, came into this world [Dan 2:34]. This is what "without hands" means, that his coming into this world was not by the work of human hands (that is, of men who do stone cutting). Joseph had no part in it, except for cooperating with Mary in the pre-arranged plan. . . . (3:21,7)

For as by one man's disobedience sin entered, and death prevailed because of sin; so also the obedience of one man, since righteousness has been introduced, will bring life to those who before were dead [Rom 5:19]. The first-formed himself, Adam, received his substance from untilled and as yet virgin soil ("for the LORD God had not caused it to rain upon the earth, and there was no one to till the ground" [Gen 2:5]), and was formed by the hand of God (that is, by the Word of God, for "all things came into being through him" [John 1:3]), for the Lord took dust from the earth and formed man. The same was true of the Word, who recapitulated Adam in himself and received a genuine birth, so that he could gather up Adam into himself from Mary, who was still a virgin. If, then, the first Adam had a man for his father and was born of human seed, it would have been appropriate to say that the second Adam was begotten of Joseph. But if the former was taken from the dust and God was his maker, it was incumbent that the latter also, making a recapitulation in himself, should be formed as man by God himself, to have an analogy with the former as to his origin. . . . (3:21,10)

So, those who allege that he took nothing from the virgin[11] err greatly. . . . For if the one from the earth was formed and received his substance from the handiwork of God himself, but the other did not, then he who was made after the image and likeness of the former did not actually replicate what the first was. In that case, he would have to be viewed as an inconsistent piece of work, ill-suited to his task and calling.

---

11. Cf. 1:7,2 (above) and 3:22,2 (immediately below).

... If he did not receive the substance of flesh from a human being, he never became man or the son of man, and if he did not become what we were, what does it matter if he suffered and endured? Everyone will admit that we are bodies taken from the earth and souls receiving spirit from God. This is what the Word of God became, recapitulating his own handiwork in himself. . . . The apostle Paul, moreover, in the Letter to the Galatians, declares plainly, "God sent his Son, born of a woman" [Gal 4:4]. Again, in the Letter to the Romans, he writes of "his Son, who was descended from David according to the flesh and was declared to be the Son of God with power according to the spirit of holiness by the resurrection from the dead, Jesus Christ our Lord" [Rom 1:3–4]. (3:22,1)

By what the heretics teach, his descent into Mary would have been superfluous: why did he come down into her if he was going to take nothing from her? . . . (3:22,2)

In due course, Mary the virgin was found obedient, saying, "Here am I, the servant of the Lord; let it be with me according to your word" [Luke 1:38]. Eve had been disobedient, for she did not obey when she was still a virgin. (To be sure, she had a husband, Adam, but she was still a virgin. In paradise "the man and his wife were both naked, and were not ashamed" [Gen 2:25], since they had only been created a short time previously and at that point had no understanding of the procreation of children. It was necessary that they should first come to adult age, and then they would begin to multiply [Gen 1:28].) Becoming disobedient, Eve became the cause of death, both for herself and for the entire human race[12]; but Mary, engaged to a man but still a virgin, yielded obedience and so became the cause of salvation, both for herself and for the whole human race. . . .

The Lord, as "the first-born of the dead" [Rev 1:5], has embraced the ancients and regenerated them into the life of God, for he made himself the beginning of those that live, as Adam became the beginning of those who die [1 Cor 15:20–22]. This is why, in tracing the genealogy of the Lord, Luke carried it back to Adam [Luke 3:23–28], thus indicating that Jesus Christ was the one who regenerated them into the gospel of life, and not they him. This is also how the knot of Eve's disobedience was untied by the obedience of Mary: what the virgin Eve had bound fast through unbelief, the virgin Mary set free through faith. (3:22,4)

12. Here Irenaeus probably had in mind the declaration, "From a woman sin had its beginning, and because of her we all die" (Sir 25:24).

Consequently, it was necessary that the Lord, coming to his lost sheep, recapitulating human history, and seeking his own handiwork, should save the very man who had been created after his image and likeness (that is, Adam). The Lord fulfilled the period of condemnation which had been incurred through disobedience, the period "that the Father had set by his own authority" [Acts 1:7]. In this way, the entire economy of salvation for humankind came to pass according to the good pleasure of the Father, so that God might not be defeated nor his wisdom lessened in the estimation of his creatures. If humanity, created by God for life but injured by the tempting serpent, lost life and could not return to it but was utterly abandoned to death, then God would have been conquered, and the wickedness of the serpent would have prevailed over the will of God. . . . Promising that they should be "like God" [Gen 3:5]—something out of their reach—the serpent worked death in them. The one who had led humankind captive was justly captured in his turn by God, and humanity, which had been led captive, was released from the bonds of condemnation. (3:23,1)

This Adam was truly the first-formed man, about whom Scripture says that the Lord said, "Let us make humankind in our image, according to our likeness" [Gen 1:26]. We have all descended from him and have all inherited his title. But since humanity is saved in Jesus Christ, it is fitting that he who was created the original man was saved, as well. For it would be absurd to maintain that he who was so gravely injured by the enemy and was the first taken captive was not rescued by him who conquered the enemy, but that his descendants were whom he had begotten in that captivity. Further, the enemy would hardly have been conquered if the most ancient spoils had remained in his control. . . . (3:23,2)

After Adam transgressed, as Scripture relates, God pronounced no curse upon Adam, but upon the ground, which he was to work. . . . As the punishment of his transgression, man received the toilsome task of tilling the earth; in the sweat of his face, he would eat bread, and he would return to the dust from which he had been taken [Gen 3:17, 19]. Similarly, the woman received her share of toil—specifically, labor, groans, the pain of childbirth, and a state of subjection in which she would serve her husband [Gen 3:16]. In this way they would neither perish altogether under God's curse nor, if they had not been reprimanded, would they be led to despise God.

But the curse in all its fulness fell upon the serpent, which had beguiled them: "The LORD God said to the serpent, 'Because you have done this, cursed are you among all animals and among all wild creatures'" [Gen 3:14]. And the Lord says the same thing in the gospel to those who are found at his left hand: "You that are accursed, depart from me into the eternal fire prepared for the devil and his angels" [Matt 25:41]. In these words he indicated that eternal fire was not originally prepared for humanity, but for the one who beguiled humanity and caused them to sin—for the one who led the apostasy and for those angels who became apostate along with him. But those human beings will justly endure this fire who, like him, persevere in works of wickedness, without repentance, and without retracing their steps. (3:23,3)

The case of Adam was not like what happened later with Cain; it was altogether different. Having been beguiled by another through the false promise of immortality, Adam was immediately seized with terror and hid himself—not as if he were able to escape from God, but, in a state of confusion at having transgressed his command, he felt unworthy to appear before God and converse with him. Since "the fear of the Lord is the beginning of wisdom" [Prov 9:10], the sense of sin leads to repentance. God shows compassion to the repentant. Adam showed his repentance by his conduct, in making a covering for himself out of fig leaves, when there were many other leaves which would have irritated his body to a lesser degree. However, he chose a covering which suited his disobedience, since he was awed by the fear of God. Resisting the erring and lustful propensity of his flesh (since he had now lost his natural disposition and childlike mind, and had come to the knowledge of evil), the covering he made for himself and his wife served continence, since he feared God and waited for his coming. By his actions, he thus indicated his thoughts, which must have been something like this: "Since by disobedience I have lost the robe of sanctity which I had from the Spirit, I now acknowledge that I deserve a covering of this sort, which allows no sensual gratification, but gnaws and irritates the body." And he would probably have retained this clothing afterwards, so as to humble himself, had not God, who is merciful, clothed them with tunics of skins instead of fig leaves. . . .

God detested the one who had led humanity astray, but by degrees—little by little—he showed compassion to the ones who had been beguiled. (3:23,5)

For this reason, God drove them out of paradise, separating them from the tree of life—not because he wanted to protect the tree of life from them, as some teach, but because God pitied them. He did not want them to continue to live forever as sinners, or for the sin which had engulfed them to last forever, or for evil to have no end or remedy. So, God set a bound to sin by interposing death, thus causing sin to cease [Rom 6:7], putting an end to it by the dissolution of the flesh into the earth. Thus humankind, eventually ceasing to live to sin, and dying to it, might begin to live to God. (3:23,6)

For this reason he put enmity between the serpent and the woman and her seed, which would continue. The one whose foot's sole would be bitten would have power to tread on the enemy's head; but the other would bite, kill, and impede the steps of humanity [Gen 3:15] until the seed appointed to tread on his head would come—the one born of Mary, of whom the prophet declared, "You will tread on the lion and the adder, the young lion and the serpent you will trample under foot" [Ps 91:13]. . . . (3:23,7)

. . . The preaching of the Church is consistent everywhere, continues on an even course, and has its authentication from the prophets, the apostles, and all the disciples. It covers the entire history of God's merciful dealing with humanity and presents a sure path to human salvation—namely, our faith. What we have received from the Church we preserve. By the Spirit of God it is always renewing its youth, as if it were some precious deposit in an excellent vessel, which renews the vessel containing it, as well. This gift of God has been entrusted to the Church, as breath was to the first created man, for this purpose, that all members receiving it may be given life. The Church enjoys communion with Christ through the Holy Spirit, the sure pledge of incorruption, who confirms our faith. . . . Where the Church is, there is the Spirit of God; and where the Spirit of God is, there is the Church, and every kind of grace; but the Spirit is truth [1 John 5:6]. . . . (3:24,1)

. . . The Father excels all in wisdom, humans and angels alike, because he is Lord, judge, just, and ruler over all. He is good, merciful, patient, and saves whom he will. Goodness does not desert him when he exercises justice, nor is his wisdom lessened, for he saves those whom he should save and judges those worthy of judgment. . . . (3:25,3)

God, who benevolently causes his sun to rise upon all and sends rain upon the just and unjust alike [Matt 5:45], will judge those who, enjoying his equally distributed kindness, have lived their lives in disregard of his gifts, spending their days in wantonness and luxury, in opposition to his benevolence, even blaspheming him who has conferred such great benefits on them. (3:25,4)

. . . We pray for them, loving them better than they seem to love themselves. Because our love is true, it will benefit them, if they will only receive it. To be sure, it is a severe remedy, scraping out the proud and putrid flesh from a wound, since it puts an end to their pride and haughtiness. We will not become weary of trying with all our might to stretch out a hand to them, though. . . . May we succeed in persuading them to abandon their error and to stop blaspheming their creator, who is the only true God and the Father of our Lord Jesus Christ. (3:25,7)

OOK 4 | *The Christian Faith, as Drawn from the Words Spoken by Christ*

B Y SENDING YOU THE fourth book of this work entitled, *The Detection and Refutation of What Is Falsely Called Knowledge*, I intend to strengthen what I have already sent you by carefully considering the words of the Lord. By this you will receive what you need to confute all these heretics and keep them from launching out further into the deep of error or being drowned in the sea of ignorance. May you turn them instead into the haven of the truth and help them find salvation. (4:pref,1)

Anyone who wants to convert these heretics to the truth needs to have a good understanding of their systems or schemes of teaching. It is impossible for anyone to heal the sick if he has no knowledge of the disease afflicting the patient. Because my predecessors—whom I consider superior to myself—did not know the Valentinians' system, they were unable to refute these heretics satisfactorily. (4:pref,2)

. . . In the preceding book, I set out the ideas of the apostles on various points, showing that they "who from the beginning were eyewitnesses and servants of the word" [Luke 1:2] of truth, held none of the opinions of these heretics, but that they warned us to shun such teachings [2 Tim 2:23], since they foresaw by the Spirit that weak-minded persons would be led astray by them. (4:pref,3)

The serpent beguiled Eve, by promising her what he did not have himself. This is also what these heretics do with their pretensions to superior knowledge and acquaintance with ineffable mysteries. . . . The aim

85

of him who envies our life is to get people to disbelieve their own salvation, and to get them to blaspheme against God the creator. For whatever the various heretics have advanced, even with utmost solemnity, they eventually come to the point that they blaspheme the creator and deny the salvation of the body, which is God's handiwork.... (4:pref,4)

Since the writings of Moses are the words of Christ, he himself declares to the Jews, as John recorded in the gospel, "If you believed Moses, you would believe me, for he wrote about me. But if you do not believe what he wrote, how will you believe what I say?" [John 5:46–47]. He thus indicates in the clearest way that the writings of Moses are his words. If, then, this was the case with Moses, then beyond a doubt, the words of the other prophets are also his, as I have pointed out. And again, the Lord himself presented Abraham as saying to the rich man with regard to those who were still alive, "If they do not listen to Moses and the prophets, neither will they be convinced even if someone rises from the dead" [Luke 16:31]. (4:2,3)

With that story, he not only told us about a poor man and a rich one. He also warned us against leading a luxurious life, one of worldly pleasures and constant feasting, lest we become slaves to our lusts and forget God: he said, "There was a rich man who was dressed in purple and fine linen and who feasted sumptuously every day" [Luke 16:19]. Through Isaiah the Spirit warned about being the kind of people "whose feasts consist of lyre and harp, tambourine and flute and wine, but who do not regard the deeds of the LORD, or see the work of his hands" [Isa 5:12]. Lest we incur the same punishment as these people did, the Lord reveals their end, showing at the same time that if they had obeyed Moses and the prophets, they would believe in him whom Moses and the prophets had preached. The one they thus preached was the Son of God, who rose from the dead, and bestows life upon us.... Many who are of the circumcision do believe in him: these have rightly heard Moses and the prophets announcing the coming of the Son of God.... (4:2,4)

All those who feared God and were zealous for his law ran to Christ and were saved. He commanded his disciples, "Go ... to the lost sheep of the house of Israel" [Matt 10:6] who are perishing. Further, many Samaritans, in the two days when the Lord stayed among them, "believed because of his word" and said to the woman, "It is no longer because of what you said that we believe, for we have heard for ourselves, and we know that this is truly the Savior of the world" [John 4:41].

Paul declares, "And so all Israel will be saved" [Rom 11:26]. He also said that the law was our pedagogue to bring us to Christ Jesus [Gal 3:24]. So they must not blame the law for their unbelief. The law never kept anyone from believing in the Son of God; indeed, it exhorted them to do so [Num 21:8], urging that the only way to be saved from the wound of the serpent was by believing in him who, in the likeness of sinful flesh, was lifted up from the earth on the tree of martyrdom, thus drawing all things to himself [John 3:14], who gives life to the dead. (4:2,7)

The heretics malignantly assert that, if heaven is the throne of God and earth his footstool, and if Scripture teaches heaven and earth shall pass away, then when these pass away the God who sits above them must also pass away, so that he cannot be the God who is over all. We respond, first of all, by pointing out that they do not understand what the expression "heaven is his throne and earth his footstool" means if they imagine that God sits as humans do, contained in the limits of a chair. Further, they do not understand what the "passing away of heaven and earth" means; Paul was not ignorant of it when he declared, "the present form of this world is passing away" [1 Cor 7:31]. David's words respond to their question, for he says that when the fashion of this world passes away, not only will God remain, but so will his servants also: "Long ago you laid the foundation of the earth, and the heavens are the work of your hands. They will perish, but you endure; they will all wear out like a garment. You change them like clothing, and they pass away; but you are the same, and your years have no end. The children of your servants shall live secure; their offspring shall be established in your presence" [Ps 102:25–28]; he thus points out plainly what will pass away, and who endures for ever—God and his servants. Similarly, Isaiah says, "Lift up your eyes to the heavens, and look at the earth beneath; for the heavens will vanish like smoke, the earth will wear out like a garment, and those who live on it will die like gnats; but my salvation will be forever, and my deliverance will never be ended" [Isa 51:6]. (4:3,1)

The heretics also declare, in regard to Jerusalem and the Lord, that if it had been "the city of the great King" [Matt 5:35] it would not have been deserted. This is like saying that if straw is a creation of God it would never part company with the wheat, or that if vine twigs had been made by God they would never be lopped off and lose their clusters. But vine branches were not originally made for their own sake, but for the sake of the fruit that would grow on them; when the fruit comes to maturity and is taken away, the vine branches are left behind and the ones which did not produce fruit are lopped off. That was the situation with Jerusalem. . . , when those who had the power to produce fruit had been carried away from her and scattered throughout the world. Isaiah said about this, "In days to come Jacob shall take root, Israel shall blossom and put forth shoots, and fill the whole world with fruit" [Isa 27:6]. Since that fruit has been sent throughout the world, Jerusalem was deservedly forsaken, and what had formerly brought forth fruit abundantly was taken away—meaning Christ and the apostles, who were able to bring forth fruit. . . . (4:4,1)

The law originated with Moses but terminated with John. Christ had come to fulfil it: "the law and the prophets were in effect until John" [Luke 16:16]. Therefore Jerusalem, which had received its commencement with David [2 Sam 5:7] but had fulfilled its purpose, was eclipsed when the new covenant was revealed. God does all things by measure and in order [Wis 11:20; cf. 1 Cor 14:33]; nothing is unmeasured with him, nothing out of order. . . . (4:4,2)

But why should we focus on Jerusalem, since the fashion of the whole world must pass away when the time for its disappearance has come, so that the fruit may be gathered into the granary, but the chaff left behind, to be consumed by fire? "See, the day is coming, burning like an oven, when all the arrogant and all evildoers will be stubble; the day that comes shall burn them up" [Mal 4:1]. John the Baptist points out who this Lord is who brings this about when he says of Christ, "He will baptize you with the Holy Spirit and fire. His winnowing fork is in his hand, and he will clear his threshing floor and will gather his wheat into the granary; but the chaff he will burn with unquenchable fire" [Matt 3:11–12]. The one who makes the chaff and the one who makes the wheat are not different persons, but one and the same, the one who judges them—that is, separates them.

Now, wheat and chaff are by nature inanimate and irrational. But human beings are endowed with reason; in this respect they are like God. Free to choose and with power over themselves, human beings themselves are to blame if some become chaff while others become wheat. Since this is so, any human being who loses genuine rationality by living irrationally—that is, in opposition to divine righteousness, submitting to various evil spirits and serving all lusts—will be justly condemned, as the prophet says, "Mortals cannot abide in their pomp; they are all like the animals that perish" [Ps 49:12]. (4:4,3)

So it is the same God who rolls up the heaven as a book and renews the face of the earth; who made things that are consumed for human beings, so that coming to full age by using these things appropriately, they might produce the fruit of immortality; and who in his kindness also grants eternal goods, "that in the ages to come he might show the immeasurable riches of his grace" [Eph 2:7]; who was announced by the law and the prophets; and whom Christ confessed as his Father. He is the creator, the God who is over all, as Isaiah says, "You are my witnesses, says the LORD, and my servant whom I have chosen, so that you may know and believe me and understand that I am he. Before me no god was formed, nor shall there be any after me. I, I am the LORD, and besides me there is no Savior. I declared and saved and proclaimed" [Isa 43:10–12]. He also declared: "I, the LORD, am first, and will be with the last" [Isa 41:4]. He does not say these things in an ambiguous or arrogant or boastful manner, but since it was impossible to come to a knowledge of God without God, he teaches people to know him through his Word. ... (4:5,1)

Our Lord and master, in the answer which he gave to the Sadducees (who said that there is no resurrection, and who thus dishonored God and lessened the credibility of the law) both indicated a resurrection and revealed God when he said to them, "You are wrong, because you know neither the scriptures nor the power of God. As for the resurrection of the dead, have you not read what was said by God, 'I am the God of Abraham, the God of Isaac, and the God of Jacob?' He is God not of the dead, but of the living" [Matt 22:29, 31]. By these arguments He made it unquestionably clear that the one who spoke to Moses out of the burning bush and declared himself to be the God of the fathers is the God of the living. ...

He who was adored by the prophets as the living God is the God of the living. His Word is the one who also spoke to Moses and silenced the Sadducees: he is the one who himself bestowed the gift of resurrection, thus revealing both the resurrection and the true God to those who were blind. For if he was not the God of the dead but of the living, and yet he was called the God of the fathers who had died, then they certainly live before God and have not passed out of existence, since they are children of the resurrection. But our Lord is himself the resurrection, as he himself declares, "I am the resurrection and the life" [John 11:25]. . . . So, Christ himself, together with the Father, is the God of the living—the one who spoke to Moses and who was also manifested to the fathers. (4:5,2)

And that is what he taught to the Jews: "Your ancestor Abraham rejoiced that he would see my day; he saw it and was glad" [John 8:56]. What was intended? "Abraham believed God, and it was reckoned to him as righteousness" [Rom 4:3]. In the first place, he believed that God was the maker of heaven and earth, the only God; and secondly, he believed that God would make his seed as numerous as the stars in heaven. (Paul alludes to this when he says, "like stars in the world" [Phil 2:15].) So, leaving his earthly kindred, he righteously followed the Word of God, living as a pilgrim with the Word, so that he might have his abode with the Word. (4:5,3)

Righteously also the apostles, who were descended from Abraham, left the ship and their father and followed the Word [Mark 1:20]. Righteously also do we, possessing the same faith as Abraham and taking up the cross as Isaac did the wood [Gen 22:6], follow him. For in Abraham humankind had learned beforehand and had been accustomed to follow the Word of God. According to his faith, Abraham followed the command of the Word of God, and willingly offered his only-begotten and beloved son as a sacrifice to God, in order that God also might be pleased to offer up for all his seed his own beloved and only-begotten Son as a sacrifice for our redemption. (4:5,4)

Since, therefore, Abraham was a prophet and by the Spirit saw the day of the Lord's coming and the dispensation of his suffering—through whom he himself and all who, following the example of his faith, trust in God, would be saved—he rejoiced greatly. So, the Lord was certainly not unknown to Abraham, for he desired to see his day [John 8:56]; neither was the Lord's Father unknown to him, for he had learned from the Word of the Lord and believed him. This was accounted to him by the Lord for righteousness. Faith towards God justifies one. . . . (4:5,5)

The Lord, who revealed to his disciples that he himself is the Word who grants knowledge of the Father, and who reproved the Jews who imagined that they had God but nevertheless rejected his Word, through whom God is made known, declared: "No one knows the Son except the Father, and no one knows the Father except the Son and anyone to whom the Son chooses to reveal him" [Matt 11:27; cf. Luke 10:22]. This is the way Matthew put it; Luke and Mark do so in similar words; John omits this passage. The heretics, however, who would be wiser than the apostles, explain the verse . . . as if the true God were known to no one before our Lord's advent, and that the God who was announced by the prophets was not the Father of Christ. (4:6,1)

But if Christ only began to have existence when he came into the world as human, and if the Father only remembered to provide for human beings' needs in the time of Tiberius Caesar, and if his Word has not always coexisted with his creatures, then it was not necessary for another God to be proclaimed; instead, the reasons for such great carelessness and neglect on his part should be made the subject of investigation. No question like that should even arise and gather enough force both to alter God and destroy our faith in the creator who supports us through his creation. For as we direct our faith towards the Son, so also should we possess a firm and immoveable love towards the Father. . . . (4:6,2)

No one can know the Father unless the Son reveals him; neither can anyone know the Son, except by the good pleasure of the Father. But the Son accomplishes the good pleasure of the Father, for the Father sends and the Son is sent. The Word knows, as far as regards us, that his Father is invisible and infinite. Since he cannot be declared by anyone else, he himself declares him to us; on the other hand, it is the Father alone who knows his own Word. Our Lord declared both these truths. So, the Son reveals the knowledge of the Father through his own manifestation: indeed, this constitutes the knowledge of the Father, for all things are made known through the Word. Therefore, so that we might know that the Son who came is the one who grants to those who believe in him a knowledge of the Father, he said to his disciples, "No one knows the Son except the Father, and no one knows the Father except the Son, and anyone to whom the Son chooses to reveal him" [Matt 11:27]. In this way, he presented himself and the Father, so that we may not receive any other Father except the one who is revealed by the Son. (4:6,3)

. . . The Lord taught us that no one is capable of knowing God, unless that person is taught by God; that is, God cannot be known without God. And this is the express will of the Father, that God should be known. For those to whom the Son has revealed him will know him. (4:6,4)

This is why the Father revealed the Son, that through him he might be manifested to all and might receive into incorruption and everlasting enjoyment the righteous ones who believe in him. To believe in him is to do his will. But those who do not believe and consequently avoid his light he will righteously shut out into the darkness which they have chosen for themselves. So, the Father has revealed himself to all by making his Word visible to all; conversely, the Word has declared the Father and the Son to all, since he has become visible to all. Therefore the righteous judgment of God will fall upon all who like others have seen but unlike others have not believed. (4:6,5)

The Word reveals God the creator through the creation itself: through the world he declares the Lord the maker of the world, through the formation of man the artificer who formed him, and through the Son the Father who begat the Son. All these things address all people in the same manner, but all do not in the same way believe them. By the law and the prophets the Word preached both himself and the Father to all; all the people heard him alike, but all did not alike believe. And the Father was shown forth through the Word himself who had been made visible and palpable, although all did not equally believe in him, even though all saw the Father in the Son—for the Father is the invisible of the Son, but the Son the visible of the Father. . . . Even the demons, on beholding the Son, exclaimed: "We know who you are, the Holy One of God" [cf. Mark 1:24]; the devil himself, looking at him and tempting him, said, "If you are the Son of God" [Matt 4:3; Luke 4:3]. All of these saw and spoke about the Son and the Father, but they all did not believe. (4:6,6)

It was fitting that the truth receive testimony from all and should thus become a means of judgment for the salvation of those who believe, but for the condemnation of those who do not believe. In this way, all will be fairly judged, and faith in the Father and Son will be established by all as the one means of salvation, receiving testimony from all—both from those belonging to it as its friends, and from those who have no connection with it as its enemies. That evidence is true and cannot be rejected which elicits even from its adversaries striking testimonies in its behalf, for they are convicted regarding the matter in hand by their own plain contemplation of it and what they have said about it. . . .

The Son, administering all things for the Father, works from the beginning of creation to the end of time. Without him no one can attain the knowledge of God. The Son is the knowledge of the Father, but the knowledge of the Son is in the Father and has been revealed through the Son. This was the reason why the Lord declared, "No one knows the Father except the Son, and no one knows the Son except the Father and anyone to whom the Son chooses to reveal him" [Matt 11:27]. "Chooses to reveal" refers not to the future alone, as if the Word had only begun to manifest the Father when he was born of Mary; rather, it applies through-out all time. The Son, present with his handiwork from the beginning, reveals the Father to all—to whom he wills, and when he wills, and as the Father wills. So, in all things and through all things, there is one God the Father, one Word the Son, and one Spirit—and one salvation for all who believe in Him. (4:6,7)

Abraham also, knowing the Father through the Word who made heaven and earth, confessed him to be God. When it was announced to him that the Son of God would be a man among men, by whose advent his seed would become as numerous as the stars of heaven, Abraham desired to see that day [John 8:56], so that he himself might also embrace Christ. Seeing it through the Spirit of prophecy, he rejoiced [Gen 17:17]. Simeon also, one of his descendants, completed the rejoicing of the pa-triarch and said, "Master, now you are dismissing your servant in peace, according to your word; for my eyes have seen your salvation, which you have prepared in the presence of all peoples, a light for revelation to the Gentiles and for glory to your people Israel" [Luke 2:29–32]. The angels similarly announced tidings of great joy to the shepherds who were keeping watch by night [Luke 2:8–13]. Moreover, Mary said, "My soul magnifies the Lord, and my spirit rejoices in God my Savior" [Luke 1:46–47]. Thus the rejoicing of Abraham descended on those descended from him—on those who were watching, beheld Christ, and believed in him. There was also reciprocal rejoicing which passed backwards from his descendants to Abraham, who desired to see the day of Christ's coming. This is why our Lord testified of him, saying, "Your ancestor Abraham rejoiced that he would see my day; he saw it and was glad" [John 8:56]. (4:7,1)

He said these things not only about Abraham, but also to show how all those who have known God from the beginning and have foretold the advent of Christ have received the revelation from the Son himself—who in the last times was made visible and passible, and spoke with the human race, so that he might raise up children for Abraham from the stones and fulfil the promise God gave him to make his descendants as numerous as the stars in heaven [Gen 15:5]. This is what John the Baptist meant when he said, "God is able from these stones to raise up children to Abraham" [Matt 3:9]. Indeed, this is what Jesus did: he drew us away from the religion of stones [idols] and from difficult and fruitless arguments, establishing in us instead a faith like Abraham's. As Paul testifies, we are children of Abraham through faith and so receive the promised inheritance [Gal 3:7, 29] (4:7,2)

This is one and the same God, who called Abraham and gave him the promise. But he is the creator, who through Christ also prepares lights in the world—that is, those who believe from among the Gentiles. And he says, "You are the light of the world" [Matt 5:14], like the stars in heaven. . . . But the Son reveals the Father to all those to whom he chooses to make him known, and neither without the goodwill of the Father nor without the agency of the Son can anyone know God. Therefore the Lord said to His disciples, "I am the way, and the truth, and the life. No one comes to the Father except through me. If you know me, you will know my Father also. From now on you do know him and have seen him" [John 14:6–7]. From these words it is evident that he is known by the Son—that is, by the Word. (4:7,3)

. . . Through Jesus Christ, God introduces to the kingdom of heaven both Abraham and his seed—that is, the Church [Gal 3:29], upon whom he confers adoption and the inheritance promised to Abraham [Gal 4:4–7]. (4:8,1)

The Lord vindicated Abraham's posterity by delivering them from bondage and calling them to salvation. . . . Both at Siloam and on frequent subsequent occasions he performed cures on the Sabbath, and for this reason many used to seek him out on the Sabbath days. The law commanded them to abstain from every servile work—that is, from all grasping after wealth which is procured by trading and by other worldly business—but it exhorted them to attend to the exercises of the soul (which consist in reflection) and the instruction that would enable them to serve their neighbors' benefit. This is why the Lord reproved those who unjustly blamed him for healing on the Sabbath days [Matt 12:1–13], since he did not violate but fulfilled the law by performing the work of a high priest, propitiating God for human beings, cleansing lepers, healing the sick, and himself suffering death, so that exiled humanity might escape condemnation and return without fear to its inheritance. (4:8,2)

. . . All who are righteous possess the sacerdotal rank [1 Pet 2:9], and all the apostles of the Lord are priests, who inherit here neither lands nor houses, but serve God and the altar continually. . . . Indeed, who were the ones who left father and mother and bid farewell to all their neighbors for the sake of the Word of God and his covenant, if not the disciples of the Lord? Moses said that the priests would not have any inheritance, because the Lord himself would be their inheritance [Num 18:20]. . . . The priests in the temple profaned the Sabbath, but they were blameless. Why, though, were they blameless? Because in the temple they were not engaged in secular affairs but in the service of the Lord, fulfilling the law but not going beyond it. . . . (4:8,3)

All this fits together because it comes from one and the same God. The Lord himself said to the disciples, "Therefore every scribe who has been trained for the kingdom of heaven is like the master of a household who brings out of his treasure what is new and what is old" [Matt 13:52]. He did not teach that one who brings out the old was one person but the one who brings out the new is another; they were one and the same. For the Lord is the steward of the house, who rules the entire house of his Father and delivers a law suited both to slaves and to those as yet undisciplined. He gives appropriate directives to those who are free and have been justified by faith; he also throws his own inheritance open to those who are sons and daughters. He called his disciples "scribes" and "teachers of the kingdom of heaven". . . .

By the things old and new which are brought out of the treasure, he means the two covenants: the old one was the giving of the law which took place formerly; he points out as the new the manner of life required by the gospel. David said about that, "Sing to the LORD a new song" [Ps 96:1]; and Isaiah urged, "Sing to the LORD a new song, his praise from the end of the earth! Let the sea roar and all that fills it, the coastlands and their inhabitants" [Isa 42:10]. Jeremiah says, "I will make a new covenant . . . , not like the covenant that I made with their ancestors" [Jer 31:31, 32] in Mount Horeb. One and the same householder produced both covenants—the Word of God, our Lord Jesus Christ, who spoke with both Abraham and Moses, has restored us anew to liberty, and has multiplied that grace which comes from himself. (4:9,1)

He declares, "Something greater than the temple is here" [Matt 12:6]. "Greater" and "less" are not applied to things which have nothing in common, are opposed to each other, and are mutually repugnant; they are used in the case of things of the same substance which possess common properties, but differ in number and size—such as water from water, light from light, and grace from grace. "Greater," therefore, is the legislation which has been given for liberty than that given for bondage;

it has also been diffused, not just through one nation, but over the whole world. For one and the same Lord, who is greater than the temple, greater than Solomon, and greater than Jonah, confers gifts upon humanity—his own presence and the resurrection from the dead. . . .

Paul declares, "Not that I have already obtained this or have already been made perfect. We know only in part, and we prophesy only in part; but when the complete comes, the partial will come to an end" [Phil 3:12; 1 Cor 13:9–10]. When the complete comes, we will not see some other Father: we will see him whom we now desire to see (for "blessed are the pure in heart, for they will see God" [Matt 5:8]). Neither will we look for another Christ and Son of God, but for the one of the virgin Mary, the one who suffered, in whom we trust, and whom we love—as Isaiah says, "It will be said on that day, Lo, this is our God; we have waited for him, so that he might save us. This is the LORD for whom we have waited; let us be glad and rejoice in his salvation" [Isa 25:9]; and Peter says in his letter, "Although you have not seen him, you love him; and even though you do not see him now, you believe in him and rejoice with an indescribable and glorious joy" [1 Pet 1:8]. We will not receive some other Holy Spirit than the one who is with us and who cries, "Abba, Father" [Rom 8:15]. We will grow in what we have now and will advance, and we will enjoy the gifts of God, no longer through a glass or by means of enigmas, but face to face. . . . (4:9,2)

The new covenant was known and preached by the prophets, who also proclaimed the one who was to bring it to pass through the good pleasure of the Father. These things had been revealed to them according to God's will, so that they might advance in believing in him and, through the successive covenants, should gradually attain to perfect salvation. For there is one salvation and one God, but the precepts which form humanity are numerous, and the steps which lead to God are not a few. It is allowable for an earthly and temporal king, even though he is only a human being, to grant to his subjects greater advantages at times: shall this not be lawful for God, since he is always the same, always willing to confer a greater degree of grace upon the human race, and to honor continually with many gifts those who please him? . . . (4:9,3)

What John records of the Lord speaking to the Jews fits with this: "You search the scriptures because you think that in them you have eternal life; and it is they that testify on my behalf. Yet you refuse to come to me to have life" [John 5:39–40]. How did the Scriptures testify of him, unless they were from one and the same Father, instructing humankind beforehand about the advent of his Son and foretelling the salvation he would bring? "If you believed Moses, you would believe me, for he wrote about me" [John 5:46]: by this he indicated that the Son of God is implanted everywhere throughout his writings—at one point speaking with Abraham, when about to eat with him; at another Noah, giving him the dimensions of the ark; at another, inquiring after Adam; at another, bringing down judgment upon the Sodomites; when he became visible and directed Jacob on his journey; and when he spoke with Moses from the bush. Indeed, it would be endless to recount the occasions when the Son of God was shown forth by Moses. Of his coming passion, too, Moses was not ignorant: he foretold him figuratively by the name given to the Passover; at that very festival, proclaimed such a long time previously by Moses, our Lord suffered, thus fulfilling the Passover. Moses not only wrote about the day, but also the place and the time of day when the sufferings would cease—by the setting of the sun: "You are not permitted to offer the Passover sacrifice within any of your towns that the LORD your God is giving you. But at the place that the LORD your God will choose as a dwelling for his name, only there shall you offer the Passover sacrifice, in the evening at sunset" [Deut 16:5–6]. (4:10,1)

. . . When chiding the ingratitude of the people, Moses said, "Do you thus repay the LORD, O foolish and senseless people?" [Deut 32:6]. He indicates that the one who established and created them from the beginning, the Word who also redeems us and gives us life in the last times, was to hang on a tree, but they would not believe on him: he said, "Your life shall hang in doubt before you; night and day you shall be in dread, with no assurance of your life" [Deut 28:66], and "Is not he your father, who created you, who made you and established you?" [Deut 32:6]. (4:10,2)

Not only the prophets, but many righteous people, foreseeing his advent through the Holy Spirit, prayed to attain that period in which they might see their Lord face to face and hear his words. The Lord made this clear when he said to his disciples, "Many prophets and righteous people longed to see what you see, but did not see it, and to hear what you hear, but did not hear it" [Matt 13:17]. In what way did they thus desire to hear and to see, unless they had foreknowledge of his future advent? But how could they have foreknown it, unless they had previously received foreknowledge from himself? And how do the Scriptures testify of him, unless everything that had ever been revealed and shown to believers came from one and the same God through the Word? . . . (4:11,1)

In this respect God differs from humans, in that God makes but humans are made. He who makes is always the same; but that which is made must receive beginning, middle, addition, and increase. And God creates in a skillful manner, while humans are created skillfully. God also is perfect in all things, equal and similar to himself, since he is all light, all mind, all substance, and the fount of all good; but human beings receive advancement and increase towards God. As God is always the same, so also humans, when found in God, will always go on towards God. God never stops conferring benefits upon and enriching humankind, and humanity never ceases to receive those benefits and to be enriched by God. The receptacle of his goodness and the instrument of his glorification is the person who is grateful to him who made him, but the receptacle of his righteous judgment is the ungrateful person, who despises his maker and is not subject to his Word. . . . (4:11,2)

. . . The Lord remains the same, and the same Father is revealed. By his advent, one and the same Lord granted a greater gift of grace to those of a later period than what he had granted to those under the Old Testament dispensation. For they indeed used to hear, by means of his servants, that the king would come, and they rejoiced to a certain extent, since they hoped for his coming. But those who have beheld him actually present have obtained liberty and have partaken of his gifts; they possess a greater amount of grace and a higher degree of exultation, rejoicing because of the king's arrival. . . . (4:11,3)

. . . He has brought down liberty to those who serve him lawfully and willingly, with all their hearts. But to scoffers and those not subject to God, who follow outward purifications for the praise of other humans (following observances which had been given as a type of future things, since the law typified certain things as a shadow, delineating eternal things by temporal and celestial by terrestrial), and to those who pretend that they observe more than what has been prescribed (as if preferring their own zeal to God himself, although they are full of hypocrisy, covetousness, and all wickedness), he has assigned everlasting perdition by cutting them off from life. (4:11,4)

In both the law and the gospel, the first and greatest commandment is to love the Lord God with the whole heart, and then there follows a commandment like it, to love one's neighbor as oneself [Deut 6:5; Lev 19:18; Matt 22:37–40]; in this, the author of the law and the gospel is shown to be one and the same. The precepts of an absolutely perfect life, since they are the same in each testament, have pointed out the same God, who promulgated particular laws adapted for each. The more prominent and greatest, though, without which salvation cannot be attained, he has presented in both. (4:12,3)

... Isaiah says, "These people draw near me with their mouths and honor me with their lips, while their hearts are far from me, and their worship of me is a human commandment learned by rote" [Isa 29:13]. He does not call the law given by Moses "human commandments"— by that he intended the traditions which the elders had invented and which, when observed, ended up making the law of God of no effect [Mark 7:13], so that they were not submissive to his Word. This is what Paul says concerning these people: "Being ignorant of the righteousness that comes from God, and seeking to establish their own, they have not submitted to God's righteousness. For Christ is the end of the law so that there may be righteousness for everyone who believes" [Rom 10:3–4]. And how is Christ the end of the law, if he was not also the one in whom it finds its meaning? The one who brought in the end has also worked the beginning.... (4:12,4)

The Lord tells us that he did not abrogate the law known by nature, by which one can be justified [Rom 2:27]—that law by which those who were justified by faith and who pleased God observed before the law was given (through Moses)—but that he extended and fulfilled it: "You have heard that it was said, 'You shall not commit adultery.' But I say to you that everyone who looks at a woman with lust has already committed adultery with her in his heart" [Matt 5:27–28]. And again, "You have heard that it was said to those of ancient times, 'You shall not murder'.... But I say to you that if you are angry with a brother or sister, you will be liable to judgment" [Matt 5:21–22]. And, "You have heard that it was said to those of ancient times, 'You shall not swear falsely'.... But I say to you, Do not swear at all.... Let your word be 'Yes, Yes' or 'No, No'" [Matt 5:33, 34, 37]. He makes other statements like these.

These do not contain or imply an opposition to or an overturning of the precepts of the past, as Marcion's followers strenuously maintain; rather, they proclaim a fulfillment and an extension of them, as he himself declares: "Unless your righteousness exceeds that of the scribes

and Pharisees, you will never enter the kingdom of heaven" [Matt 5:20].
What is meant by this "exceeding"? In the first place, we must believe not
only in the Father, but also in his Son now revealed; he is the one who
leads humankind into fellowship and unity with God. In the next place,
we must not only say, but we must do; for they said, but did not. And we
must not only abstain from evil deeds, but even from desires for them.
He did not teach us all this as something opposed to the law, but as its
fulfillment, something which would implant the manifold righteousness
of the law within us. It would have been contrary to the law if he had
instructed his disciples to do anything which the law prohibited. What
he commanded—not only to abstain from things forbidden by the law,
but even from yearning for them—is not contrary to the law or the utterance of someone destroying the law, but of one fulfilling, extending,
and affording greater scope to it. (4:13,1)

The law, since it was laid down for those in bondage, instructed
by means of physical objects of an external nature, thus drawing souls
to obey the commandments by a bond, so that people might learn to
serve God. But the Word set the soul free and taught that through it the
body should be willingly purified. With this accomplished, it followed
as a matter of course that the bonds of slavery to which human beings
had by then become accustomed were removed, and that they should
follow God without fetters. With this, the laws of liberty were appropriately extended and subjection to the king increased, so that no one who
is converted would appear unworthy to him who set him free, but that
the piety and obedience due to the master of the household should be
rendered by servants and children alike. . . . (4:13,2)

This is why the Lord forbade lust in place of the commandment,
"You shall not commit adultery" and prohibited anger in place of "You
shall not commit murder." As well, in place of the requirement to give
a tithe, he commanded us to share all our possessions with the poor
[Matt 19:21]; and not to love our neighbors only, but even our enemies
[Matt 5:43–44]. Further, he called us to be liberal in our giving, even presenting gratuitous gifts to those who would take away our goods: "From
anyone who takes away your coat do not withhold even your shirt. . . . If
anyone takes away your goods, do not ask for them again. Do to others
as you would have them do to you" [Luke 6:29–31]. So, we should not
grieve like those who are unwilling to be defrauded, but should even
rejoice as those who have given willingly, since we have conferred a favor

on our neighbors instead of just yielding to necessity. Moreover, he said, "If anyone forces you to go one mile, go also the second mile" [Matt 5:41]; if you do this, you are not following him like a slave but accompanying him as someone free, thus showing yourself kindly disposed and useful to your neighbor—not regarding their evil intentions, but performing your kind offices, thus becoming more like the Father who "makes his sun rise on the evil and on the good, and sends rain on the righteous and on the unrighteous" [Matt 5:45].

All these instructions were not the commandments of someone abrogating the law, but of one fulfilling, extending, and widening it among us. It is as if one said that a much wider grant of liberty implants within us a greater subjection to and affection for our liberator. He did not set us free so that we should depart from him, . . . but that the more we receive his grace, the more we should love him. . . . (4:13,3)

. . . To submit to God and follow his Word, to love him above all and one's neighbor as oneself, and to abstain from everything evil, and all other similar commands are common to both covenants and reveal one and the same God. Our Lord, the Word of God, in the first instance drew slaves to God, but afterwards he freed those who were subject to him, as he himself declared to his disciples: "I do not call you servants any longer, because the servant does not know what the master is doing; but I have called you friends, because I have made known to you everything that I have heard from my Father" [John 15:15]. When he said, "I do not call you servants any longer," he indicated in the most marked manner that he was the one who had originally established human bondage in respect to God through the law, but who later granted them freedom. When he said, "The servant does not know what the master is doing," he points out, by referring to his own advent, the ignorance of those who are in a servile condition. But when he calls his disciples "friends," he clearly shows himself as the Word of God, whom Abraham followed voluntarily, without compulsion, in his noble faith and so became "the friend of God" [Jas 2:23]. The Word of God did not accept the friendship of Abraham as if he needed it, for he was perfect from the beginning—he said, "Before Abraham was, 'I am'" [John 8:58]). Rather, he accepted it so that in his goodness he might grant eternal life to Abraham, for friendship with God imparts immortality to those who embrace it. (4:13,4)

In the beginning, God formed Adam, not as if he needed humanity, but so that he might have someone upon whom to confer his benefits. Not only before Adam, but even before all the rest of creation, the Word glorified his Father, remaining in him—and he himself was glorified by the Father, as he later indicated when he prayed, "Father, glorify me in your own presence with the glory that I had in your presence before the world existed" [John 17:5]. He did not need our service when he ordered us to follow him, but in this way he granted us salvation—for to follow the savior is to be a partaker of salvation, and to follow light is to receive light.

Those who are in light do not themselves illumine the light; they are illumined and revealed by it. They certainly contribute nothing to it; rather, receiving the benefit, they are illumined by the light. So also the service we render to God profits him nothing, and God does not need our obedience. He grants life and incorruption and eternal glory to those who follow and serve him, bestowing benefits on those who serve him because they serve him and on his followers because they follow him. He does not receive any benefit from them, though, for he is rich, perfect, and in need of nothing. The reason God demands service from human beings is so that, since he is good and merciful, he may benefit those who continue in his service. While God needs nothing, humans need fellowship with God, and this is the glory of a human being, to continue and remain permanently in God's service. The Lord said to his disciples, "You did not choose me but I chose you" [John 15:16]. This indicates that they did not glorify him when they followed him, but that in following the Son of God they were glorified by him. This is also why he prayed to his Father, "I desire that those also, whom you have given me, may be with me where I am, to see my glory" [John 17:24]; in this he did not vainly boast, for he desired his disciples to share in his glory.... (4:14,1)

The munificence of God is also the reason God formed humanity in the beginning: he chose the patriarchs for salvation; he prepared a people ahead of time, teaching the willful to follow God; he raised up prophets upon earth, so as to accustom human beings to bear his Spirit and to have communion with God—needing nothing himself, but granting communion with himself to those needed it; and he sketched out, like an architect, the plan of salvation for those who pleased him. He himself furnished guidance to those who did not behold him in Egypt, while to those who became unruly in the desert he promulgated a suitable law. Then he granted a noble inheritance to the people who entered into the good land, and he killed the fatted calf for those who turned to the Father, and presented them with the finest robe [Luke 15:22–23]. Thus, in a variety of ways, he prepared the human race to agree to salvation. . . . (4:14,2)

He also thus had the Jewish people construct the tabernacle and build the temple, chose the Levites and appointed sacrifices, offerings, legal admonitions, and all the other service of the law. He certainly needs none of these things, for he is always full of all good and already had within himself all the odor of kindness and every perfume of sweet-smelling savors, long before Moses even existed. Furthermore, by repeated appeals he instructed the people who were prone to turn to idols instead to persevere and serve God. In all this, he called them to what is of primary importance through those which are secondary—that is, to things that are real, by means of those that are typical; by things temporal, to eternal; by the carnal to the spiritual; and by the earthly to the heavenly. This was the reason he said to Moses, "See that you make them according to the pattern of what was shown you on the mountain" [Exod 25:40]. . . . (4:14,3)

So, the Jews had a law, a course of discipline, and a prophecy of future things. At first, God warned them through natural precepts, which he had implanted in humankind from the beginning (that is, the Decalogue—which if any one does not observe, that person has no salvation), imposing no other demands on them. As Moses said in Deuteronomy, "These words the Lord spoke . . . to your whole assembly at the mountain . . . , and he added no more. He wrote them on two stone tablets, and gave them to me" (Deut 5:22). . . . (4:15,1)

Not only that, the Lord also showed that certain precepts were enacted for them by Moses because of their hardness of heart and their unwillingness to be obedient. When they challenged him, "Why then did Moses command us to give a certificate of dismissal and to divorce her?" He answered them, "It was because you were so hard-hearted that Moses allowed you to divorce your wives, but from the beginning it was not so" [Matt 19:7–8]. . . .

Even in the New Testament, the apostles ended up granting certain concessions out of consideration for human weakness because of the inability of some to control themselves [cf. 1 Cor 7:1–6], lest becoming stubborn and coming to despair altogether of their salvation, they should apostatize from God. So, it should occasion no surprise if in the Old Testament the same God permitted similar indulgences for the sake of his people, drawing them on by the ordinances already mentioned, so that they might obtain the gift of salvation through them—while they obeyed the Decalogue and, restrained by him, did not revert to idolatry nor apostatize from God, but learned to love him with the whole heart. ... (4:15,2)

Furthermore, we learn from Scripture itself that God gave circumcision, not as the fulfillment of righteousness, but as a sign of it, so that the race of Abraham might continue recognizable: God said to Abraham, "Every male among you shall be circumcised. You shall circumcise the flesh of your foreskins, and it shall be a sign of the covenant between me and you" [Gen 17:10–11]. Ezekiel the prophet said the same with regard to the Sabbaths: "I gave them my sabbaths, as a sign between me and them, so that they might know that I the LORD sanctify them" [Ezek 20:12]. And in Exodus, God said to Moses, "You shall keep my sabbaths, for this is a sign between me and you throughout your generations" [Exod 31:13].

These things were all given as signs, but these signs were not empty; they had meaning and purpose, since they were given by a wise artist. Circumcision in the flesh typified the circumcision after the Spirit: the apostle said, "You were circumcised with a spiritual circumcision" [Col 2:11], and the prophet declared, "Circumcise your hard heart" [Deut 10:16 LXX]. The sabbaths taught that we should be steadfast in God's service every day: the apostle Paul said, "All day long we are accounted as sheep to be slaughtered" [Rom 8:36]—that is, we are consecrated to God, ministering continually to our faith and persevering in it, abstaining from all love of money and not seeking treasures upon earth [Matt 6:19]. Moreover, the sabbath of God—that is, the kingdom—was, as it were, indicated by created things; in that kingdom, the one who will have persevered in serving God will enjoy a state of rest and partake of God's table. (4:16,1)

No one was justified by these things; rather, they were given as signs to the people. Abraham's case shows that, for he had not yet received circumcision and was offering no sabbath observance, but he "believed God, and it was reckoned to him as righteousness, and he was called the friend of God" [Jas 2:23]. Similarly, Lot was not circumcised, but he was brought out of Sodom, receiving salvation from God. So also Noah pleased God although he was uncircumcised, and he received the dimensions of the ark, resulting in the world of the second race of humanity. Enoch too, pleasing God without circumcision, discharged the office of God's spokesperson to the angels although he was a man: he was translated and is being preserved until now as a witness of the righteous judgment of God, for the angels who transgressed fell to the earth in judgment, but this man who pleased God was translated for salvation[1 Enoch 6–7, 12–13[1]]. . . . (4:16,2)

Why did not the Lord form the covenant for the fathers? Because "the law is laid down not for the innocent" [1 Tim 1:9], but the righteous fathers already had the meaning of the Decalogue written in their hearts and souls. They loved the God who made them, and did no injury to their neighbor. . . . But when this righteousness and love to God had passed into oblivion and became extinct in Egypt, out of his great good-will toward humankind, God revealed himself by a voice and powerfully led the people out of Egypt, so that human beings might again become disciples and followers of God. He punished those who were disobedient, so that they would not despise their creator. . . . And the Word of God through Moses commanded love to God and taught just dealing with our neighbor. He did this so that we should neither be unjust nor unworthy of God, who prepares humankind for his friendship and for agreement with neighbors by the Decalogue. By this, humanity benefitted greatly, but God did not; he did not need anything from humankind. (4:16,3)

That is why Scripture says, "These words the Lord spoke with a loud voice to your whole assembly . . . , and he added no more" [Deut 5:22]: as I have already observed about this, he needed nothing from them. Again, Moses says, "So now, O Israel, what does the LORD your God require of you? Only to fear the LORD your God, to walk in all his ways, to love him, to serve the LORD your God with all your heart and with all your soul" [Deut 10:12]. These things indeed made humankind glorious, by supplying what they needed—namely, God's friendship; but they did not profit God at all, since he did not need humanity's love. The only way humans could enjoy the glory of God was by serving him; therefore, Moses said to them again, "Choose life so that you and your descendants may live, loving the LORD your God, obeying him, and holding fast to him; for that means life to you and length of days" [Deut 30:19–20].

---

1. The book of *1 Enoch*, cited in Jude 14–16, was eventually included as canonical only in the Ethiopic OT, but its echoes are found in several early Christian authors; it is available in *OTP* 13–89.

Preparing human beings for this life, the Lord himself spoke the words of the Decalogue to all of them. In similar manner, they remain permanently with us, since they are extended and increased, but not abrogated, by his advent in the flesh. (4:16,4)

However, the laws of bondage were promulgated one by one to the people by Moses; they were directed for their instruction or for their punishment, as Moses himself declared: "And the LORD charged me at that time to teach you statutes and ordinances" [Deut 4:14]. These things, given for bondage and for a sign to them, he cancelled by the new covenant of liberty. But he has increased and widened those laws which are natural, noble, and common to all. Further, he has abundantly and ungrudgingly granted humankind to know God as Father by adoption, to love him with the whole heart, and to follow his word unswervingly, while they abstain not only from evil deeds, but even from the desire after them. . . . We must remember that we will give account to God not only of our deeds, as if we were slaves, but also of our words and thoughts [Matt 12:36], as those who have truly received the power of liberty, in which one is more severely tested, to see whether he will respect, fear, and love the Lord. And for this reason Peter says that we must not use our freedom as a cover for evil [1 Pet 2:16], but to examine and show faith. (4:16,5)

Moreover, the prophets abundantly indicate that God did not need slavish obedience, but that it was for their benefit that he enjoined certain observances in the law. And the Lord clearly taught that God did not need their sacrifices but called for them in order to benefit the one who offers them, as I have pointed out. When he saw them neglecting righteousness, failing to love God, and imagining that God could be propitiated by sacrifices and the other typical observances, Samuel spoke to them: "Has the LORD as great delight in burnt offerings and sacrifices, as in obeying the voice of the LORD? Surely, to obey is better than sacrifice, and to heed than the fat of rams" [1 Sam 15:22]. David also said, "Sacrifice and offering you do not desire, but you have given me an open ear. Burnt offering and sin offering you have not required" [Ps 40:6]. He thus teaches them that God desires obedience, which renders them secure, rather than sacrifices and offerings, which will not make them righteous; thus he also prophesies the new covenant at the same time. He speaks even more clearly of these things: "For you have no delight in sacrifice; if I were to give a burnt offering, you would not be pleased.

The sacrifice acceptable to God is a broken spirit; a broken and contrite heart, O God, you will not despise" [Ps 51:16–17].

Since God needs nothing, he declares in the preceding Psalm: "I will not accept a bull from your house, or goats from your folds. For every wild animal of the forest is mine, the cattle on a thousand hills. I know all the birds of the air, and all that moves in the field is mine. If I were hungry, I would not tell you, for the world and all that is in it is mine. Do I eat the flesh of bulls, or drink the blood of goats?" [Ps 50:9–12]. Then, so that no one might conclude that in his anger he refuses these things, he continues: "Offer to God a sacrifice of thanksgiving, and pay your vows to the Most High. Call on me in the day of trouble; I will deliver you, and you shall glorify me" [Ps 50:14–15]. With these words he rejects those things by which sinners imagined they could propitiate God and shows that he needs nothing, but he encourages and advises those things through which one can be justified and draw near to God.

Isaiah says the same: "What to me is the multitude of your sacrifices? says the LORD; I have had enough" [Isa 1:11]. And when he had repudiated burnt offerings, sacrifices, and oblations, as well as observances of new moons, sabbaths, festivals, and all the services accompanying these, he called them to be concerned with the things that relate to salvation: "Wash yourselves; make yourselves clean; remove the evil of your doings from before my eyes; cease to do evil, learn to do good; seek justice, rescue the oppressed, defend the orphan, plead for the widow. Come now, let us argue it out, says the LORD" [Isa 1:16–18]. (4:17,1)

It was not because, like a mere man, he was angry (as many dare to say) that he rejected their sacrifices; rather, he did so out of compassion for their blindness, and with a view to pointing them to the true sacrifice, by offering which they would appease God and thus receive life from him. Elsewhere he also declared, "The sacrifice acceptable to God is a broken spirit; a broken and contrite heart, O God, you will not despise" [Ps 51:19]. If he had repudiated these sacrifices of theirs because he was angry, as if they were persons unworthy to obtain his compassion, he certainly would not have urged these same things upon them as the way by which they could be saved. But since God is merciful, he did not fail to give them good counsel. For after he had said by Jeremiah, "Of what use to me is frankincense that comes from Sheba, or sweet cane from a distant land? Your burnt offerings are not acceptable, nor are your sacrifices pleasing to me" [Jer 6:20], he went on to say, "Hear the word of the

LORD, all you people of Judah. Thus says the LORD of hosts, the God of Israel: Amend your ways and your doings, and let me dwell with you in this place. Do not trust in deceptive words, 'This is the temple of the LORD, the temple of the LORD, the temple of the LORD'" [Jer 7:2–3]. (4:17,2)

Again, he points out that he had not led them out of Egypt so that they might offer sacrifice to him, but that, forgetting the idolatry of the Egyptians, they should be able to hear the voice of the Lord, which would be their salvation and glory. This he declared by Jeremiah: "Thus says the LORD, Add your burnt offerings to your sacrifices, and eat the flesh. For in the day that I brought your ancestors out of the land of Egypt, I did not speak to them or command them concerning burnt offerings and sacrifices. But this command I gave them, 'Obey my voice, and I will be your God, and you shall be my people; and walk only in the way that I command you, so that it may be well with you.' Yet they did not obey or incline their ear, but, in the stubbornness of their evil will, they walked in their own counsels, and looked backward rather than forward" [Jer 7:21–24]. He also declared through the same man: "But let those who boast boast in this, that they understand and know me, that I am the LORD; I act with steadfast love, justice, and righteousness in the earth" [Jer 9:24]. Immediately after this, he explained: "For in these things I delight, says the LORD"—but not in sacrifices, or in burnt offerings, or in oblations. The people did not receive these precepts as of primary importance, but as secondary, and for the reason already alleged, as Isaiah also says, "You have not brought me your sheep for burnt offerings or honored me with your sacrifices. I have not burdened you with offerings, or wearied you with frankincense. You have not bought me sweet cane with money, or satisfied me with the fat of your sacrifices. But you have burdened me with your sins; you have wearied me with your iniquities" [Isa 43:23–24]. He says, therefore, "This is the one to whom I will look, to the humble and contrite in spirit, who trembles at my word" [Isa 66:2]. . . . "Is not this the fast that I choose: to loose the bonds of injustice, to undo the thongs of the yoke, to let the oppressed go free, and to break every yoke? Is it not to share your bread with the hungry, and bring the homeless poor into your house; when you see the naked, to cover them, and not to hide yourself from your own kin? Then your light shall break forth like the dawn, and your healing shall spring up quickly; your vindicator shall go before you, the glory of the LORD shall be your rear guard. Then you shall call, and the LORD will answer; you shall cry for help, and he will say, 'Here I am'" [Isa 58:6–9].

From among the twelve prophets, Zechariah also pointed out to the people the will of God: "Thus says the LORD of hosts: Render true judgments, show kindness and mercy to one another; do not oppress the widow, the orphan, the alien, or the poor; and do not devise evil in your hearts against one another" [Zech 7:9–10]. He said further, "These are the things that you shall do: Speak the truth to one another, render in your gates judgments that are true and make for peace, do not devise evil in your hearts against one another, and love no false oath; for all these are things that I hate, says the LORD" [Zech 8:16–17]. Moreover, David said similarly, "Which of you desires life, and covets many days to enjoy good? Keep your tongue from evil, and your lips from speaking deceit. Depart from evil, and do good; seek peace, and pursue it" [Ps 34:12–14]. (4:17,3)

From all this it is clear that God did not seek sacrifices and burnt offerings from them, but faith and obedience and righteousness, all for their salvation. When teaching them his will in Hosea the prophet, God said, "I desire steadfast love and not sacrifice, the knowledge of God rather than burnt-offerings" [Hos 6:6]. Besides this, our Lord exhorted them to the same effect when he said, "But if you had known what this means, 'I desire mercy and not sacrifice,' you would not have condemned the guiltless" [Matt 12:7]. Thus he testifies that the prophets preached the truth, but he accuses those who heard him of being foolish through their own fault. (4:17,4)

He also directed his disciples to offer God the first-fruits of what he had made—again, not as if he needed them, but so that the disciples might themselves be neither unfruitful nor ungrateful—when he took a created thing, bread, and gave thanks, and said, "This is my body" [Matt 26:26]. He took the cup, which is also part of the creation to which we belong, acknowledged it as his blood, and taught the new oblation of the new covenant—which the Church has received from the apostles and offers to God throughout all the world, who gives us the first-fruits of his own gifts in the New Testament to sustain us. From among the twelve prophets, Malachi prophesied about this: "I have no pleasure in you, says the LORD of hosts, and I will not accept an offering from your hands. For from the rising of the sun to its setting my name is great among the nations, and in every place incense is offered to my name, and a pure offering; for my name is great among the nations, says the LORD of hosts" [Mal 1:10–11]. In the plainest manner this indicates that the former people [the Jews] would cease to make offerings to God, but that in every place a pure sacrifice would be offered to him, and that his name would be glorified among the nations. (4:17,5)

But what other name is there which is glorified among the Gentiles than that of our Lord, by whom both the Father and humanity are glorified? Since it is the name of his own Son, whom he made human, he calls it his own.... Thus the Father confesses the name of Jesus Christ, which is glorified in the Church throughout all the world, to be his own, since it belongs to his Son, and also because the one who thus uses it gave him for the salvation of humankind. So, since the name of the Son belongs to the Father, and since in the omnipotent God the Church makes offerings through Jesus Christ, he appropriately declares, "And in every place incense is offered to my name, and a pure offering." Now John, in the Apocalypse, declares that the incense is "the prayers of the saints" [Rev 5:8]. (4:17,6)

The oblation of the Church, which the Lord gave instructions to be offered throughout all the world, is accounted with God a pure sacrifice and is acceptable to him—again, not that he needs a sacrifice from us, but so that the one who offers may be glorified in what he offers, if his gift is accepted. By the gift both honor and affection are shown forth towards the king.... (4:18,1)

Oblations, as a class in general, have not been set aside, for there were both oblations among the Jews and there are oblations among the Christians. The Jews had sacrifices; so does the Church. However, the species has been changed, since the offering is now made by freemen, not slaves. The Lord is always one and the same; however, the character of a servile oblation is different from that of freemen, so that the very oblations might indicate the liberty now granted. With him nothing is without purpose or signification or design. This is why the Jews consecrated the tithes of their goods to him; whereas those who have received liberty set aside all their possessions for the Lord's purposes, bestowing joyfully and freely the valuable portions of their property, since they expect to receive better things hereafter, like the poor widow who cast all her living into the treasury of God [Luke 21:4]. (4:18,2)

In the beginning God respected the gifts of Abel, because he offered them with singlemindedness and righteousness, but he had no respect for Cain's offering [Gen 4:4–5], because his heart was divided by the envy and malice which he cherished against his brother. This was shown when God reproved his hidden thoughts, "If you do well, will you not be accepted?" [Gen 4:7]. God is not appeased by sacrifice. If any one tries to offer a sacrifice as an outward show, unexceptionably, in due order, and according to regulation, but in his soul does not grant his neighbor the fellowship which is right and proper, and he is not under the fear of God—one who thus cherishes secret sin does not deceive God by the sacrifice which is offered correctly in outward appearance, nor will such an oblation profit him anything. Instead, that one must give up the evil which he has conceived within himself, so that sin may not, by his hypocritical action, make him his own destroyer. For this reason the Lord also declared, "Woe to you, scribes and Pharisees, hypocrites! For you are like whitewashed tombs, which on the outside look beautiful, but inside they are full of the bones of the dead and of all kinds of filth. So you also on the outside look righteous to others, but inwardly you are full of hypocrisy and lawlessness" [Matt 23:27–28]. As far as outward appearance went, they seemed to offer correctly, but within themselves they had jealousy like Cain's. That is why they killed the righteous one, dismissing the counsel of the Word, as Cain did.

Consequently, sacrifices do not sanctify anyone, for God does not need sacrifice. What moves God to accept an offering is the conscience of the offerer, which sanctifies the sacrifice when it is pure. But he says, "Whoever sacrifices a lamb [is] like one who breaks a dog's neck" [Isa 66:3]. (4:18,3)

But since the Church offers with singlemindedness, her gift is appropriately reckoned a pure sacrifice by God. . . . It is indeed right for us to make an oblation to God, and in all things to be grateful to God our maker—in a pure mind, in faith without hypocrisy, in well-grounded hope, and in fervent love, offering the first-fruits of his own created things. Only the Church offers this pure oblation to the creator, offering to him, with thanksgiving, the things taken from his creation. . . . (4:18,4)

. . . Our view accords with the Eucharist, which in turn establishes our view. For we offer him his own, faithfully proclaiming the fellowship and union of flesh and Spirit. For as the bread, which is produced from the earth, when it receives the invocation of God, is no longer common bread, but the Eucharist, consisting of two realities, earthly and heavenly, so also our bodies, when they receive the Eucharist, are no longer corruptible, since they now have the hope of the resurrection to eternity. (4:18,5)

So we make offering to him, not as if he needed it, but rendering thanks for his gift and thus sanctifying what has been created. For while God does not need our possessions, we need to offer something to God. Solomon said, "Whoever is kind to the poor lends to the LORD, and will be repaid in full" [Prov 19:17]: God, who needs nothing, takes our good works to himself so that he may grant us a reward out of his abundant goodness. Our Lord says in this regard, "Come, you that are blessed by my Father, inherit the kingdom prepared for you from the foundation of the world; for I was hungry and you gave me food, I was thirsty and you gave me something to drink, I was a stranger and you welcomed me, I was naked and you gave me clothing, I was sick and you took care of me, I was in prison and you visited me" [Matt 25:34–36]. . . . (4:18,6)

As Scripture itself suggests, one may justly ask the heretics, How high above God do you lift up your imaginations, you rashly elated people? You have heard that the heavens are measured in the palm of his hand [Isa 40:12]: tell me the measure, and recount the endless number of cubits, explain to me the fulness—the breadth, length, height, beginning and end of the measurement. The human mind cannot understand or comprehend them, for the heavenly treasuries are great. God cannot be measured in the heart, and he is incomprehensible by the mind; he holds the earth in the hollow of his hand. Who can measure his right hand? Who even knows his finger? Who understands his hand—that hand which encompasses immensity; that hand which, by its own measure, spreads out the whole of the heavens and which enfolds the earth with all its abysses in its palm? . . . God is "far above all rule and authority and power and dominion, and above every name that is named" [Eph 1:21] of all the things which have been created and established. And this one, who fills the heavens and views the abysses, is also present with every one of us: he says, "Am I a God near by, says the LORD, and not a God far off? Who can hide in secret places so that I cannot see them?" [Jer 23:23]. . . . (4:19,2)

But if no human being can comprehend the fulness and the greatness of his hand, how will anyone be able to understand or know in his heart so great a God? . . . It is clear to all that no one can fully declare the goodness of God from the things he has made. And that his greatness is not defective, but contains all things, and extends even to us, and is with us, everyone who entertains worthy conceptions of God will confess. (4:19,3)

As to his greatness, it is not possible to know God, for it is impossible to measure the Father; but as to his love, which is what leads us to God by his Word when we obey him, we always learn that there is so great a God, and that he himself established, selected, adorned, and contains all things—including us and our world. We were made, along with those things which are contained by him. He is the one who Scripture says formed humankind by taking clay of the earth and breathing into his face the breath of life [Gen 2:7]. It was not angels who made or formed us; neither angels nor anything else had the power to make an image of God, except the Word of the Lord. God did not need their assistance to do what he had already determined to do, as if he needed hands. With him the Word and Wisdom, the Son and the Spirit, were always present, by whom and in whom he freely and spontaneously made all things—to whom he said, "Let us make humankind in our image, according to our likeness" [Gen 1:26]. . . . (4:20,1)

Consequently, Scripture declared truth when it said, "First of all, believe that God is one, who created all things and set them in order, and made out of what did not exist everything that is."[2] He contains all things and is himself contained by no one. Among the prophets, Malachi rightly urged, "Have we not all one father? Has not one God created us?" [Mal 2:10]. In agreement with this the apostle says, "There is . . . one God and Father of all, who is above all and through all and in all" [Eph 4:4, 6]. The Lord likewise says, "All things have been handed over to me by my Father" [Matt 11:27]—obviously meaning him who made all things, since he did not deliver to him someone else's things, but his own. "All things" indicates that nothing has been kept back from him. That is why the same one is the judge of the living and the dead, the one "who has the key of David, who opens and no one will shut, who shuts and no one opens" [Rev. 3:7]. For no one in heaven or in earth or under the earth was able to open the book of the Father or to behold him, except the Lamb who was slain [Rev 5:3–6] and has redeemed us with his own blood.

---

2. Irenaeus is here citing *The Shepherd of Hermas*, Mandate 1; written c. 95–100 CE, this document was considered by a number of leaders of the early Church to be Scripture; it is available in *AposFrs* 334–527.

When "the Word became flesh" [John 1:14], he received power over all things from the same God who made all things by the Word and adorned them by his Wisdom, so that just as the Word of God had sovereignty in the heavens, so also he might have sovereignty in earth, since he was a righteous man who "committed no sin, and no deceit was found in his mouth" [1 Pet 2:22], and that he might have pre-eminence over those things under the earth, since he himself became "the first-born from the dead" [Col 1:18]. This was so that all things might behold their king, as I have already urged, and that the paternal light might meet with and rest upon the flesh of our Lord. From his resplendent flesh it would come to us, so that humanity might attain immortality, having been invested with the paternal light. (4:20,2)

So there is one God, who by the Word and Wisdom created and arranged all things. This is the creator who has granted this world to the human race and who, as to his greatness, is unknown to all whom he has made—for no one has searched out his height, whether among the ancients who have gone to their rest or any of those who are now alive. But in his love, he is always known through him by whose means he ordained all things. This Word is our Lord Jesus Christ, who in the last times was made a human among humankind, so that he might join the end to the beginning—that is, humanity to God.

The prophets, who received the prophetic gift from the same Word, announced his advent in the flesh, in which the blending and communion of God and humanity took place according to the Father's good pleasure. The Word of God thus foretold from the beginning that God would be seen by humans and converse with them on earth, confer with them, and be present with his own creation—saving it, becoming capable of being perceived by it, freeing us from the hands of all who hate us (that is, from every spirit of wickedness), and enabling us to serve him in holiness and righteousness all our days [Luke 1:71, 75], so that human beings, having embraced the Spirit of God, might pass into the glory of the Father. (4:20,4)

The prophets declared these things in a prophetic manner. They did not teach, as some allege, that the one foreseen by the prophets was a different god, since the Father of all is invisible. That is what these heretics teach, but they totally misconstrue the nature of prophecy. Prophecy is a prediction of future things, a setting forth ahead of time of what will happen later. The prophets indicated beforehand that God would be seen by humans, as the Lord also says, "Blessed are the pure in heart, for they will see God" [Matt 5:8]. In respect to his greatness and his awesome glory, "no one shall see me [God] and live" [Exod 33:20], for the Father is incomprehensible. But with regard to his infinite power, in his love and kindness he grants to those who love him to see God—something which the prophets also predicted. "What is impossible for mortals is possible for God" [Luke 18:27]: no human can see God by his own powers, but when God pleases he is seen by humans, by whom and when and as he wills. God is powerful in all things: seen prophetically at that time through the Spirit, and seen adoptively through the Son, he shall also be seen paternally in the kingdom of heaven. The Spirit prepares humanity in the Son of God, and the Son leads humanity to the Father, while the Father confers incorruption for eternal life, which comes to all those who see God. . . .

Those who see God receive life. That is why, although he is beyond comprehension and boundless and invisible, he made himself visible and comprehensible and within the capacity of those who believe, so that he might give life to those who receive and behold him through faith. For as his greatness is past finding out, so also his goodness is beyond expression; having been seen through his goodness, he grants life to those who see him. Without life it is impossible to live, and the means of life is found in fellowship with God. But fellowship with God is to know God and to enjoy his goodness. (4:20,5)

Human beings therefore shall see God so that they may live: they will be made immortal by that sight and will attain even unto God. As I already said, this was declared figuratively by the prophets, that God would be seen by those who bear his Spirit in them and wait patiently for his coming. Moses said in Deuteronomy, "Today we have seen that God may speak to someone and the person may still live" [Deut 5:24]. Some of these people saw the prophetic Spirit and his active influences being poured forth in all kinds of gifts; others, again, beheld the advent of the Lord and that dispensation which held sway from the beginning, by which he accomplished the will of the Father regarding things both celestial and terrestrial; and others beheld paternal glories adapted to the times and to those who saw and heard them then, and to all who were subsequently to hear them. In this way God was revealed; God the Father was shown forth through all these operations, with the Spirit working and the Son ministering, while the Father was approving—and thus salvation for humankind was being achieved. . . .

As to the questions of what nature and how great he is, God is invisible and indescribable to all things which he has made. Even so, he is by no means unknown: all things learn through his Word that there is one God the Father, who contains all things and gives life to all, as is written in the gospel: "No one has even seen God. It is God the only Son, who is close to the Father's heart, who has made him known" [John 1:18]. (4:20,6)

The Son of the Father makes him known from the beginning, since he was with the Father from the beginning. At appropriate times, for the benefit of humankind, he showed the human race prophetic visions, diversities of gifts, his own ministrations, and the glory of the Father, in regular order and connection. Where there is a regular succession, there is also fixedness; and where fixedness, there suitability to the period; and where suitability, there also utility. For this reason, the Word became the one who dispensed paternal grace for the benefit of humanity, for whom he made such great dispensations, revealing God to humanity, but presenting humanity to God, all while preserving the invisibility of the Father, lest anyone should ever come to despise God, and so that he should always possess something towards which humankind might advance. On the other hand, he revealed God to humanity through many dispensations, lest they should cease to exist by falling away from God altogether.

The glory of God is a human being fully alive, and the life of a human being consists in beholding God. If what the creation shows of God grants life to all living in the earth, then much more does the revelation of the Father which comes through the Word give life to those who see God. (4:20,7)

. . . Of old, prophecies came not by word alone but in visions also, and in the prophets' mode of life and the actions which they performed, as led by the Spirit. In this invisible way they saw God, as Isaiah said, "My eyes have seen the King, the LORD of hosts" [Isa 6:5]—by which he pointed out that human beings should behold God with their eyes and hear his voice. In this way they also saw the Son of God as a man conversant with human beings: they prophesied what would happen, saying that he who was had not yet come but was nonetheless present, proclaiming also the impassible as subject to suffering, and declaring that he who was then in heaven had descended into the dust of death [Ps 22:15]. As to the rest of what he would accomplish, some of this they beheld through visions, some they proclaimed by word, while some they indicated in types, by means of outward actions, showing visibly things which were to be seen; heralding by word of mouth those which should be heard; and performing by actual operation what should take place by action; but all the while announcing them all prophetically. That is why Moses declared to the people who transgressed the law that God was a consuming fire [Deut 4:24], thus threatening that God would bring a day of fire upon them; but to those who feared God he said, "The LORD, a God merciful and gracious, slow to anger, and abounding in steadfast love and faithfulness, keeping steadfast love for the thousandth generation, forgiving iniquity and transgression" [Exod 34:6–7]. (4:20,8)

The Word spoke to Moses, appearing before him just as any one might speak to his friend [Num 12:8]. But Moses desired to see openly the one who was speaking with him, and God said to him, "You cannot see my face; for no one shall see me and live. . . . See, there is a place by me where you shall stand on the rock; and while my glory passes by I will put you in a cleft of the rock, and I will cover you with my hand until I have passed by; then I will take away my hand, and you shall see my back, but my face shall not be seen" [Exod 33:20–24]. This shows us two truths: it is impossible for a human being to see God, but in the wisdom of God, human beings would see him in the last times, in the depth of a rock—that is, in his coming as a man. That is why the Lord conferred with Moses face to face on the top of a mountain, with Elijah also present, as the gospel relates [Matt 17:3]; in the last days, he thus made good the ancient promise. (4:20,9)

The prophets did not behold the actual face of God: they saw the dispensations and mysteries through which humankind afterwards would come to see God, similar to what was said to Elijah: "'Go out and stand on the mountain before the LORD, for the LORD is about to pass by.' Now there was a great wind, so strong that it was splitting mountains and breaking rocks in pieces before the LORD, but the LORD was not in the wind; and after the wind an earthquake, but the LORD was not in the earthquake; and after the earthquake a fire, but the LORD was not in the fire; and after the fire a sound of sheer silence" [1 Kgs 19:11–12]. In this way, the prophet—who was very indignant, because of the transgression of the people and the slaughter of Baal's prophets—was both taught to act in a gentler manner, and the Lord's advent as a man was pointed out, that it would be subsequent to the law given by Moses, mild and tranquil, in which he would neither break the bruised reed, nor quench the smoking flax [Isa 42:3]. The mild and peaceful repose of his kingdom was also thus indicated: after the wind which rent the mountains, the earthquake, and the fire come the tranquil and peaceful times of his kingdom, in which the Spirit of God, in the most gentle manner, gives life to and increases humankind. . . . (4:20,10)

If, then, neither Moses nor Elijah nor Ezekiel, who all had many celestial visions, saw God, but if what they saw were similitudes of the splendor of the Lord and prophecies of things to come, then it is clear that the Father is invisible, of whom the Lord declared: "No one has ever seen God" [John 1:18a]. But, as he himself willed for the benefit of those who beheld, the Word showed the Father's brightness and explained his purposes—as the Lord also said, "It is God the only Son, who is close to the Father's heart, who has made him known" [John 1:18b]. He himself also shows that the Word of the Father is both rich and great: he did not appear to those who saw him in only one figure or character, but in accordance with the reasons and effects aimed at in his dispensations, as it is written in Daniel. For at one time he was seen present with Hananiah, Mishael, and Azariah in the furnace of fire, preserving them from the effects of fire: Nebuchadnezzar exclaimed, "The fourth has the appearance of a god" [Dan 3:25]. At another time he was represented as "a stone cut from the mountain not by hands" [Dan 2:45], who would smite all temporal kingdoms, driving them away, and himself filling the whole earth. The same one was beheld as the son of man coming in the clouds of heaven, and drawing near to the Ancient of Days, and receiving from him all power and glory, and a kingdom: "His dominion is an everlasting dominion that shall not pass away, and his kingship is one that shall never be destroyed" [Dan 7:14]. . . . (4:20,11)

However, he was beheld by the prophets, not only by visions seen and words proclaimed, but also in actual works, through them prefiguring future events. That is why Hosea the prophet took "a wife of whoredom," showing thus that "the land commits great whoredom by forsaking the LORD" [Hos 1:2–3]—meaning those who are on the earth. From people of this sort it would be God's good pleasure to take out [Acts 15:14] a Church which would be sanctified by fellowship with his Son, just as that woman was sanctified by intercourse with the prophet. This is the reason Paul declares that "the unbelieving wife is made holy through her husband" [1 Cor 7:14]. Further, the prophet named his children, "Not pitied" and "Not my people" [Hos 1:6, 9], so that, as the apostle says, "Those who were not my people I will call 'my people,' and her who was not beloved I will call 'beloved.' And in the very place where it was said to them, 'You are not my people,' there they shall be called children of the living God" [Rom 9:25–26]. The apostle thus shows that what had been done typically by the prophet's actions was done truly by Christ in the Church....

Thus also Rahab the harlot, while condemning herself as a Gentile guilty of all sins, nevertheless received the three spies and hid them at her home. These three were a type of the Father and the Son, together with the Holy Spirit. When the entire city in which she lived fell to ruins at the blast of the seven trumpets, by believing the scarlet sign Rahab the harlot and all her family were preserved when all was over. This is what the Lord intended when he declared to those who did not receive his advent, the Pharisees who undoubtedly nullified the sign of the scarlet thread (which meant the Passover and the redemption and exodus of the people from Egypt), when he said, "The tax collectors and the prostitutes are going into the kingdom of God ahead of you" [Matt 21:31]. (4:20,12)

The apostle has abundantly taught that our faith was prefigured in Abraham, that he was the patriarch of our faith and, as it were, the prophet of it: "Does God supply you with the Spirit and work miracles among you by your doing the works of the law, or by your believing what you heard? Just as Abraham 'believed God, and it was reckoned to him as righteousness' [Gen 15:6], so, you see, those who believe are the descendants of Abraham. And the scripture, foreseeing that God would justify the Gentiles by faith, declared the gospel beforehand to Abraham, saying, 'All the Gentiles shall be blessed in you' [Gen 12:3]. For this reason, those who believe are blessed with Abraham who believed" [Gal 3:5–9]. This is why the apostle declared that this man was not only the prophet of faith, but also the father of those who from among the Gentiles believe in Jesus Christ, because his faith and ours are one and the same: he believed in things future as if they were already accomplished, because of the promise of God; similarly, by faith we behold our inheritance in the future kingdom because of the promise of God. (4:21,1)

The history of Isaac also has a symbolic character. In the Letter to the Romans, the apostle declares: "Rebecca when she had conceived children by one husband, our ancestor Isaac," received answer from the

Word "that God's purpose of election might continue, not by works but by his call" [Rom 9:10–11], it was said unto her, "Two nations are in your womb, and two peoples born of you shall be divided; the one shall be stronger than the other, the elder shall serve the younger" [Gen 25:23]. From this it is clear that there were not only prophecies about the patriarchs, but also that the children brought forth by Rebecca were a prediction of two nations; that one would be greater, the other less; that one would be servant, the other free; but that both should come from one and the same father. Our God, one and the same, is also their God, who knows hidden things, who knows all things before they can come to pass. For this reason he said, "I have loved Jacob, but I have hated Esau" [Rom 9:13; Mal 1:2–3]. (4:21,2)

Furthermore, if anyone examines Jacob's life, he will find it full of symbolic significance. In the first place, at his birth he took hold of his brother's heel [Gen 25:26] and so was called Jacob (that is, the supplanter—one who holds, but is not held, struggling and conquering), grasping in his hand his adversary's heel—that is, victory. This is why the Lord was born, the type of whose birth he showed ahead of time, about whom John says in the Apocalypse, "He came out conquering and to conquer" [Rev 6:2]. Next, Jacob took the rights of the firstborn when his brother despised them, just as the younger nation received Christ when the older one rejected him, saying, "We have no king but the emperor" [John 19:15].

In Christ all this is fulfilled: the latter people who believe in him have snatched away the blessings of the former from the Father, just as Jacob took away the blessing of Esau. Because of this Jacob suffered the plots and persecutions of his brother, just as the Church does from the Jews. The twelve tribes—the race of Israel—were born in a foreign country; Christ was also born in a strange country, to generate the twelve-pillared foundation of the Church. Various colored sheep were allotted to this Jacob as his wages; the wages of Christ are human beings, who from various and diverse nations come together into one cohort of faith, as the Father promised him, saying, "Ask of me, and I will make the nations your heritage, and the ends of the earth your possession" [Ps 2:8].

And since from the multitude of his children the prophets of the Lord afterwards arose, it was necessary that Jacob beget children from the two sisters, even as Christ did from the two laws of one and the same Father. Similarly, Jacob had children by the handmaids, indicating that

Christ would raise up children of God, both from those who are free and from those who are slaves, granting all of them in the same way the gift of the Spirit, who brings us to life. . . . For with God nothing is without purpose or due significance. (4:21,3)

Now in the last days, when the fulness of the time of liberty had arrived, the Word himself "washed away the filth of the daughters of Zion" [Isa 4:4] when he washed the disciples' feet with his own hands [John 13:5]. This was the goal of the human race, inheriting God: that as in the beginning through our first parents we were all brought into bondage, becoming subject to death, so at last through the last Adam all who from the beginning were his disciples, being cleansed and washed from the defilement of death, should come to life in God—for he who washed the feet of the disciples sanctified the entire body, and rendered it clean. . . . (4:22,1)

It was not only for those who believed on him in the time of Tiberius Caesar that Christ came; nor did the Father direct his providence only for those who are alive now; but for all those who from the beginning, according to their capacity, in their generation have feared and loved God, have practiced justice and piety towards their neighbors, and have earnestly desired to see Christ and hear his voice. Therefore, at his second coming he will first awake from their sleep in death all persons of this description and will raise them up—as well as the rest who will be judged—and give them a place in his kingdom. For truly "God is one" who directed the patriarchs toward his dispensations and "justifies the circumcised on the ground of faith and the uncircumcised through that same faith" [Rom 3:30]. . . . (4:22,2)

. . . When Joseph became aware that Mary was pregnant and had decided to break off their engagement quietly, the angel said to him in sleep, "Do not be afraid to take Mary as your wife, for the child conceived in her is from the Holy Spirit. She will bear a son, and you are to name him Jesus, for he will save his people from their sins" [Matt 1:20–21]. Exhorting him further, he added: "All this took place to fulfill what had been spoken by the Lord through the prophet: 'Look, the virgin shall conceive and bear a son, and they shall call him Emmanuel'" [Matt 1:22]. In this way, the angel influenced him by the words of the prophet, warding off blame from Mary and pointing out that she was the virgin spoken of by Isaiah beforehand who would give birth to Immanuel. So, when Joseph was convinced beyond all doubt, he took Mary and gladly obeyed in regard to all the rest of the training of Christ, the journey into Egypt and back again, and then to Nazareth. But those who did not know the Scriptures, the promise of God, or the dispensation of Christ, later called Joseph the father of the child [Luke 3:23; John 6:42]. . . . (4:23,1)

Philip came upon the eunuch of the Ethiopians' queen reading the words which had been written, "Like a sheep he was led to the slaughter, and like a lamb silent before its shearer, so he does not open his mouth. In his humiliation justice was denied him" [Acts 8:32–33; Isa 53:7–8], and all the rest which the prophet related about his passion and his coming in the flesh, and how he would be dishonored by those who did not believe him. Philip easily persuaded the eunuch to believe that the one spoken of was Christ Jesus, who was crucified under Pontius Pilate and suffered all that the prophet had predicted, and that he was the Son of God, who gives eternal life to human beings. And immediately after Philip had baptized him, he departed from him. For nothing else but baptism was lacking for one who had already been instructed by the prophets: he was not ignorant of God the Father nor of the rules about how to live, but only of the advent of the Son of God. When he had come to know that, in a short space of time he went on his way rejoicing, to be the herald in Ethiopia of Christ's advent. So Philip did not have a hard time with him, since he was already trained by the prophets in the fear of God. For this reason, too, the apostles could gather the sheep from the house of Israel and speak to them out of the Scriptures, proving that this crucified Jesus was the Christ, the Son of the living God. They persuaded a great multitude who already feared God, and in one day about 3,000 persons were baptized [Acts 2:41; 4:4]. (4:23,2)

This is why Paul, the apostle of the Gentiles, says, "I worked harder than any of them" [1 Cor 15:10]: the instruction of the former [the Jews] was a comparatively easy task, since the other apostles could cite proofs from the Scriptures, and because the Jews, in the habit of hearing Moses and the prophets, could thus readily receive the first-born from the dead and the Prince of life from God. . . . As I have pointed out in the preceding book, the apostle first instructed the Gentiles to turn away from the superstition of idols and to worship one God, the creator of heaven and earth, and the maker of the whole creation; and that his Son was his Word, by whom he founded all things; and that in the last times he became a human among humankind; that he reformed the human race, but destroyed and conquered the enemy of humanity and gave to his handiwork victory against the adversary. . . . (4:24,1)

. . . So, the one who became apostle to the Gentiles had to work harder than those who preached the Son of God among those of the circumcision, for the latter had the assistance of the Scriptures, which the Lord confirmed and fulfilled in coming as he had been announced. But among the Gentiles, Paul brought a foreign erudition, a new doctrine that the gods of the nations not only were no gods at all, but even the idols of demons; and that there is only one God, who is "far above all rule and authority and power and dominion, and above every name that is named" [Eph 1:21]; and that his Word, invisible by nature, became palpable and visible among humankind and descended "to the point of death—even death on a cross" [Phil 2:8]; and that those who believe in him will be incorruptible and delivered from suffering and will receive the kingdom of heaven. These things were preached to the Gentiles by word, without the Scriptures: therefore, also, those who preached among the Gentiles had to work harder. . . . (4:24,2)

Anyone who reads the Scriptures attentively will find in them an account of Christ and a foreshadowing of the new calling, for Christ is the treasure hidden in the field [Matt 13:44]—that is, in this world (for "the field is the world" [Matt 13:38]). The treasure hid in the Scriptures is Christ, who was pointed out by types and parables. His human nature could not be understood before the things predicted took place (that is, the advent of Christ). . . . Every prophecy, before its fulfilment, is enigmatic and ambiguous, but when its time of fulfillment has arrived and the prediction has come to pass, then the prophecies have a clear and certain exposition.

For this reason, to this day when the law is read to the Jews, it is like a fable to them, since they do not embrace the explanation of all things which accords with the coming of the Son of God in human nature. But when it is read by Christians, it is a treasure, hidden indeed in a field but brought to light and expounded by the cross of Christ; it thus enriches human understanding, manifests the wisdom of God, declares his dealing with humankind, forms the kingdom of Christ ahead of time, preaches by anticipation the inheritance of the holy Jerusalem, and proclaims beforehand that those who love God will be greatly privileged to see God. They hear his word, and from the hearing of his discourse they will be glorified so greatly that others will be unable to behold the glory of their countenance, as was said by Daniel: "Those who are wise shall shine like the brightness of the sky, and those who lead many to righteousness, like the stars forever and ever" [Dan 12:3]. This is what happens to those who rightly read the Scriptures. This is the way the Lord himself taught his disciples after his resurrection from the dead, arguing from the Scriptures, "Was it not necessary that the Christ should suffer ... and then enter into his glory, ... and that repentance and forgiveness of sins be proclaimed in his name to all nations?" [Luke 24:26, 47].... (4:26,1)

That is why it is necessary to obey the presbyters who are in the Church. They have the succession from the apostles; together with the succession of the episcopate, they have received the certain gift of truth, according to the good pleasure of the Father. We need to view with suspicion those who turn from the primitive succession and assemble themselves together elsewhere, for they are either heretics of perverse minds, schismatics puffed up and self-pleasing, or hypocrites who act this way for money or vainglory; all these have fallen from the truth. Heretics, who bring strange fire to the altar of God (that is, strange doctrines), will be burned up by the fire from heaven, as Nadab and Abihu were [Lev 10:1–2]. Those who rise up in opposition to the truth and exhort others against the Church of God will remain among those in hell, as it were swallowed up by an earthquake, like Korah, Dathan, and Abiram [Num 16:33]. But those who split the Church and rend her unity will receive the same punishment from God as Jeroboam did [1 Kgs 14:10]. (4:26,2)

There are some whom many believe to be presbyters; however, these people serve their own lusts and do not place the fear of God supreme in their hearts, but conduct themselves with contempt towards others, exult in holding a place of prominence, and do evil in secret, saying, "No one sees us." They will be convicted by the Word, who does not judge by outward appearances or look at the countenance, but who examines the heart [1 Sam 16:7]; they will hear the words found in Daniel the prophet: "You offspring of Canaan and not of Judah, beauty has beguiled you and lust has perverted your heart. You old relic of wicked days, your sins have now come home, which you have committed in the past, pronouncing unjust judgments, condemning the innocent and acquitting the guilty, though the Lord said, 'You shall not put an innocent and righteous person to death'" [Sus 56, 52–53]. This is the sort of person about whom the Lord said, "But if that wicked slave says to himself, 'My master is delayed,' and he begins to beat his fellow slaves, and eats and drinks with drunkards, the master of that slave will come on a day when he does not expect him and at an hour that he does not know. He will cut him in pieces and put him with the unfaithful" [Matt 24:48–51; cf. Luke 12:45–46]. (4:26,3)

So it behooves us to turn away from all such people but to hold fast to those who hold the doctrine of the apostles. With the order of priesthood, these people display sound speech and blameless conduct which serves to confirm and correct others. Moses was entrusted with such leadership and could say in good conscience before God, "I have not taken one donkey from them, and I have not harmed anyone of them" [Num 16:15]. . . . (4:26,4)

The Church treasures such presbyters; the prophet says about them, "I will appoint Peace as your overseer and Righteousness as your taskmaster" [Isa 60:17]. The Lord also declared about them, "Who then is the faithful and wise slave, whom his master has put in charge of his household, to give the other slaves their allowance of food at the proper time? Blessed is that slave whom his master will find at work when he arrives" [Matt 24:45–46]. Paul advises us where we can find such people: "God has appointed in the church first apostles, second prophets, third teachers" [1 Cor 12:28]. So where the gifts of the Lord have been placed, there it behooves us to learn the truth—namely, from those who possess that succession of the Church which is from the apostles, and among whom exists what is sound and blameless in conduct, as well as what is unadulterated and incorrupt in speech. These people preserve this faith of ours in one God who created all things; and they increase our love for the Son of God, who accomplished such marvelous dispensations for our sake; and they expound the Scriptures to us without danger, neither blaspheming God, nor dishonoring the patriarchs, nor despising the prophets. (4:26,5)

The Lord descended into the regions beneath the earth to preach his advent and to proclaim remission of sins for all who believe in him [1 Pet 3:19–20]. All those believed in him, who had hoped for him—that is, those who had proclaimed his coming advent and submitted to his dispensations (the righteous ones, the prophets, and the patriarchs)—their sins he remitted in the same way as he does ours. So, we should not hold against them whatever sins they committed, if we would not despise the grace of God. . . . For "all have sinned and fall short of the glory of God" [Rom 3:23], and are not justified by what they have done, but only through the coming of the Lord—those, that is, who earnestly turn their eyes toward his light. Their actions were committed to writing for our instruction, so that we might know, first of all, that our God and theirs is one and that sins do not please him even if they were committed by renowned people, and that, secondly, we should turn away from all wickedness. For if these men of long ago, who received these gifts before we received them, became objects of disgrace when they committed any sin and served fleshly lusts, what will people in the present day have to endure if they despise the Lord's coming and become the slaves of their own lusts? Truly, the death of the Lord became healing and remission of sins to the former, but Christ will not die again in behalf of those who now commit sin [Heb 6:46], for "death no longer has dominion over him" [Rom 6:9]. Instead, the Son shall come in the glory of the Father, requiring from his stewards the money which he had entrusted to them, with interest [Matt 25:19–27]—and from those to whom he had given most he will demand most [Luke 12:48]. So, we should not puff ourselves up or be severe in our assessments of those long ago; instead, we should pay attention to ourselves, lest having come to know Christ we nonetheless do things displeasing to God and receive no further forgiveness of sins, but be shut out of his kingdom. That was what Paul warned against when he said, "If God did not spare the natural branches, perhaps he will not spare you, [who were] a wild olive shoot [but] were grafted in their place to share the rich root of the olive tree" [Rom 11:21, 17]. (4:27,2)

You will notice, too, that the transgressions of the common people were described in the same way—not for the sake of those who transgressed then, but as instruction for us. We should understand that it is one and the same God against whom these people long ago sinned and against whom some people now transgress who claim to have believed in him. But Paul also plainly declared about this: "I do not want you to be unaware, brothers and sisters, that our ancestors were all under the cloud, and all passed through the sea, and all were baptized into Moses in the cloud and in the sea, and all ate the same spiritual food, and all drank the same spiritual drink. For they drank from the spiritual rock that followed them, and the rock was Christ. Nevertheless, God was not pleased with most of them, and they were struck down in the wilderness. Now these things occurred as examples for us, so that we might not desire evil as they did. Do not become idolaters as some of them did; as it is written, 'The people sat down to eat and drink, and they rose up to play.' We must not indulge in sexual immorality as some of them did, and 23,000 fell in a single day. We must not put Christ to the test, as some of them did, and were destroyed by serpents. And do not complain as some of them did, and were destroyed by the destroyer. These things happened to them to serve as an example, and they were written down to instruct us, on whom the ends of the ages have come. So if you think you are standing, watch out that you do not fall." [1 Cor 10:1–12]. (4:27,3)

. . . So the unrighteous, the idolaters, and fornicators perished then. It is the same now, for the Lord declares that such persons are sent into eternal fire [Matt 13:42; 25:41], and the apostle says, "Do you not know that wrongdoers will not inherit the kingdom of God? Do not be deceived! Fornicators, idolaters, adulterers, male prostitutes, sodomites, thieves, the greedy, drunkards, revilers, robbers—none of these will inherit the kingdom of God" [1 Cor 6:9–10]. And since he did not say this to those outside the Church, but to us (lest we be cast out of the kingdom of God for engaging in any such thing), he went on to say, "And this is what some of you used to be. But you were washed, you were sanctified, you were justified in the name of the Lord Jesus Christ and in the Spirit of our God" [1 Cor 6:11]. As was the case long ago, that those who led evil lives and led others astray were condemned and cast out, so also now the offending eye is plucked out, and the foot and the hand cut off, lest the rest of the body perish in like manner [Matt 18:8–9].

Further, we have the directive: "I am writing to you not to associate with anyone who bears the name of brother or sister who is sexually immoral or greedy, or is an idolater, reviler, drunkard, or robber. Do not even eat with such a one" [1 Cor 5:11]. The apostle also says, "Let no one deceive you with empty words, for because of these things the wrath of God comes on those who are disobedient. Therefore do not be associated with them" [Eph 5:6–7]. And as then the condemnation of sinners included others who approved of them and associated with them, so it is the case now: "a little yeast leavens the whole batch of dough" [1 Cor 5:6]. . . . (4:27,4)

Both testaments reveal the same righteousness of God who exacts vengeance—in the earlier case, he did so in types, temporarily, and more moderately; but in the latter, really, enduringly, and more sternly. The fire is eternal, and the wrath of God which will be revealed from heaven . . . entails a heavier punishment for those who incur it. . . . (4:28,1)

Since in the New Testament what we believe about God has been enriched by the coming of the Son of God, so that human beings might become partakers in God [2 Pet 1:4], our lives must become even more circumspect than of old: we are directed not only to abstain from evil actions, but even from evil thoughts, idle words, empty talk, and vulgar language [Eph 5:4]. The punishment of those who do not believe the Word of God, despise his advent, and turn away from it is increased, since it will be not just temporal but also eternal. All those to whom the Lord says, "You that are accursed, depart from me into the eternal fire" [Matt 25:41] will be damned forever; but all those to whom he will say, "Come, you that are blessed by my Father, inherit the kingdom prepared for you from the foundation of the world" [Matt 25:34] will receive the kingdom forever and continually experience its blessings. There is one and the same God the Father and his Word, who has always been with the human race through various dispensations, has accomplished many things, from the beginning has saved those who are saved (those who love God and follow the Word of God according to the group to which they belong), and has judged those who are judged (that is, those who forget God, blaspheme him, and transgress his word). (4:28,2)

. . . To those who contradict us and say, "If the Egyptians had not been afflicted with plagues and, when pursuing Israel, had not been drowned in the sea, God could not have saved his people," we give this answer: unless the Jews had become the slayers of the Lord (by which eternal life was taken away from them) and, by also killing the apostles and persecuting the Church, had fallen into an abyss of wrath, we could not have been saved. For as they were saved through the blindness of the Egyptians, so we too are saved by that of the Jews, since the death of the Lord is the condemnation of those who nailed him to the cross and did not believe his advent, but the salvation of those who believe in him. For the apostle also says, "We are the aroma of Christ to God among those who are being saved and among those who are perishing; to the one a fragrance from death to death, to the other a fragrance from life to life" [2 Cor 2:15–16]. To whom, then, is there the savor of death unto death? To those who neither believe nor are subject to the Word of God. And who are the ones who gave themselves over to death? Undoubtedly, those who neither believe nor submit to God. Again, who are the ones who have been saved and received the inheritance? Those, doubtless, who believe God and have continued in his love—like Caleb the son of

Jephunneh, Joshua the son of Nun [Num 14:30], and innocent children who have had no sense of evil [Jonah 4:11]. But who are the ones who are saved now and receive eternal life? Is it not those who love God, believe his promises, and are "infants in evil" [1 Cor 14:20]? (4:28,3)

. . . The same God inflicts blindness on those who do not believe and give him no thought, just as the sun, his creature, affects those who because of their weak eyes cannot behold its light. But to those who believe in him and follow him he grants a fuller and greater illumination of mind. This squares with what the apostle says: "In their case the god of this world has blinded the minds of the unbelievers, to keep them from seeing the light of the gospel of the glory of Christ, who is the image of God" [2 Cor 4:4]. Again, he declares, "Since they did not see fit to acknowledge God, God gave them up to a debased mind and to things that should not be done" [Rom 1:28]. Speaking about Antichrist, too, he asserts, "For this reason God sends them a powerful delusion, leading them to believe what is false, so that all who have not believed the truth but took pleasure in unrighteousness will be condemned" [2 Thess 2:11–12]. (4:29,1)

So, if in the present time also, God—who knows the number of those who will not believe (since he foreknows all things)—has given over to unbelief and turned his face away from people like this, if he leaves them in the darkness which they have chosen for themselves, what is surprising if long ago he also gave over to their unbelief both Pharaoh, who never would have believed, and those who were with him? As the Word declared to Moses from the bush: "I know . . . that the king of Egypt will not let you go unless compelled by a mighty hand" [Exod 3:19]. . . . (4:29,2)

Those who criticize and find fault because by God's command the people [of Israel], just before they departed, accepted all sorts of vessels and clothing from the Egyptians [Exod 3:21–22; 11:2] and then left—vessels and clothing from which the tabernacle was prepared in the wilderness—show that they are ignorant of the righteous way God deals with humanity. As a presbyter has remarked,[3] if God had not directed things this way in the exodus which served as a type, no one could now be saved in the ultimate exodus—that is, in the faith in which we have been established, and by which we have come out from among the

---

3. Charles Hill has presented a persuasive argument that this presbyter must have been Polycarp; see his *From the Lost Teaching of Polycarp*.

number of the Gentiles. In some cases a small but in other cases a large amount of property, acquired from the mammon of unrighteousness, comes to the service of the Church. From what source do we derive the houses in which we dwell, the garments in which we are clothed, the vessels we use, and everything else we need for everyday life, if not from those things which, when we were Gentiles, we acquired by avarice or received from our heathen parents, relations, or friends who obtained them unrighteously? Indeed, even now we acquire such things when we are in the faith. For who sells and does not wish to make a profit from the one who buys? Or who purchases anything, and does not wish to obtain good value from the seller? Or who carries on a trade without desiring to earn his livelihood by it? And with regard to those in the royal palace who believe [cf. Phil 4:23], do they not derive the utensils they employ from the property which belongs to Caesar? And does not each of these Christians give to the poor according to his ability? The Egyptians were debtors to the Jewish people, not just in regard to property, but also for their very lives, because of the kindness of the patriarch Joseph long before. But in what way are the heathen debtors to us, from whom we receive both gain and profit? Whatever they amass with labor we make use of without labor, though we are in the faith. (4:30,1)

. . . So how did the Israelites act unjustly, if out of many things they took a few, when they might have possessed much property if they had not served them [the Egyptians]? They might then have gone forth wealthy; whereas they received only an insignificant payment for their heavy servitude and went away poor. . . . (4:30,2)

If we and they were compared, who would seem to have received their worldly goods in the fairer manner? Would it not be the Jewish people from the Egyptians, who were indebted to the Jewish people, rather than we who receive property from the Romans and other nations, who are under no similar obligation to us? Moreover, because of the Romans' accomplishments the world is at peace, and so we walk on the highways without fear and sail where we will. . . . It is for this sort of thing that the Lord said, "Do not judge, so that you may not be judged. For with the judgment you make you will be judged" [Matt 7:1–2]. By this he did not mean that we should not find fault with sinners, or that we should consent to those who act wickedly; instead, he intends that we should not pronounce an unfair judgment on the dispensations of God, who has ordained all things so that they turn out for good [Rom 8:28], in a way consistent with justice. . . .

We are shown to be righteous by whatever else we do well, since we thus redeem, as it were, our property from strange hands. But when I say, "from strange hands," this is not as if the world were not God's possession. We have gifts of this sort and receive them from others in the same way as the Israelites of old received them from the Egyptians who did not know God. By these gifts we erect in ourselves the tabernacle of God, for God dwells in those who act uprightly, as the Lord says: "Make friends for yourselves by means of dishonest wealth" [Luke 16:9]. . . . (4:30,3)

. . . The whole exodus of the people out of Egypt, which took place under divine guidance, was a type and image of the exodus of the Church which would later take place from among the nations. In the fullness of time, he led it out from this world to be his own inheritance. Moses the servant of God could not bestow it, but Jesus the Son of God gives it. And if anyone devotes close attention to what is stated by the prophets about the end and to what John the disciple of the Lord saw in the Apocalypse [Rev 15–16], he will find that the nations are to receive the same plagues universally as Egypt then did particularly. (4:30,4)

When recounting matters of this kind about those who lived long ago, the presbyter [before mentioned] was in the habit of instructing us in this fashion: "With respect to those misdeeds for which the Scriptures themselves blame the patriarchs and prophets, we should not denounce them or become like Ham, who ridiculed the shame of his father and so fell under a curse; rather, we should give thanks to God for them, since their sins have been forgiven them through the advent of our Lord, for he said that they gave thanks for us and gloried in the coming salvation. Again, with regard to those actions on which the Scriptures pass no censure but are simply recorded, we should not become accusers, since we are not more exacting than God and we are not greater than our master. Instead, we should search for types in them, for nothing which was recorded in Scripture without being condemned is without deeper significance. . . ." (4:31,1)

This is the way a presbyter who had been a disciple of the apostles dealt with the two testaments, proving that both were from one and the same God. He maintained that there was no other God besides the one who made and fashioned us, and that the instruction of those who teach that this world of ours was made by angels or by some other power or by another God was baseless. If one turns away from the creator of all things and grants that this creation to which we belong was formed by or through any other than the one God, that person will necessarily fall into a great deal of inconsistency and many contradictions of this kind, for which he will be unable to provide explanations which could be regarded as either probable or true.... But if anyone believes in the one God who made all things by the Word—as Moses says, "God said, 'Let there be light'; and there was light" [Gen 1:3]; and as we read in the Gospel, "All things came into being through him, and without him not one thing came into being" [John 1:3]; and as the apostle Paul says in like manner, "One God and Father of all, who is above all and through all and in all" [Eph 4:6]—that person will first of all "hold fast to the head, from whom the whole body, nourished and held together by its ligaments and sinews, grows with a growth that is from God" [Col 2:19]. And then every word will also be consistent for him, if he diligently reads the Scriptures in company with those who are presbyters in the Church—among whom we find the apostolic doctrine, as I have pointed out. (4:32,1)

That all the apostles taught that there were two testaments among the two peoples, but that one and the same God gave both testaments for the benefit of those who were to believe in God, I have proved from the apostles' teaching in the third book. The first testament was not given without reason or purpose or accidentally: it was given for the benefit of those whom it subdued to the service of God (even though God needs no service from human beings). It exhibited types of heavenly things, since humankind was not yet able to see the things of God directly. It thus foreshadowed the images of those things which now actually exist in the Church, so that our faith might be firmly established. It contained a prophecy of coming things, so that humankind might learn that God has foreknowledge of all things. (4:32,2)

A spiritual disciple, one who has genuinely received the Spirit of God—who was from the beginning and has been present with human-kind in all the dispensations of God, announced things future, revealed things present, and narrated things past—such a person indeed judges all others but is himself judged by no one [1 Cor 2:15]. That person judges the nations "who serve the creature rather than the Creator" [Rom 1:25] and with a reprobate mind devote themselves to what has no lasting existence. That person also judges the Jews, who do not accept the word of liberty and are thus unwilling to go forth free, although they have a deliverer. They pretend to serve God, who needs nothing, by going beyond the requirements of the law, but they neither recognize the advent of Christ, which he accomplished for the salvation of humanity, nor are willing to understand that all the prophets announced his two advents. In the first, he became a man who experienced suffering and weakness [Isa 53:3], sat upon the foal of a donkey [Zech 9:9], was the stone rejected by the builders [Ps 118:22], was led as a sheep to the slaughter [Isa 53:7], and by the stretching forth of his hands destroyed Amalek [Exod 17:11]. In this first advent he gathered into his Father's fold, from the ends of the earth, the children who had been scattered abroad [Isa 11:12], and he remembered his own who had died and descended to them so that he might deliver them [1 Pet 3:19–20]. But in the second he will come on the clouds [Dan 7:13], bringing on the day which burns like an oven [Mal 4:1], striking the earth with the rod of his mouth [Isa 11:4], slaying the unrighteous with the breath of his lips, having a winnowing fork in his hands and clearing his floor and gathering the wheat into his granary, but burning the chaff with unquenchable fire [Matt 3:12; Luke 3:17]. (4:33,1)

He will also examine the doctrine of Marcion. . . . Why did the Lord call himself the son of man, if he had not experienced human birth? And how could he forgive us sins, for which we are answerable to our maker and God? Further, if he were not truly flesh, but only appeared to be human, how could he have been crucified, and how could blood and water issue from his pierced side [John 19:34]? Moreover, what body was it that those who buried him put in the tomb? And what was it that rose again from the dead? (4:33,2)

He will also judge all the followers of Valentinus, because, while they confess with the tongue one God the Father from whom everything derives its existence, they maintain that he was the result of an apostasy or defect. Further, while they also confess with the tongue one Lord Jesus Christ, the Son of God, they assert a distinct generation of the only-begotten, another for the word, another for Christ, and still another for the savior. . . . The spiritual man will also judge the vain teachings of the rest of the perverse Gnostics, showing that they are the disciples of Simon Magus. (4:33,3)

He [the truly spiritual person] will also judge the Ebionites[4]: how can they be saved unless it was God who accomplished their salvation

---

4. The Ebionites were a Jewish Christian group who taught that Jesus was the Messiah [i.e., Christ] but that he was only human, the son of Joseph and Mary.

on earth? Or how shall a human being pass into God, unless God has first become human? And how can a human being escape from the generation which ends in death, except through a new generation, given in a wonderful and unexpected manner, as a sign of salvation by God—that new birth which flows from the virgin through faith? . . . How, too, could he have subdued [Luke 11:21–22] the one who was stronger than humanity (who had not only overcome humankind but also retained it under his power) and conquer him who had conquered, while liberating humanity which had been conquered, unless he had been greater than the humanity which had thus been vanquished? But who else is superior to and more eminent than that humankind formed after the likeness of God, except the Son of God, after whose image humanity was created? It was for this reason that in these last days he exhibited that image: the Son of God became human, assuming the ancient production into himself, as I have shown in the immediately preceding book. (4:33,4)

He will also judge those who speak of Christ as if his humanity were only an opinion held by some. How can they think they are carrying on a real discussion, if their master was only imaginary? How can they receive anything real from him if he was only an imaginary being, not a genuine one? How can they partake of salvation, if the one in whom they claim to believe only presented himself as a phantasm? . . . (4:33,5)

He will also judge false prophets who, although they have not received the gift of prophecy from God and do not fear God, but—whether for pride, or for some personal advantage, or acting under the influence of a wicked spirit—pretend to utter prophecies, while they actually lie about God. (4:33,6)

He will also judge those who cause schisms, people destitute of the love of God, who desire their way more than the unity of the Church, and who for trifling reasons or any kind of reason which occurs to them cut in pieces and divide the great and glorious body of Christ and, as far as lies in them, destroy it. People like that speak about peace but bring on war; they strain out a gnat but swallow a camel [Matt 23:24]. They will not be able to achieve any reformation adequate to make up for the mischief they cause by their schism. He will also judge all those who are beyond the pale of the truth—that is, who are outside the Church.

But he himself will be judged by no one. To him all things are consistent: he has a complete faith in one God Almighty, from whom are all things; and in the Son of God, Jesus Christ our Lord, by whom are all things, and in the dispensations connected with him, by means of which the Son of God became man; and a firm belief in the Spirit of God, who grants us a knowledge of the truth, and has set forth the dispensations of the Father and the Son, through which he dwells with every generation of humanity, according to the will of the Father. (4:33,7)

True knowledge is the doctrine of the apostles, which is the ancient constitution of the Church throughout the entire world. The body of Christ is clearly manifest by the successions of bishops, by whom the Church existing in every place has been faithfully taught, so that the truth has come down also to us. It has been guarded and preserved by a thorough presentation of doctrine, without any spurious scriptures and without receiving either addition or subtraction. It consists in reading the Word of God without falsification, a legitimate and diligent exposition in harmony with the Scriptures, without either danger or blasphemy, and the pre-eminent gift of love [1 Cor 13:13], which is more precious than knowledge, more glorious than prophecy, and which excels all the other gifts of God. (4:33,8)

Because of her love for God, the Church in every place and through all time sends forward a multitude of martyrs to the Father.... The Church alone sustains with purity the reproach of those who suffer persecution for righteousness' sake, endure all sorts of punishments, and are put to death because of their love for God and their confession of his Son.... Thus the Church endures something similar to the ancient prophets, as the Lord declares, "In the same way they persecuted the prophets who were before you" [Matt 5:12], since in a new fashion she suffers persecution from those who do not receive the Word of God, while the same Spirit rests upon her [1 Pet 4:14] as upon the ancient prophets. (4:33,9)

The prophets, along with other things they predicted, also foretold that all those on whom the Spirit of God would rest and who would obey the word of the Father and serve him according to their ability would endure persecution, be stoned, and be slain. The prophets prefigured all these things in themselves because of their love to God and on account of his Word. Since they themselves were each members of Christ, one of them prophesied this, but all of them prefigured and proclaimed him. This comports with the way a human body works: as the working of the whole body is shown by its members, even though the complete human being is not displayed by any single member but by all taken together, so also all the prophets prefigured the one [Christ], while each of them, in his special place as a member, served to shadow forth beforehand the particular work of Christ associated with that member. (4:33,10)

Some of them, beholding him in glory, saw his glorious life at the Father's right hand [Isa 6:1; Ps 110:1]. Others beheld him coming on the clouds as the son of man [Dan 7:13]. Those who declared regarding him, "They look on the one whom they have pierced" [Zech 12:10], indicated his second advent—about which he himself said, "When the Son of Man comes, will he find faith on earth?" [Luke 18:8]. Paul also refers to this advent when he says, "It is indeed just of God to repay with affliction those who afflict you, and to give relief to the afflicted as well as to us, when the Lord Jesus is revealed from heaven with his mighty angels in flaming fire" [2 Thess 1:6–8]. Others speak of him as a judge and say, referring to the day of the Lord as a burning furnace, "[he] will gather his wheat into the granary; but the chaff he will burn with unquenchable fire" [Matt 3:12]. Thus they threatened the unbelieving, concerning whom the Lord himself also declares, "Depart from me into the eternal fire prepared for the devil and his angels" [Matt 25:41]. Similarly the apostle says, "These will suffer the punishment of eternal destruction, separated from the presence of the Lord and from the glory of his might, when he comes to be glorified by his saints and to be marveled at on that day among all who have believed" [2 Thess 1:9–10]. Others declare, "You are the most handsome of men"; and "God, your God, has anointed you with the oil of gladness beyond your companions" [Ps 45:2, 7]; and, "Gird your sword on your thigh, O mighty one, in your glory and majesty. In your majesty ride on victoriously for the cause of truth and to defend the right" [Ps 45:3–4]. The numerous other similar affirmations spoken about him indicate the beauty and magnificence which exist in his kingdom, along with the transcendent and pre-eminent exaltation granted to all those under his sway, so that those who hear these things might desire to be found there, doing what is pleasing to God.

As well, there are those who said, "He is a man, and who will know him?" [Jer 17:9 LXX], and "I went to the prophetess, and she conceived and bore a son" [Isa 8:3], and "he is named Wonderful Counselor, Mighty God" [Isa 9:6]. Those who proclaimed him as Immanuel from the virgin [Isa 7:14] pointed out the union of the Word of God with his own workmanship, declaring that the Word would become flesh and the Son of God the son of man—the pure one opening purely that pure womb which regenerates humanity unto God, and which he himself made pure.

Even so, having become what we are, he is nevertheless the Mighty God, whose generation cannot be explained. Some said, "The Lord roars from Zion, and utters his voice from Jerusalem" [Joel 3:16], and "In Judah God is known" [Ps 76:1], pointing to his advent which took place in Judea. . . . Those, again, who declare that at his coming "the lame shall leap like a deer, and the tongue of the speechless sing for joy, and the eyes of the blind shall be opened, and the ears of the deaf unstopped" [Isa 35:6, 5], that weak hands and feeble knees will be strengthened [Isa 35:3], that the dead who are in the grave will arise [Isa 26:19], and that he himself "has borne our infirmities and carried our diseases" [Isa 53:4]—all these proclaimed the works of healing which he accomplished. (4:33,11)

Moreover, some of them proclaimed that as a weak and inglorious man, who knew what it was to bear infirmity [Isa 53:3], and sitting upon the foal of an ass [Zech 9:9], he would come to Jerusalem and would give his back to stripes [Isa 50:6] and his cheeks to palms [which struck him], would be led like a sheep to the slaughter [Isa 53:7], would have vinegar and gall given him to drink [Ps 69:21], would be forsaken by his friends and those nearest to him [Ps 38:11], would stretch forth his hands the whole day long [Isa 65:2], would be mocked and maligned by those who looked upon him [Ps 22:7], that his garments would be parted and lots cast for his raiment [Ps 22:18], and that he would be brought down to the dust of death [Ps 22:15], with things of a similar nature. They thus prophesied his coming and entrance into Jerusalem as a man, who by his passion and crucifixion endured all the things which have been mentioned. Others, again, when they said, "The holy Lord remembered his own dead ones who slept in the dust, and came down to them to raise them up, that he might save them,"[5] tell us thus why he suffered all these things. As well, some taught, "On that day, says the Lord God, I will make the sun go down at noon, and darken the earth in broad daylight. I will turn your feasts into mourning, and all your songs into lamentation" [Amos 8:9–10]. By this they plainly foretold the darkening of the sun during his crucifixion from the sixth hour onwards, and that after this event those days which were their festivals according to the law and their songs would be changed into grief and lamentation when they were handed over to the Gentiles. Jeremiah also makes this point still clearer

---

5. Irenaeus cites this passage three times in *AH* (at 3:20,4, attributing it to Isaiah; at 4:22,1, attributing it to Jeremiah; and here, without attribution); however, it is not found anywhere in the OT or any extant versions of any of the prophetic books.

when he says about Jerusalem, "She who bore seven has languished; she has swooned away; her sun went down while it was yet day; she has been shamed and disgraced. And the rest of them I will give to the sword before their enemies, says the LORD" [Jer 15:9]. (4:33,12)

Further, those who spoke of his slumbering and sleeping, and of his rising again because the Lord sustained him [Ps 3:5], and who called the principalities of heaven to open the everlasting doors so that the king of glory might go in [Ps 24:7] proclaimed beforehand his resurrection from the dead by the Father's power and his ascension into heaven. And when they declared, "Its rising is from the end of the heavens, and its circuit to the end of them; and nothing is hid from its heat" [Ps 19:6], they announced that he would be taken up again to the place from which he had come down, and that there is no one who can escape his righteous judgment. And those who said, "The Lord is king; let the peoples tremble! He sits enthroned upon the cherubim; let the earth quake" [Ps 99:1], were thus predicting, in part, the wrath from all nations which fell on those who believed in him after his ascension, with the movement of the whole earth against the Church; and, in part, the fact that when he comes from heaven with his mighty angels, the whole earth shall be shaken, as he himself declares, "There will be great suffering, such as has not been from the beginning" [Matt 24:21]. As well, it is asked, "Who will contend with me? Let us stand up together. Who are my adversaries? Let them confront me" [Isa 50:8], and declared, "All of them will wear out like a garment; the moth will eat them up" [Isa 50:9], and "The pride of everyone shall be brought low; and the LORD alone will be exalted on that day" [Isa 2:17]. This indicates that after his passion and ascension God would cast beneath his feet all who were opposed to him, and he would be exalted above all, and there would be no one who can be either excused or compared to him. (4:33,13)

And those who declare that God would make a new covenant [Jer 31:31–32] with humankind, not like the one he had made with the fathers at Mount Horeb, and would give to humans "a new heart and a new spirit" [Ezek 36:26], and again, "Do not remember the former things, or consider the things of old. I am about to do a new thing; now it springs forth, do you not perceive it? I will make a way in the wilderness and rivers in the desert ..., to give drink to my chosen people, the people whom I formed for myself so that they might declare my praise" [Isa 43:18–21], thus clearly announced the liberty which marks the new covenant, and the new wine which is put into new bottles [Matt 9:17]—namely, the faith which is in Christ. By it he proclaimed the way of righteousness sprung up in the desert, and the streams of the Holy Spirit in a dry land, to give water to the elect people of God, whom he has acquired so that they might show forth his praise.... (4:33,14)

...His people always know the same God, and always acknowledge the same Word of God, although he has only recently been manifested to us. They also acknowledge at all times the same Spirit of God—who, although he has been poured out upon us in a new way in these last times, has descended upon the human race from the creation of the world to its end—from whom those who believe God and follow his word receive salvation. On the other hand, those who depart from him and despise his precepts, and by their deeds dishonor him who made them, and by their opinions blaspheme him who nourishes them, heap up against themselves most righteous judgment [Rom 2:5].... (4:33,15)

...Read carefully the gospel conveyed to us by the apostles. Read the prophets the same way, and you will find that they predicted his entire way of life, all his teaching, and all his sufferings. But if you then ask, "What did the Lord bring to us by his advent?", realize that by bringing himself, the one who had been announced, he brought everything new. This was proclaimed beforehand, that something new would come to renew humankind and give it life. The king's advent was announced ahead of time by servants sent to prepare and equip those who are to entertain their Lord. But now that the king has actually come, his subjects have been filled with the joy proclaimed beforehand, have received the liberty which he bestows, share in the sight of him, have listened to his words, and have enjoyed the gifts which he confers. So no one in his right mind will now ask what new thing the king has brought: he has brought himself, and has bestowed on humanity those good things which were announced beforehand, things which the angels desire to look into [1 Pet 1:12]. (4:34,1)

But the servants would have turned out to be false, and not sent by the Lord, if Christ in his advent had not fulfilled their words and been exactly what had been promised. That is why he said, "Do not think that I have come to abolish the law or the prophets; I have come not to abolish but to fulfil. For truly I tell you, until heaven and earth pass away, not one letter, not one stroke of a letter, will pass from the law until all is accomplished" [Matt 5:17–18]. By his advent he fulfilled all things, and in the Church he still fulfills the new covenant foretold by the law and will do so until the consummation. To this effect also Paul, his apostle, says in the Letter to the Romans, "But now, apart from law, the righteousness of God has been disclosed, and is attested by the law and the prophets," for "the one who is righteous will live by faith" [Rom 3:21; 1:17]. This fact, that the righteous shall live by faith, had been previously announced by the prophets [Hab 2:4]. (4:34,2)

But how could the prophets have had power to predict the advent of the king, proclaim beforehand the liberty which he would bestow, announce ahead of time all that was done by Christ—his words, works, and sufferings—and predict the new covenant, if they had received prophetical inspiration from some other God, who was ignorant (as the heretics allege) of the ineffable Father, his kingdom, and his dispensations which the Son of God fulfilled when he came upon earth in these last times? The heretics cannot claim that these things came to pass by chance, as if they were spoken by the prophets regarding someone else, but that only similar events happened to the Lord, for all the prophets prophesied these same things, but they never came to pass in the case of any of the ancients. If these things had happened to anyone among them in ancient times, those who lived subsequently would certainly not have prophesied that these events would come to pass in the last times. Moreover, there is no one among the fathers, prophets, or ancient kings in whose case any of these things properly and specifically took place. All of them prophesied about the sufferings of Christ, but they themselves never endured sufferings like what was predicted, and the points connected with the passion of the Lord which were foretold were realized in no one else. It did not happen at the death of anyone among the ancients that the sun set at midday, or the veil of the temple was torn, or the earth quaked, or the rocks split, or the dead were raised up. None of these ancients were raised up on the third day, or received into heaven, or at his assumption had the heavens opened; nor did the nations believe in the name of any other; nor did any of them, having been dead and rising again, lay open the new covenant of liberty. Therefore the prophets spoke of no one else but the Lord, in whom all these things transpired. (4:34,3)

However, if any one, advocating the cause of the Jews, maintains that this new covenant was fulfilled by the temple built under Zerubbabel (after the emigration to Babylon, and in the return of the people after seventy years), let that person know that the temple constructed of stones was certainly rebuilt then. . . . Even so, no new covenant was given then, for they used the Mosaic law until the coming of the Lord. However, with the Lord's advent, the new covenant which brings back peace and the law which gives life have gone forth over the whole earth, as the prophets said: "For out of Zion shall go forth the law, and the word of the Lord from Jerusalem. He shall judge between the nations, and shall decide for many peoples; they shall beat their swords into plowshares, and their spears into pruning hooks; nation shall not lift up sword against nation, neither shall they learn war any more" [Isa 2:3–4 RSV; Mic 4:2–3]. If some other law and word went forth from Jerusalem and brought in such peace among the Gentiles who received it and convinced many a nation of its folly, then it appears that the prophets spoke about someone else. But if the law of liberty—that is, the Word of God—preached by the apostles (who went forth from Jerusalem throughout all the earth) caused such a change in the state of things that these nations beat their swords and war lances into plowshares, and changed them into pruning hooks for reaping the corn (that is, into instruments used for peaceful purposes), and that they are now unaccustomed to fighting, but when smitten offer also the other cheek [Matt 5:39], then the prophets spoke these things of no other person but him who brought them to pass. This person is our Lord, and in him that declaration is fulfilled, since he himself was the one who has made the plow and introduced the pruning hook . . . , and the gathering in of the produce in the last times by the Word. For this reason, since he joined the beginning to the end, and is the Lord of both, he has finally displayed the plow, in that the wood has been joined to the iron, and has thus cleansed his land because the Word, having been firmly united to flesh and fixed with nails, has reclaimed the savage earth. In the beginning, he prefigured the pruning hook through Abel, pointing out that a righteous race of humankind would be gathered in. For he said, "The righteous perish, and no one takes it to heart; the devout are taken away, while no one understands" [Isa 57:1]. . . . (4:34,4)

These arguments are sufficient to answer those who maintain that the prophets were inspired by a different God, and that our Lord came from another Father—perhaps enough to get them finally to desist from their extreme folly. This is what I genuinely hope for in adducing these scriptural proofs—that confuting these heretics as far I can by these passages, I may restrain them from their great blasphemy, and from insanely fabricating a multitude of gods. (4:34,5)

When the savior came to this earth, he sent his apostles into the world to proclaim his advent faithfully and to teach the Father's will.... If he sent forth his own apostles in the Spirit of truth, not in that of error, then he did the same with the prophets; for the Word of God was always one and the same.... (4:35,2)

...The heretics, numerous as they are, all differ with each other, holding many different opinions about the same thing, all carrying around their clever notions secretly within themselves. However, even if they should come to agree among themselves about the things predicted in the Scriptures, we would still confute them. Now, though, they convict themselves of holding wrong opinions, since they do not agree in what they teach. But we follow for our teacher the one and only true God, and possess his words as the rule of truth. That is why we all speak alike about the same things, knowing only one God, the creator of this universe—who sent the prophets, who led the people out of the land of Egypt, and who in these last times manifested his own Son [Heb 1:2], so that he might put the unbelievers to confusion and search out the fruit of righteousness. (4:35,4)

...As one coming from the Father with supreme authority, the Son used to express himself thus: "But I say to you" [Matt 5:22, 28, 32, 34, 39, 44]. His servants, who came from their Lord, spoke as servants should when they declared, "Thus says the Lord." (4:36,1)

The one they proclaimed as Lord to the unbelievers was the one about whom Christ taught. The God who called those in the earlier dispensation is the same one who receives those of the later one. The one who at first used the law which leads to bondage is the same one who later on called his people by means of adoption. For God planted the vineyard of the human race when he formed Adam and chose the fathers; then he leased it out to tenant workers when he set up the Mosaic dispensation; he put a fence around it (that is, he gave particular instructions about their worship); he built a tower (that is, he chose Jerusalem); he dug a winepress (that is, he prepared a receptacle of the prophetic Spirit) [Mark 12:1]. He also sent prophets before the migration to Babylon, and after that sent others in greater number than before, to seek the fruits, saying to them (the Jews): "Thus says the Lord of hosts, 'Amend your ways and your doings, render true judgments, show kindness and mercy to one another; do not oppress the widow, the orphan, the alien, or the poor; and do not devise evil in your hearts against one another; love no false oath. Wash yourselves; make yourselves clean; remove the evil of your doings from before my eyes; cease to do evil, learn to do good; seek justice, rescue the oppressed, defend the orphan, plead for the widow. Come now, let us argue it out,' says the Lord" [Jer 7:3; Zech 7:9–10; 8:17; Isa 1:16–18]. And again: "Keep your tongue from evil, and your lips from speaking deceit. Depart from evil, and do good; seek peace, and pursue it" [Ps 34:13–14]. In preaching these things, the prophets sought the fruits of righteousness. Last of all he sent to those unbelievers his own Son, our Lord Jesus Christ, whom the wicked tenant workers cast out of the vineyard when they had slain him. Therefore the Lord God gave it up (no longer fenced in but opened wide to all the world) to other tenant workers, who would render the fruits in their seasons [Mark 12:2–9]. The beautiful elect tower is now also raised everywhere, for the illustrious Church is now everywhere, and everywhere the winepress has been dug—for those who receive the Spirit are everywhere. Since the former rejected the Son of God and cast him out of the vineyard when they killed him, God has justly rejected them and given to the Gentiles outside the vineyard the fruits of its cultivation. This agrees with what Jeremiah says, "The Lord has rejected and forsaken the generation that provoked his wrath. For the people of Judah have done evil in my sight, says the LORD" [Jer 7:29–30]. Similarly, Jeremiah says, "I raised up sentinels for you: 'Give heed to the sound of the trumpet!' But they said, 'We will not give heed.' Therefore hear, O nations" [Jer 6:17–18]. It is one and the same Father who planted the vineyard, led forth the people, sent the prophets, sent his own Son, and gave the vineyard to those other tenant workers who render the fruits in their season. (4:36,2)

That is why, to make us good workmen, the Lord said to his disciples, "Be on guard so that your hearts are not weighed down with dissipation and drunkenness and the worries of this life, and that day catch you unexpectedly, like a trap. For it will come upon all who live on the face of the whole earth" [Luke 21:34–35]; and, "Be dressed for action and have your lamps lit; be like those who are waiting for their master to return from the wedding banquet" [Luke 12:35–36]; and, "Just as it was in the days of Noah, so it will be in the days of the Son of Man. They were eating and drinking, and marrying and being given in marriage, until the day Noah entered the ark, and the flood came and destroyed all of them. Likewise, just as it was in the days of Lot: they were eating and drinking, buying and selling, planting and building, but on the day that

Lot left Sodom, it rained fire and sulphur from heaven and destroyed all of them—it will be like that on the day that the Son of Man is revealed" [Luke 17:26–30]; and, "Keep awake therefore, for you do not know on what day your Lord is coming" [Matt 24:42]. He declares one and the same Lord, who in the times of Noah brought the flood because of humanity's disobedience, who in the days of Lot rained fire from heaven because of the multitude of sinners among the inhabitants of Sodom, and who, on account of this same disobedience and similar sins, will bring on the day of judgment at the end of time. He declares that on that day it will be more tolerable for Sodom and Gomorrah than for any city and house which did not receive the word of his apostles: "And you, Capernaum, will you be exalted to heaven? No, you will be brought down to Hades. For if the deeds of power done in you had been done in Sodom, it would have remained until this day. But I tell you that on the day of judgment it will be more tolerable for the land of Sodom than for you" [Matt 11:23–24]. (4:36,3)

Since the Son of God is always one and the same, he gives to those who believe on him a well of water springing up to eternal life [John 4:14], but he causes the unfruitful fig tree immediately to dry up [Matt 21:19–20]. In the days of Noah he justly brought on the flood to extinguish the infamous race of humans existing then, who could not bring forth fruit to God (since the angels that sinned had commingled with them [Gen 5:2]), and to put a check on the sins of these men, while still preserving the archetype, the formation of Adam. He rained fire and brimstone from heaven on Sodom and Gomorrah in the days of Lot as an example of the righteous judgment of God [Jude 7], that all might know that "every tree . . . that does not bear good fruit is cut down and thrown into the fire" [Matt 3:10]. He is the one who says that it will be more tolerable for Sodom in the general judgment than for those who beheld his wonders but did not believe on him or receive his doctrine [Matt 11:24; Luke 10:12]. As by his advent he gave a greater privilege to those who believed on him and do his will, so also he pointed out that those who did not believe on him will face a more severe punishment in the judgment—thus extending equal justice to all, and intending to exact more from those to whom he gives more. . . . (4:36,4)

. . . All human beings are the property of God, for "the earth is the Lord's, and all that is in it, the world, and those who live in it" [Ps 24:1].

. . . Everyone, then, as a creature is his workmanship, even if that person is ignorant of God. For he gives existence to all. . . . (4:36,6)

. . . The parable of the workmen sent into the vineyard at different periods of the day declares one and the same God who called some in the beginning, when the world was first created; but others afterwards; and others during the intermediate period; others after a long lapse of time; and others at the end of time [Matt 20:1–16]. So there are many workers in their generations, but only one householder who calls them together. There is only one vineyard, since there is also only one righteousness; and there is only one administrator, for there is one Spirit of God who arranges all things. Similarly, there is only one hire, for they all received a penny, each one having the royal image and superscription [cf. Matt 22:20]—the knowledge of the Son of God, which is eternal life. That is why he began by giving their pay to those who worked last, because it was in the last times, when the Lord was revealed, that he presented himself to all. (4:36,7)

. . . If, then, those who believe in him through the preaching of his apostles throughout the east and west shall recline with Abraham, Isaac, and Jacob in the kingdom of heaven, partaking with them of the banquet [Matt 8:11], one and the same God is set forth as the one who chose the patriarchs, visited the people, and called the Gentiles. (4:36,8)

This expression of our Lord, "How often have I desired to gather your children together . . . , and you were not willing" [Matt 23:37], sets forth the ancient law of human liberty: God made human beings free from the beginning, possessing their own power, even as they do their own souls, to obey the commands of God voluntarily, and not by divine compulsion. For there is no coercion with God, but he always bears goodwill towards humankind. That is why he gives good counsel to all. And in all human beings, as well as in angels, he has placed the power of choice (for angels are rational beings), so that those who yield obedience might justly possess what is good, given indeed by God but preserved by themselves. On the other hand, those who have not obeyed will with justice not be found in possession of the good and will receive appropriate punishment, for God kindly bestowed on them what was good but they did not diligently keep it or count it something precious, but showed contempt for his abundant goodness. Since they reject the good, and as it were spit it out, they will all deservedly incur the just judgment of God. . . . God has given what is good, as the apostle tells us in the Letter to the Romans, and those who do good will receive glory and honor [Rom 2:4, 5, 7] because they have done what is good when they had it in their power not to do it; but those who do not do it will receive the just judgment of God, because they did not do good when they had it in their power to do so. (4:37,1)

If some had been made bad by nature and others good, the latter would not deserve praise for being good, for that is the way they were created; nor would the former be reprehensible, for that would be the way they were made. But since all humanity has the same nature, able both to retain and do what is good, as well as the power to cast it from them and not do it, some justly receive praise, even among those who are guided by good laws (and much more from God), and obtain deserved testimony for their good choices in general and for persevering in them. But the others are blamed and receive a just condemnation because they rejected what is fair and good. That is why the prophets used to exhort people to what was good, to act justly and to work righteousness, as I have abundantly shown, because it is in our power to do so, and because by our excessive negligence we might become forgetful. We need that good counsel which the good God has granted us to know through the prophets. (4:37,2)

For this reason the Lord also said, "Let your light shine before others, so that they may see your good works and give glory to your Father in heaven" [Matt 5:16]; and "Be on guard so that your hearts are not weighed down with dissipation and drunkenness and the worries of this life" [Luke 21:34]; and "Be dressed for action, and have your lamps lit; be like those who are waiting for their master to return from the wedding banquet, so that they may open the door for him as soon as he comes and knocks. Blessed are those slaves whom the master finds alert when he comes" [Luke 12:35–37]; and again, "That slave who knew what his master wanted, but did not prepare himself or do what was wanted, will receive a severe beating" [Luke 12:47]; and "Why do you call me 'Lord, Lord,' and do not do what I tell you?" [Luke 6:46]; and again, "But if that wicked slave says to himself, 'My master is delayed,' and he begins to beat his fellow slaves, and eats and drinks with drunkards, the master of that slave will come on a day when he does not expect him and at an hour that he does not know. He will cut him in pieces and put him with the hypocrites" [Matt 24:48–51]. All such passages indicate the independence of human will, as well as the counsel which God conveys to them, by which he exhorts us to submit to him and seeks to turn us away from unbelief against him—without, however, in any way coercing us. (4:37,3)

No doubt, if any one is unwilling to follow the gospel itself, it is in his power to reject it, but that is hardly wise. It is in one's power to disobey God and to forfeit what is good, but that will result in no small amount of injury and mischief. . . . (4:37,4)

God has maintained human wills free and under their own control, not only for actions but also for faith: "According to your faith let it be done to you" [Matt 9:29]. This shows that faith is under the control of each human being. Again, "All things can be done for the one who believes" [Mark 9:23]; and "Go; let it be done for you according to your faith" [Matt 8:13]. All such expressions indicate that a person is in his own power as regards faith: because of this, "Whoever believes in the Son has eternal life; whoever disobeys the Son will not see life, but must endure God's wrath" [John 3:36]. In the same way the Lord, showing both his own goodness and indicating that humans are in their own free will and power, said to Jerusalem, "How often have I desired to gather your children together as a hen gathers her brood under her wings, and you were not willing! See, your house is left to you, desolate" [Matt 23:37–38]. (4:37,5)

Those who maintain the opposite present a God destitute of power, as if he were unable to accomplish what he willed. . . . They say, "He should not have created angels with a nature that could transgress or human beings, who so quickly showed themselves ungrateful towards him. For he made them rational beings, endowed with the power of examining and judging, and not like things which are irrational or of an animal nature: they can do nothing of their own will, but are drawn by necessity and compulsion to what is good. In them there is the same instinct and practice, working mechanically in one groove, and they are incapable of being anything else but what they were created to be."

But on this approach not even what is good could make them grateful, nor would communion with God be precious, nor would the good be worthy of being sought after, since it would present itself without humanity's endeavor, care, or study, but would be implanted of its own accord and without their concern. Their being good would be thus of no consequence, because they were good by nature rather than by will, and because they possess good spontaneously, not by choice. For this reason they would not understand that good is beautiful, and so they would not take pleasure in it. How can those who are ignorant of good enjoy it? What credit is it to those who have not aimed at it? How could it be a crown for those who have not pursued it, like the crowns received by victors in a contest? (4:37,6)

... Things which come spontaneously are not esteemed as highly as are those attained by strenuous effort. Since, then, this power has been conferred on us, both the Lord has taught and the apostle has enjoined us the more to love God, so that we may reach this prize for ourselves by striving after it. ... The ability to see would not appear so desirable, unless we had known what a loss it would be to lose our sight; and health is esteemed much more highly if one has been ill—as is light contrasted with darkness, and life with death. In the same way the heavenly kingdom is desirable to those who have known the earthly one. ...

The Lord endured all these things for us so that we, instructed by them all, might in all respects be careful in the time to come, and that, having been rationally taught to love God, we might continue in his perfect love. God has displayed long-suffering in the face of humanity's apostasy, while humans have been instructed by it, as the prophet says, "Your apostasies will convict you" [Jer 2:19]. God thus determined all things ahead of time for the purpose of bringing humankind to perfection, for their edification, and to reveal his dispensations, so that goodness might be manifest and righteousness completed, so that the Church might be fashioned after the image of his Son, and so that humans might finally be brought to maturity at some future time, becoming ripe through such privileges to see and know God. (4:37,7)

If, however, anyone asks, "But could not God have made humankind perfect from the beginning?", let that person know that since God is always the same and unbegotten, all things are possible to him. But created things must be inferior to him who created them, from the very fact of their later origin—for it was not possible for things recently created to have been uncreated. But since they are not uncreated, they come short of being perfect: as those who come into being, they are like infants, unaccustomed to and unexercised in perfect discipline. A mother may be able to give strong food to her infant, but the child is not able to receive such substantial nourishment: so also, it was possible for God to have made humankind perfect from the first, but humanity could not receive this, since they were still like infants. This is why our Lord in these last times, having summed up all things in himself, came to us, not as he might have come but as we were capable of beholding him. He might easily have come to us in his immortal glory, but in that case we could never have endured its greatness. So he who was the perfect bread of the Father offered himself to us as milk, because we were like infants. He did this when he appeared as a man, so that we, being nourished, as it were, from the breast of his flesh, and by such a course of nourishment having become accustomed to eat and drink the Word of God, might be able to contain in ourselves the bread of immortality, which is the Spirit of the Father. (4:38,1)

. . . Similarly, God had power to grant perfection to humankind at the beginning, but since they had only recently been created, they could not possibly have received it; or if they had received it, they could not have contained it; or if they had contained it, they could not have retained it. This was why the Son of God, although he was perfect, passed through the state of infancy in common with the rest of humankind, partaking of it not for his own benefit, but for the infantile stage of human existence, so that humankind might be able to receive him. There was nothing impossible to or deficient in God in that humankind was not an uncreated being. The only limitation was on the humanity just created. (4:38,2)

Power, wisdom, and goodness are simultaneously exhibited by God—his power and goodness in this, that of his own will he called into being and fashioned things which had no previous existence; his wisdom in making all created things parts of one harmonious and consistent whole. Those things which, through his abounding kindness, grow and last a long time, reflect the glory of the uncreated one, the God who bestows good ungrudgingly. Since these things were created, they are not uncreated; by continuing to exist throughout a long course of ages, though, they receive a certain quality of the uncreated, for God generously grants them eternal existence.

So, in all things God has the pre-eminence, who is the only uncreated, the first of all things, and the primary cause of the existence of everything, while all other things remain under God's control. But being in subjection to God is the way to immortality, and immortality is the glory of the uncreated one. By this arrangement and these harmonies, by this sequence, a human being, created and organized, is made according to the image and likeness of the uncreated God—the Father planning everything well and giving his commands, the Son carrying

them out and doing the work of creating, and the Spirit nourishing and
increasing what is made, but humankind making progress day by day
and ascending thus towards the perfect (that is, approximating to the
uncreated one), for the uncreated (that is, God) is perfect. It was necessary that humankind should in the first instance be created; and having
been created, should grow; and having grown, should be strengthened;
and being strengthened, should abound; and abounding, should recover
from the disease of sin; and having recovered, should be glorified; and
being glorified, should see his Lord. For God is the one who is yet to be
seen, and beholding God leads to immortality, but immortality brings
one near to God. (4:38,3)

   ...According to his great kindness he graciously conferred good on
us and made human beings like himself, in their own power. At the same
time by his prescience he knew the weakness of human beings and the
consequences which would flow from it. But by love and power he would
overcome the limitations of created nature. It was necessary, first, for
nature to be exhibited; then, for what was mortal to be conquered and
swallowed up by immortality, and the corruptible by incorruptibility
[1 Cor 15:53], and for human beings to be made after the image and likeness of God, having received the knowledge of good and evil. (4:38,4)

   Humankind has received the knowledge of good and evil. It is good
to obey God, to believe in him, and to keep his commandment: indeed,
this is the life of humanity, just as not to obey God is evil—indeed, it
is death. Since God, therefore, gave such mental power, humans knew
both the good of obedience and the evil of disobedience, that the eye of
the mind, experiencing both, might use good judgment and choose the
better things; that they might never become lazy or neglect God's command; and learning by experience that it is an evil thing which deprives
them of life (that is, disobedience to God), might never attempt it at
all, but, knowing that what preserves life (namely, obedience to God) is
good, might diligently and eagerly keep it. So humanity has had a twofold experience, possessing knowledge of both kinds, that with discipline
they might choose the better things.

   But if they had no knowledge of the opposite, could they have had
instruction in what is good? We have a more certain and clearer understanding in this way than we would from merely mental suppositions
about what would happen. Just as the tongue experiences sweet and
bitter by tasting, and the eye discriminates between black and white by

vision, and the ear recognizes distinct sounds by hearing, so also the mind, by experiencing both, comes to know what is good and becomes more devoted to good by obeying God. In the first place, through repentance it turns from disobedience as something disagreeable and nauseous; then it comes to understand what disobedience really is, that it is opposed to goodness and sweetness, so that the mind may never even attempt to taste disobedience to God. But if anyone shuns the knowledge of both these kinds of things and the twofold perception of knowledge, that person unwittingly divests himself of the character of a human being. (4:39,1)

. . . At the beginning, it is necessary for you to hold the rank of a human being, and only afterwards to partake of the glory of God. You do not make God; God makes you. If you are God's workmanship, await the hand of your maker who creates everything in due time—"in due time" as far as you are concerned, whose creation is being carried out. Offer your heart to him in a soft and pliable state, preserving the form in which the creator fashioned you, having moisture in yourself—so that you do not, by becoming hardened, lose the impressions of his fingers. But by preserving your framework you will ascend to what is perfect, for the moist clay which is in you is hidden there by the workmanship of God. His hand fashioned your substance; he will cover you over, inside and outside, with pure gold and silver, and he will adorn you to such a degree that even "the king will desire your beauty" [Ps 45:11]. . . . (4:39,2)

If, though, you will not believe in him and flee from his hands, the reason for your imperfection will be in you who did not obey, not in him who called. . . . The skill of God is not defective, for he can raise up children for Abraham from stones [Matt 3:9]; the one who does not obtain it is the cause of his own imperfection. Light has not ceased just because people have blinded themselves: it remains the same as ever, but those who are thus blinded are wrapped up in darkness by their own fault. . . . So, those who have apostatized from the light given by the Father and transgressed the law of liberty have done so through their own fault, since they were created as free agents, possessing power over themselves. (4:39,3)

But since God foreknows all things, he prepared fit habitations for both, kindly conferring the light which they desire on those who seek after the light of incorruption and turn toward it, but preparing darkness suitable to those who oppose the light for the despisers and mockers who avoid and turn away from this light and who, as it were, blind themselves. He has thus inflicted an appropriate punishment on those who try to avoid being subject to him. Submission to God is eternal rest, but those who shun the light receive a place worthy of their flight, and those who fly from eternal rest find a place suited to their fleeing. Since all good things are with God, those who by their own determination fly from God rob themselves of all good things. Having been thus robbed of all good things with respect to God, they consequently fall under the just judgment of God. Those who shun rest will justly incur punishment, and those who avoid the light will justly dwell in darkness. ... Those who fly from the eternal light of God, which contains all good things in itself, are themselves the reason they inhabit eternal darkness, destitute of all good things. It is their own fault they are consigned to such an abode. (4:39,4)

... The Father, who has prepared the kingdom for the righteous, into which the Son has received those worthy of it, is also the one who has prepared the furnace of fire, into which the angels commissioned by the son of man will send those persons who deserve it, according to God's command. (4:40,2)

For the Lord sowed good seed in his own field, and "the field is the world" [Matt 13:38], he says. "But while everybody slept, an enemy came and sowed weeds among the wheat, and then went away" [Matt 13:25]. From this we learn that this was the apostate angel: the enemy, envious of God's workmanship [Wis 2:24], sought to make humanity God's enemy. That is why God banished from his presence the one who stealthily and deliberately sowed the tares (that is, the one who brought about the transgression). But God took compassion on humankind who—no doubt carelessly, but still wickedly—disobeyed him. God turned the enmity by which the apostate angel tried to make humanity God's enemy against its author: instead of being angry with humankind, God turned his anger in another direction, settling it instead on the serpent. As the Scripture tells us, God said to the serpent, "I will put enmity between you and the woman, and between your offspring and hers; he will strike your head, and you will strike his heel" [Gen 3:15]. And the Lord fulfilled this in himself when he was made man from a woman and trod upon the serpent's head, as I pointed out in the preceding book. (4:40,3)

Since the Lord has said that there are certain angels of the devil, for whom eternal fire is prepared, and since, further, he declares that "the weeds are the children of the evil one" [Matt 13:38], it must be acknowledged that he has ascribed all who belong to this apostasy to the one who is the ringleader of this transgression. He did not make either angels or human beings that way by nature. The devil did not create anything whatsoever: he is himself a creature of God, like the other angels. God made all things, as David says with regard to everything: "He spoke, and it came to be; he commanded, and it stood firm" [Ps 33:9]. (4:41,1)

Since, then, all things were made by God, and since the devil became the cause of apostasy for himself and others, the Scripture justly terms those who remain in a state of apostasy "children of the devil" and "angels of the wicked one." For "children," as one before me has observed, has a twofold meaning: one according to the order of nature, being born as a child; the other, being accepted and counted as a child, even though there is a difference between being born a child and being made one. The first is born from the person referred to, but the second is made so, either by creation or by the teaching of his doctrine. When anyone has been taught from the mouth of another, that person is deemed a child of the one who gave the instruction, and the latter is called his father. According to nature, then—that is, according to creation, so to speak—we are all children of God, because we were all created by God. But as regards obedience and doctrine, we are not all the children of God: only those are who believe in him and do his will. But those who do not believe and do not obey his will are children and angels of the devil, because they do the works of the devil.... (4:41,2)

In human society, children who disobey their fathers are disinherited. Even though they are still children by nature, by law they are disinherited and do not become heirs of their natural parents. It is the same way with God: those who do not obey him are disinherited by him and have ceased to be his children.... But if they should be converted and come to repentance, and cease from evil, they have power to become the children of God [John 1:12] and to receive the inheritance of immortality which he gives. This is why he has called those who give place to the devil and do his works his "angels" and "children of the evil one" [Matt 25:41; 13:38]. Even so, they were created by one and the same God. If they believe and submit to God and proceed to keep his doctrine, they are the children of God; but if they apostatize and fall into transgression, they are ascribed to their chief, the devil—to him who first became the cause of apostasy to himself, and afterwards to others. (4:41,3)

Since the words of the Lord are numerous, while they all proclaim one and the same Father, the creator of this world, it has been necessary for me to use many arguments to refute those who are involved in many errors—if by any means, when they are confuted by many proofs, they may be converted to the truth and saved.... (4:41,4)

BOOK 5 | *The Christian Faith, as Drawn from Further Teaching of Christ and the Apostles*

IN THE FOUR PRECEDING books, I have exposed all the heretics, brought their doctrines to light, and refuted them by adducing something from the teachings peculiar to each of them as found in their writings, as well as by using more general arguments which apply to them all. Then I have pointed out the truth and shown the preaching of the Church, which the prophets proclaimed (as I have shown), but which Christ brought to perfection and the apostles have handed down. The Church has received it, she alone has preserved it in its integrity throughout all the world, and she has transmitted it to her children. Having thus disposed of all the questions the heretics pose to us, and also having presented the apostles' doctrine and clearly set forth much of what was said and done by our Lord in parables, in this fifth book of this work which exposes and refutes what is falsely called knowledge I will present further proofs from the rest of the Lord's teaching and the letters of the apostles.

In this way I hope to fulfill the request you made of me, as one who has been granted responsibility for the ministry of the Word. Further, by every means in my power I will try to furnish you with considerable assistance against the heretics' contradictions, to give you what you need to reclaim the wanderers and convert them to the Church of God and, at the same time, to confirm the minds of the neophytes. That way they too will steadfastly preserve the faith they have received, which has been guarded by the Church in its integrity, so that they may not be even slightly turned aside by those who try to teach them false doctrines and lead them away from the truth.

It will be incumbent on you, though, and all who read this work to attend carefully to what I present, so that you will obtain a knowledge of the subjects against which I am contending. That way you will be prepared to answer these false teachers appropriately and to use the arguments brought forward against them. Then with the heavenly faith you will be able to repudiate their teachings as refuse. You must follow the only true and steadfast teacher, the Word of God, our Lord Jesus Christ, who through his transcendent love became what we are, that he might make us to be what he is. (5:pref)

There is no other way we could have learned the things of God, unless our master, who is the Word, had become human. No other being had the power to reveal to us the things of the Father except his own proper Word. For what other person "has known the mind of the Lord" or who else "has been his counselor?" [Rom 11:34]. We could have learned in no other way than by seeing our teacher and hearing his voice with our own ears. Now, having become imitators of his works and doers of his words, we may have communion with him, receiving benefit from the perfect one, who is prior to all creation. We have only recently been created by the only best and good being, who alone has immortality: we were formed after his likeness, predestined according to the foreknowledge of the Father, so that we (who as yet did not exist) might come into being and be made the first-fruits of creation. At his appointed time we received the blessings of salvation through what the Word has done, who as the mighty Word is perfect in all things and is genuine man. Redeeming us by his own blood in a fitting manner, he gave himself as a ransom for those who had been led into captivity. The apostasy tyrannized over us unjustly: though by nature we belonged to the omnipotent God, the fall alienated us contrary to nature, turning us into its own disciples. The Word of God, powerful and thoroughly just in all things, righteously turned against that apostasy and redeemed from it what belonged to him. He did not do so by violent means, even though that apostasy had obtained dominion over us at the beginning by greedily snatching away what was not its own; he did so through persuasion, as was fitting for a God of counsel who does not use violence to obtain what he desires. In this way, justice was not infringed on and the ancient handiwork of God was not allowed to go to destruction. The Lord has redeemed us through his own blood, giving his soul for our souls and his flesh for our flesh, and has poured out the Spirit of the Father for the union and communion of God and humankind, imparting God to humanity by means of the Spirit. On the other hand, he has united humanity to God by his own incarnation and, through communion with God, genuinely and lastingly bestowed immortality on us by his coming. With this, all the teachings of the heretics fall to ruin. (5:1,1)

Those who allege that he merely seemed to appear in the flesh speak falsehood. These things were not done only in appearance, but in actuality. . . . He would not have truly possessed flesh and blood, by which he redeemed us, unless he had summed up in himself the ancient formation of Adam. . . . (5:1,2)

. . . The Holy Spirit came upon Mary, and the power of the Most High overshadowed her, so that what was generated was a holy child, the Son of the Most High God the Father of all [Luke 1:35], who accomplished this incarnation. He thus showed forth a new kind of generation—that, as through the former generation we inherited death, so by this new generation we might inherit life. . . . So in these last times, the Word of the Father and the Spirit of God, having become united with the ancient substance of Adam's formation, formed man living and perfect, receptive of the perfect Father—so that, as in the natural Adam we were all dead, so in the spiritual Adam we may all be made alive [1 Cor 15:22]. For at no time did Adam escape from the hands of God [that is, the Son and the Spirit], to whom the Father said, "Let us make humankind in our image, according to our likeness" [Gen. 1:26]. (5:1,3)

. . . He could not have truly redeemed us by his own blood, if he had not really become human, restoring to his own handiwork what was said about it in the beginning—that humanity was made after the image and likeness of God. He did not steal what belonged to someone else by stratagem; he took possession again of what belonged to him, in a righteous and gracious manner. As to the apostasy, he redeems us righteously from it by his own blood; as regards us who have been redeemed, he does this graciously. We have given nothing to him previously, and he does not desire anything from us, as if he needed something. But we need fellowship with him. This is why he graciously poured himself out, that he might gather us into the bosom of the Father. (5:2,1)

But deluded in every respect are those who despise the way God has accomplished all this, disallow the salvation of the flesh, and treat its regeneration with contempt, maintaining that it is not capable of incorruption. If the flesh cannot be saved, then the Lord did not redeem us with his blood—nor is the cup of the Eucharist the communion of his blood, nor the bread which we break the communion of his body [1 Cor 10:16]. Blood can only come from veins and flesh and whatever else makes up the human substance, and this is the way the Word of God was actually made. By his own blood he redeemed us, as his apostle also declares, "In whom we have redemption [through his blood], the forgiveness of sins" [Col 1:14]. As his members, we are nourished by the creation which he himself grants to us, for he causes his sun to rise, and sends rain when he wills [Matt 5:45]. He has acknowledged the cup, a part of the creation, as his own blood from which he invigorates our blood, and he has established the bread, also a part of the creation, as his own body from which he gives increase to our bodies. (5:2,2)

When the mingled cup and the ground bread receive the Word of God, and the Eucharist of the blood and the body of Christ is made, through which the substance of our flesh is increased and supported, how can the heretics claim that the flesh is incapable of receiving the gift of God, which is life eternal? Flesh is nourished from the body and blood of the Lord and is a member of him. The blessed Paul declares in his Letter to the Ephesians that "we are members of his body, of his flesh and of his bones" [Eph 5:30]. He does not say these words about some spiritual and invisible man, for a spirit does not have bones or flesh [Luke 24:39]; rather, he refers to the way the Lord became an actual man, with flesh, nerves, and bones—that flesh which is nourished by the cup which is his blood and receives increase from the bread which is his body. A cutting from a vine planted in the ground bears fruit in its season. A grain of wheat, falling into the earth and decomposing, rises with plentiful increase through the Spirit of God who contains all things. Through the wisdom of God, that grain serves for our use. Grain also, receiving the Word of God, becomes the Eucharist, which is the body and blood of Christ. So also our bodies, nourished by it but deposited in the earth and suffering decomposition there, shall rise at their appointed time. The Word of God will grant them resurrection to the glory of God the Father, who freely gives to this mortal immortality, and to this corruptible incorruption [1 Cor 15:53]. The strength of God is thus made perfect in weakness [2 Cor 12:9], so that we may never, with ungrateful minds, become puffed up (as if we had life from ourselves) and exalted against God. . . . (5:2,3)

... God's power is made perfect in weakness [2 Cor 12:9], rendering that person better who comes to know the power of God through his own weakness.... There is nothing wrong about learning one's infirmities by endurance; rather, it has the beneficial effect of preventing one from forming an undue opinion of himself.... (5:3,1)

The heretics set aside the power of God and do not consider what the Word declares when they focus on the weakness of the flesh but do not take into consideration the power of him who raises it from the dead. If he does not give life to what is mortal and does not bring back the corruptible to incorruption, he is not a God of power. But from our origin we ought to perceive that he is powerful in all regards, since God, taking dust from the earth, formed humankind. Surely it is much more difficult and incredible to bring humanity into existence as living and thinking creatures out of non-existent bones, nerves, veins, and all the rest of what is included than it is to bring together again what had been created but had afterwards decomposed into dust and become again the material from which humanity was first formed. If in the beginning, as God pleased, he gave being to humanity, which had never previously existed, then he can easily bring back to life those who formerly lived when it pleases him. Flesh will then again be found fit for and capable of receiving the power of God, which at the beginning received the skillful touch of God.... (5:3,2)

... Since the Lord has power to infuse life into what he has fashioned, and since the flesh is capable of being brought to life, what can keep it from participating in incorruption, which is a blissful and never-ending life granted by God? (5:3,3)

... Neither the nature of any created thing nor the weakness of the flesh can prevail against the will of God. God is not subject to created things, but created things are to God, and all things obey his will [Jdt 16:18]. The Lord has declared, "What is impossible for mortals is possible for God" [Luke 18:27].... Human unbelief cannot nullify divine faithfulness [Rom 3:3–4]. (5:5,2)

God is glorified in his handiwork; he fits it so that it conforms to and is modelled after his own Son. By the hands of the Father—that is, by the Son and the Holy Spirit—human beings, not merely parts of them, were made in the likeness of God. The soul and the spirit comprise part of a human but not the entire person, for a complete human being is composed by the commingling and union of the soul which has received the spirit of the Father, plus the fleshly nature which was molded after the image of God. . . . The flesh which has been molded is not a complete human being in itself, but only part of one; neither is the soul itself, considered alone, the human being: it is part of one. Neither is the spirit a complete human being, for it is called the spirit, and not a human being. It is the commingling and union of all these which constitutes a complete human being. This is why the apostle, explaining himself, makes it clear that the saved person is complete as well as spiritual, as he says in the First Letter to the Thessalonians: "May the God of peace himself sanctify you entirely; and may your spirit and soul and body be kept complete and blameless at the coming of our Lord Jesus Christ" [1 Thess 5:23]. What was his purpose in praying that these three (soul, body, and spirit) be preserved to the coming of the Lord, unless he knew of the future reintegration and union of the three, and that they would share one and the same salvation? That is why he also declares that those are complete who present to the Lord the three component elements without blemish. Those alone are "complete" (i.e., "perfect") who have the Spirit of God remaining in them and have preserved their souls and bodies blameless, holding fast faith in God and dealing righteously with their neighbours. (5:6,1)

This is why he says that this handiwork is "the temple of God," declaring: "Do you not know that you are God's temple and that God's Spirit dwells in you? If anyone destroys God's temple, God will destroy that person. For God's temple is holy, and you are that temple" [1 Cor 3:16]. With this he clearly declares that the body is the temple in which the Spirit dwells. When the Lord said in reference to himself, "Destroy this temple, and in three days I will raise it up, . . . he was speaking of the temple of his body" [John 2:19, 21]. Not only does the apostle acknowledge our bodies to be a temple, but even the temple of Christ: "Do you not know that your bodies are members of Christ? Should I therefore take the members of Christ and make them members of a prostitute?" [1 Cor 6:15].

In this, he is not speaking to some "spiritual" person, for a being like that could have nothing to do with a prostitute. He declares that our bodies—that is, the flesh which perseveres in holiness and purity—are "the members of Christ." However, if a body is joined to a prostitute, it becomes a member of the prostitute. That is why he says, "If anyone destroys God's temple, God will destroy that person." Is it not then the height of blasphemy to allege that the temple of God, in which the Spirit of the Father dwells, the members of Christ, does not partake of salvation but is thrown into perdition? As well, to indicate that our bodies are not raised by their own power but by the power of God, he says to the Corinthians, "The body is not meant for fornication but for the Lord, and the Lord for the body. And God raised the Lord and will also raise us by his power" [1 Cor 6:13–14]. (5:6,2)

In the same way that Christ arose in the substance of his flesh and pointed out to his disciples the mark of the nails and the opening in his side [John 20:20]—which are tokens of the flesh which rose from the dead—so will he also raise us by his power. Again, he says to the Romans, "If the Spirit of him who raised Jesus from the dead dwells in you, he who raised Christ from the dead will give life to your mortal bodies" [Rom 8:11]. (5:7,1)

But we now receive a certain portion of his Spirit, who leads us towards perfection and prepares us for incorruption, as little by little we become accustomed to receive and bear God. The apostle terms this a "pledge"—that is, a first portion of what has been promised to us by God—when he says in the Letter to the Ephesians, "In him you also, when you had heard the word of truth, the gospel of your salvation, and had believed in him, were marked with the seal of the promised Holy Spirit; this is the pledge of our inheritance" [Eph 1:13–14]. This pledge, already dwelling in us, renders us spiritual even now, and the mortal is swallowed up by immortality [2 Cor 5:4]: "You are not in the flesh; you are in the Spirit, since the Spirit of God dwells in you" [Rom 8:9]. This does not come to pass by getting rid of the flesh, but by granting the Spirit: those to whom he was writing were not without flesh, but were those who had received the Spirit of God, by whom "we cry, Abba, Father" [Rom 8:15]. So, if already now we have that pledge and cry, "Abba, Father," what will it be like when, on rising again, we see him face to face, when all the members burst out in a continuous hymn of triumph, glorifying him who raised them from the dead and granted them eternal life? If the pledge authorizes us even in the present time to cry, "Abba, Father," what will the complete grace of the Spirit accomplish, which will be given by God? It will render us like him and accomplish the will of the Father, for it will remake humanity after the image and likeness of God. (5:8,1)

The apostle rightly calls those persons who have the pledge of the Spirit and are not enslaved by the lusts of the flesh but are subject to the

Spirit and who in all things live by the light of reason "spiritual," for the Spirit of God dwells in them. . . . But those who reject the Spirit's counsel are slaves to fleshly lusts, leading lives contrary to reason. Without restraint, they plunge headlong into their own desires, having no yearning for the divine Spirit, and live like swine and dogs. The apostle properly calls such people "carnal" because they take no thought for anything but carnal things [1 Cor 2:14—3:1]. (5:8,2)

. . . As I have shown, a perfect human being is composed of three things—flesh, soul, and spirit. One of these—the spirit—preserves and fashions. By another—the flesh—it is united and formed. Then there is the one which is between these two—the soul, which sometimes follows the spirit and is raised up by it, but sometimes sympathizes with the flesh and falls into carnal lusts. . . . (5:9,1)

On the other hand, all those who fear God and trust in his Son's advent, and who through faith establish the Spirit of God in their hearts, are properly called "pure," "spiritual," and "those living to God," because they have the Spirit of the Father, who purifies human beings and raises them up to the life of God. The Lord has testified that "the flesh is weak" and that "the spirit is willing" [Matt 26:41]: it is able to effect what it desires. So, if anyone allows the Spirit to become a stimulus to his weak flesh, it inevitably follows that what is strong will prevail over the weak, so that the weakness of the flesh will be absorbed by the strength of the Spirit. The one in whom this takes place cannot in that case be carnal but spiritual, because of the fellowship of the Spirit. That is the way the martyrs were able to make their witness and despise death—not through the weakness of the flesh, but by the assistance of the Spirit. . . . (5:9,2)

. . . For this reason the apostle declares, "As we have borne the image of the man of dust, we will also bear the image of the man of heaven" [1 Cor 15:49]. What, then, is "of dust"? It is what was formed out of dust. And what is "of heaven"? That is the Spirit. So when he says that we were destitute of the heavenly Spirit and walked in former times in the oldness of the flesh, not obeying God, so now let us, receiving the Spirit, walk in newness of life, obeying God. Since without the Spirit of God we cannot be saved, the apostle exhorts us through faith and chaste living to preserve the Spirit of God, lest the divine Spirit forsake us and we lose the kingdom of heaven—for he declares that flesh and blood, in themselves alone, cannot possess the kingdom of God [1 Cor 15:50]. (5:9,3)

... This is why Christ died, that the gospel covenant being manifested and known to the whole world might in the first place free the slaves who rightly belong to him; and then afterwards, as I have already shown, that he might make them his heirs, when the Spirit possesses them as his inheritance.... (5:9,4)

... This is why he says, "This perishable body must put on imperishability, and this mortal body must put on immortality" [1 Cor 15:53]; and again, "But you are not in the flesh; you are in the Spirit, since the Spirit of God dwells in you" [Rom 8:9]. He sets this forth still more plainly when he says, "Though the body is dead because of sin, the Spirit is life because of righteousness. If the Spirit of him who raised Jesus from the dead dwells in you, he who raised Christ from the dead will give life to your mortal bodies also through his Spirit that dwells in you" [Rom 8:10–11]. He goes on to say, "For if you live according to the flesh, you will die" [Rom 8:13]. By this he does not prohibit them from living their lives in the flesh, for he himself was in the flesh when he wrote to them; rather, he cuts away the lusts of the flesh which bring death. And for this reason he goes on to say, "But if by the Spirit you put to death the deeds of the body, you will live. For all who are led by the Spirit of God are children of God" [Rom 8:13–14]. (5:10,2)

Recognizing what unbelievers might say in response, he specified what he calls carnal, explaining himself so there would be no room for doubt left to those who dishonestly try to pervert his meaning. He writes in the Letter to the Galatians, "Now the works of the flesh are obvious: fornication, impurity, licentiousness, idolatry, sorcery, enmities, strife, jealousy, anger, quarrels, dissensions, factions, envy, drunkenness, carousing, and things like these. I am warning you, as I warned you before: those who do such things will not inherit the kingdom of God" [Gal 5:19–21]. He thus points out to his hearers more explicitly what he means when he declares, "Flesh and blood will not inherit the kingdom of God." Those who do these things, since they walk after the flesh, are unable to live unto God. He goes on to specify the spiritual actions which bring life, the gift of the Spirit: "By contrast, the fruit of the Spirit is love, joy, peace, patience, kindness, generosity, faithfulness, gentleness, and self-control. There is no law against such things" [Gal 5:22–23]. So, as the one who has sought the better things and has produced the fruit of the Spirit will be saved by communion in the Spirit, so also the one who has continued in the works of the flesh listed above, being rightly reckoned as carnal for not receiving the Spirit of God, will not be able to inherit the kingdom of heaven. The same apostle testifies elsewhere, writing to the Corinthians, "Do you not know that wrongdoers will not inherit the kingdom of God? Do not be deceived! Fornicators, idolaters, adulterers, male prostitutes, sodomites, thieves, the greedy, drunkards, revilers, robbers—none of these will inherit the kingdom of God. And this is what some of you used to be. But you were washed, you were sanctified, you were justified in the name of the Lord Jesus Christ and in the Spirit of our God" [1 Cor 6:9–11]. He thus shows in the clearest manner how one goes to destruction—by continuing to live after the flesh; on the other hand, he points out how one is saved—he says that the name of our Lord Jesus Christ and the Spirit of our God are what save. (5:11,1)

The breath of life by which man became a living being [Gen 2:7] is one thing, and the life-giving Spirit, which caused him to become spiritual, is another. That is the background for what Isaiah says, "Thus says God, the LORD, who created the heavens and stretched them out, who spread out the earth and what comes from it, who gives breath to the people upon it and spirit to those who walk in it" [Isa 42:5]—thus telling us that breath is given in common to all people on earth, but that the Spirit is theirs alone who tread down earthly desires.... (5:12,2)

For it is not one thing which dies and another which is given life, just as it is not one thing which is lost and another which is found: the Lord came seeking that same sheep which had been lost. What was it, then, that was dead? Without question, it was the substance of the flesh, which had lost the breath of life and had become dead. This was what the Lord came to bring to life, that as in Adam we all die, since we are of an animal nature, so in Christ we may all live [1 Cor 15:22], as being spiritual—laying aside, not God's handiwork, but the lusts of the flesh, and receiving the Holy Spirit. To this end, the apostle says in the Letter to the Colossians, "Put to death, therefore, whatever in you is earthly," which he goes on to list: "fornication, impurity, passion, evil desire, and greed (which is idolatry)" [Col 3:5]. Laying these aside is what the apostle preaches, but he declares that those who do such things, since they are only flesh and blood, cannot inherit the kingdom of heaven.... (5:12,3)

... The end result of the Spirit's work is the salvation of the flesh. What other visible fruit is there of the invisible Spirit than making the flesh mature and capable of incorruption?... (5:12,4)

The maker of all things, the Word of God, the one who formed humankind from the beginning, when he found his handiwork impaired by wickedness, worked all kinds of healing in it. Sometimes he has done so for individuals, who are his handiwork; at other times, he has done so for all, to restore humanity sound and complete in all points, working to make humankind whole for himself, in preparation for the resurrection. For what was his purpose in healing some afflictions of the flesh and restoring them to their original condition, if those parts which he had healed were not going to obtain salvation? . . . (5:12,6)

. . . Death will then be genuinely vanquished, when that flesh which it holds down finally escapes its dominion. He wrote to the Philippians, "Our citizenship is in heaven, and it is from there that we are expecting a Savior, the Lord Jesus Christ. He will transform the body of our humiliation that it may be conformed to the body of his glory, by the power that also enables him to make all things subject to him" [Phil 3:20–21]. What then is this "body of humiliation" which the Lord will transform, to conform it to "the body of his glory"? Clearly, it is the body made of flesh, which is certainly humbled when it falls into the earth. Although mortal and corruptible, it becomes immortal and incorruptible in this transformation, not through its own powers but through the mighty working of the Lord, who is able to invest the mortal with immortality and the corruptible with incorruption. (5:13,3)

The same apostle who has declaimed against the substance of flesh and blood, that it cannot inherit the kingdom of God, has everywhere adopted the term "flesh and blood" with regard to the Lord Jesus Christ—partly to establish his human nature (for he spoke of himself as the son of man), and partly to confirm the salvation of our flesh. For if the flesh were not in a position to be saved, the Word of God would certainly not have become flesh. And if the blood of the righteous were not to be inquired after, the Lord would certainly not have had blood. But blood cries out from the beginning of the world: God said to Cain, after he had killed his brother, "Your brother's blood is crying out to me from the ground!" [Gen 4:10]. And as to their blood being inquired after, he said to those with Noah, "For your own lifeblood I will surely require a reckoning: from every animal I will require it and from human beings, each one for the blood of another. . . . Whoever sheds the blood of a human, by a human shall that person's blood be shed" [Gen 9:5–6]. To the same effect the Lord said to those who would afterwards shed his blood, "The blood of all the prophets shed since the foundation of the world, from the blood of Abel to the blood of Zechariah, who perished between the altar and the sanctuary . . . will be charged against this generation" [Luke 11:50–51]. He thus points to the recapitulation which would take place in himself—the pouring out of blood, from the beginning, of all the righteous ones and the prophets, and that through himself their blood would be required. Now this blood could hardly be thus required unless it also had the capability of being saved; nor would the Lord have summed up these things in himself, unless he himself had been made flesh and blood as Adam originally was. Thus at the end of time he saved in his own person what in the beginning had perished in Adam. (5:14,1)

. . . The Word has saved what was created—namely, humanity which had perished. He accomplished this by taking it unto himself and seeking its salvation. The thing which had perished had flesh and blood. The Lord, taking dust from the earth, formed humanity; and it was for humanity that all the dispensation of the Lord's advent took place. He himself therefore had flesh and blood, so that he could recapitulate in himself, not something else, but the original handiwork of the Father, seeking out what had perished. And because of this the apostle, in the Letter to the Colossians, says, "And you who were once estranged and hostile in mind, doing evil deeds, he has now reconciled in his fleshly body through death, so as to present you holy and blameless and irreproachable before him" [Col 1:21–22]. He says, "You have been reconciled in his fleshly body," because his righteous flesh has reconciled that flesh which was kept in bondage to sin and brought it into friendship with God. (5:14,2)

If anyone alleges that in this respect the flesh of the Lord was different from ours because it did not commit sin and no deceit was found in his soul, while we, on the other hand, are sinners, that person speaks the truth. But if that person pretends that the Lord possessed a different kind of flesh, then the apostolic sayings about reconciliation will not agree with what that person says. That is reconciled which formerly had been opposed. Now, if the Lord had taken some other kind of flesh, he would not have reconciled that flesh to God which had become an enemy by transgression. But now, through communion with himself, the Lord has reconciled humankind to God the Father, reconciling us to himself by the body of his own flesh [Col 1:22] and redeeming us by his own blood, as the apostle says to the Ephesians, "In him we have redemption through his blood, the forgiveness of our trespasses" [Eph 1:7]. He also says to them, "You who once were far off have been brought near by the blood of Christ" [Eph 2:13]. And in all his letters the apostle plainly testifies that we have been saved through the flesh and blood of our Lord. (5:14,3)

So, if flesh and blood are the things in which we have life, it was not declared in the literal meaning that flesh and blood cannot inherit the kingdom of God. These words refer to the carnal deeds already mentioned, which turn human beings toward sin and rob them of life. This is why he says in the Letter to the Romans, "Do not let sin exercise dominion in your mortal bodies, to make you obey their passions. No longer present your members to sin as instruments of wickedness, but present yourselves to God as those who have been brought from death to life, and present your members to God as instruments of righteousness" [Rom 6:12–13]. With these same members in which we used to serve sin and produce fruit unto death, he desires us to be obedient unto righteousness, so that we may bring forth fruit unto life [Rom 6:13]. Remember, therefore, my beloved friend, that you have been redeemed by the flesh of our Lord, reestablished by his blood, and "holding fast to the head, from whom the whole body, nourished and held together by its ligaments and sinews, grows with a growth that is from God" [Col 2:19]—that is, acknowledging the Son of God's advent in the flesh and his divinity, and steadfastly relying on his human nature, availing yourself of these proofs drawn from Scripture. Then you will easily overthrow all those notions of the heretics which were concocted afterwards. (5:14,4)

... To the man who had been blind from birth he gave sight, not by a word, but by an outward action. He did not do this without a purpose, or just because it happened that way, but so that he might manifest the hand of God which had formed humankind at the beginning. So when his disciples asked him why the man had been born blind, whether for his own or his parents' sins, he replied, "Neither this man nor his parents sinned; he was born blind so that God's works might be revealed in him" [John 9:3]. Now "God's work" was the creation of humankind. Scripture indicates that he made humanity by a kind of process: "The LORD God formed man from the dust of the ground" [Gen 2:7]. That is why the Lord spat on the ground and made clay and smeared it upon the eyes [John 9:6]: he thus pointed out how humanity had originally been formed, showing the hand of God to those who can understand by whose hand humanity was formed out of the dust. What the artificer, the Word, had omitted to form in the womb he then supplied in public, so that God's works might be manifested in him.... (5:15,2)

The Word of God forms us in the womb, as he says to Jeremiah: "Before I formed you in the womb I knew you, and before you were born I consecrated you; I appointed you a prophet to the nations" [Jer 1:5]. Paul also writes in this manner: "God . . . had set me apart before I was born . . . , that I might proclaim him among the Gentiles" [Gal 1:15–16]. Therefore, just as we are formed by the Word in the womb, so this same Word formed the power of sight in him who had been blind from birth. In this, he showed openly who it is who fashions us in secret, since the Word himself had been revealed to humankind. He also thus set forth the original formation of Adam, the way in which he was created, and by whose hand he was fashioned, indicating the whole from a part. For the Lord who formed the visual powers is he who made the whole human being, carrying out the will of the Father.

As to that formation in Adam, humanity had fallen into transgression and needed the laver of regeneration. So the Lord said to him upon whom he had conferred sight, after he had smeared his eyes with the clay, "Go, wash in the pool of Siloam" [John 9:7]. In this way he granted him complete healing, and that regeneration which takes place by means of the laver. That is why, when he was washed, he came seeing—that he might both know him who had fashioned him and that we might learn to know him who has conferred life upon us. (5:15,3)

. . . Scripture, pointing out what should come to pass, says that when Adam had hid himself because of his disobedience, the Lord came to him in the evening, called him forth, and asked, "Where are you?" [Gen 3:9]. In the last times the very same Word of God came to call humankind, reminding them of their doings, lives which they had tried to hide from the Lord. For just as at that time God spoke to Adam in the evening, searching him out, so in the last times, by means of the same voice searching out his posterity, he has visited them. (5:15,4)

This Word was manifested again when the Word of God became human, assimilating himself to humanity and humanity to himself, so that by its resemblance to the Son humankind might become precious to the Father. For in times long past, it was said that humanity was created after the image of God. That could not be seen, though, for the Word after whose image humanity had been created remained invisible, and so humankind easily lost the similitude. However, when the Word of God became flesh, he confirmed both of these: he showed forth the image truly, since he himself became what was his image, and he re-established the image after a sure manner, by assimilating humanity to the invisible Father by the visible Word. (5:16,2)

The Lord has shown himself not only by these things, but also by his passion. He did away with that human disobedience which had taken place at the beginning through a tree: "He became obedient to the point of death—even death on a cross" [Phil 2:8], rectifying that disobedience which had occurred by reason of a tree through an obedience wrought on a tree. . . . By the tree we disobeyed God and did not believe his word, so by a tree he was obedient and yielded to his Word. By so doing, he clearly shows forth God himself, whom we had offended in the first Adam, who did not obey his commandment. In the second Adam, however, who was obedient even unto death, we are reconciled, being made obedient even unto death. For we were debtors to no one but to him whose commandment we broke at the beginning. (5:16,3)

This being is the creator: in regards to his love, he is the Father; in regard to his power, he is Lord; and in regard to his wisdom, he is our maker and fashioner. By transgressing his commandment we became his enemies. In the last times the Lord has restored us to friendship through his incarnation, having become the "one mediator between God and humankind" [1 Tim 2:5], propitiating the Father against whom we had sinned for us and cancelling our disobedience by his own obedience. In this way he also conferred upon us the gift of communion with and subjection to our maker. This is why he also has taught us to say in prayer, "And forgive us our debts" [Matt 6:12], for he is our Father, whose debtors we were, since we had transgressed his commandments. But who is this being? Is he some unknown one, a Father who gives no commandment to anyone? Or is he the God proclaimed in the Scriptures, to whom we were debtors, since we had transgressed his commandment? The commandment was given to humankind by the Word, for Adam "heard the voice of the LORD God" [Gen 3:8 LXX]. It is proper that his Word says, "Your sins are forgiven" [Mark 2:5]. The one against whom we had sinned in the beginning grants forgiveness of sins in the end. If we had disobeyed the command of any other, but it had been another being who said, "Your sins are forgiven," then such a person would be neither good, nor true, nor just. How can one be good who gives what is not his own? . . . (5:17,1)

By remitting sins, he healed humankind, while also manifesting who he was. For if no one can forgive sins but God alone, while the Lord remitted them and healed human beings, it is plain that he himself was the Word of God made the son of man, who had received from the Father the power to remit sins. He was man and God, so that, since as man he suffered for us, so as God he might have compassion on us and forgive us our debts, in which we were made debtors to God our creator. That is why David said beforehand, "Happy are those whose transgression is forgiven, whose sin is covered. Happy are those to whom the LORD imputes no iniquity" [Ps 32:1–2]. David thus points to the forgiveness of sins which comes with his advent, "erasing the record that stood against us with its legal demands" and "nailing it to the cross" [Col 2:14], so that as by means of a tree we were made debtors to God, so also by means of a tree we may obtain the remission of our debt. (5:17,3)

The Father bears the creation and his own Word simultaneously, and the Word borne by the Father grants the Spirit to all as the Father wills. To some he gives what is made according to the order of creation, but to others what is from God (i.e., regeneration) according to the order of adoption. Thus one God the Father is declared, "who is above all and through all and in all" [Eph 4:6]. The Father is above all, and he is the head of Christ; the Word is through all things and is himself the head of the Church; while the Spirit is in us all, and he is the living water [John 7:38–39], which the Lord grants to those who rightly believe in him, love him, and know that there is one Father, who is above all, and through all, and in us all. . . . (5:18,2)

The creator of the world is truly the Word of God. This is our Lord, who in the last times was made human. Existing now in this world unseen, he contains all things created and is immanent throughout the entire creation, for the Word of God governs and arranges all things. He came to his own in a visible manner, was made flesh, and hung upon the tree, so that he might recapitulate all things in himself. "His own people did not accept him" [John 1:11], as Moses had foretold: "Your life shall hang in doubt before you" [Deut 28:66]. Those who did not accept him did not receive life, "but to all who received him, who believed in his name, he gave power to become children of God" [John 1:12]. . . . (5:18,3)

It was joyfully declared that the Lord was clearly coming to what he had made and was sustaining them through that creation he always supports; that he was recapitulating the disobedience which had occurred in connection with a tree through the obedience on a tree; and that he was doing away with that deception by which that virgin Eve, who was already espoused to a man, was unhappily misled. This was joyfully announced in the angel's declaration to the virgin Mary, who was also espoused to a man. As the former was led astray by the word of an angel, so that she fled from God when she had transgressed his Word, so the latter, by an angelic communication, received the glad tidings that she should bear God, being obedient to his Word. While the former disobeyed God, the latter was persuaded to be obedient to God; thus, the virgin Mary became the patroness of the virgin Eve. And so, as the human race fell into bondage to death by means of a virgin, so it is rescued by a virgin, virginal disobedience being balanced in the opposite scale by virginal obedience. So also the sin of the first-created man receives amendment by the correction of the first-begotten, the coming of the serpent is conquered by the harmlessness of the dove, and the bonds are loosened by which we had been fast bound to death. (5:19,1)

All the heretics are unlearned and ignorant of the way God works; they are unacquainted with the plan by which he took human nature upon himself. They have thus blinded themselves from seeing the truth, with the result that what they teach makes salvation impossible. . . . (5:19,2)

All the heretics came along much later than the bishops to whom the apostles committed the Churches—a fact which I have taken much pain to demonstrate in the third book. It is no surprise, then, that these heretics, since they are blind to the truth and turn aside from the right way, walk in various paths. Because of that the footsteps of their doctrine are scattered here and there, without agreement or connection. But the path of those belonging to the Church circumscribes the whole world, since the Church possesses the sure tradition from the apostles. She thus enables us to see that the faith of all is one and the same, since all receive one and the same God the Father, believe in the same dispensation regarding the incarnation of the Son of God, know the same gift of the Spirit, recognize the same commandments, preserve the same form of ecclesiastical constitution, expect the same advent of the Lord, and await the same salvation of the total person—that is, of soul and body.

And without question the preaching of the Church is true and steadfast, in which one and the same way of salvation is shown throughout the whole world. God has entrusted the light to her.... The Church preaches the truth everywhere. She is the seven-branched candlestick which bears the light of Christ [Rev 1:20]. (5:20,1)

Therefore, those who forsake the preaching of the Church call in question the knowledge of the holy presbyters, not pausing to reflect that, even as an individual, a religious man is much more reliable than a blasphemous and impudent sophist—which is what all the heretics are, who imagine that they have hit upon something beyond the truth. Following their own ideas, proceeding on their ways variously, inharmoniously, and foolishly, not keeping always to the same opinions with regard to the same things, they are blind men led by the blind who will deservedly fall into the ditch of ignorance lying in their path [Matt 15:14], ever seeking and never finding out the truth [2 Tim 3:7]. It behooves us, therefore, to avoid their doctrines and take careful heed that we do not suffer any injury from them, but to flee to the Church, be brought up in her bosom, and be nourished with the Lord's Scriptures. For the Church has been planted as a garden in this world. That is why the Spirit of God said, "You may freely eat of every tree of the garden" [Gen 2:16]—that is, eat from all the Lord's Scriptures. But you must not eat with a proud mind or touch any heretical falsehood. These heretics profess that they themselves have the knowledge of good and evil, and they set their own impious minds above the God who made them. That is why they form opinions on what is beyond the limits of the understanding. This is why the apostle forbids us to think of ourselves more highly than we ought to think but to use careful judgment, so that we not be cast out of the garden for eating the "knowledge" of these people, knowledge which supposedly knows more than it possibly can! ... (5:20,2)

In his work of recapitulation, Christ has summed up all things, waging war against our enemy and crushing him who at the beginning led us away captive in Adam, and trampling on his head. This you can already understand from what God said to the serpent, "I will put enmity between you and the woman, and between your offspring and hers; he will strike your head, and you will strike his heel" [Gen 3:15]. From that time onwards, he who was to be born of a woman—from the virgin, after the likeness of Adam—was preached as keeping watch for the head of the serpent. This is the seed of which the apostle says in the Letter to the Galatians that "the law . . . was added . . . until the seed would come to whom the promise had been made" [Gal 3:19]. This is exhibited in a still clearer light in the same letter, where he writes: "But when the fullness of time had come, God sent his Son, born of a woman" [Gal 4:4]. The enemy would not have been vanquished fairly unless he had been conquered by a man born of a woman, since it was by means of a woman that he got the advantage over humanity at first, thus setting himself up as humanity's opponent. And so the Lord presents himself as the son of man, comprising in himself that original man out of whom the woman was fashioned, so that, as our species went down to death through a vanquished man, so we might also ascend to life again through a victorious one. As it was through a man that death received the palm of victory over us, so it was also by a man that we received the palm against death. (5:21,1)

The Lord would not have recapitulated in himself the ancient and original enmity against the serpent, fulfilling the promise of the creator and obeying his command, if he had come from another father. But since he is the same one who formed us at the beginning and sent his Son at the end, the Lord fulfilled his own Word, having been made of a woman, by destroying our adversary and perfecting humankind after the image and likeness of God. He did not draw the means of confounding him from any other source than from the words of the law; he used the Father's commandment as a help to destroy and confuse the apostate angel.

Fasting forty days, like Moses and Elijah, he was hungry afterwards—first, so that we might perceive that he was a real and substantial man (for it is natural for a human being to be hungry when fasting), and secondly, so that his opponent might have an opportunity of attacking him. At the beginning it was by means of food that the enemy persuaded humanity (which was, however, not suffering from hunger) to transgress God's commandment, but in the end he did not succeed in persuading him who was hungry to take that food which proceeded from God. For when tempting him he said, "If you are the Son of God, command these stones to become loaves of bread" [Matt 4:3]. But the Lord repulsed him by the commandment of the law, saying, "It is written, 'One does not live by bread alone'" [Matt 4:4, citing Deut 8:3]. As to those words, "If you are the Son of God," he made no remark: by thus acknowledging his human nature he baffled his adversary and exhausted the force of his first attack through his Father's word. Thus the corruption of humanity, which occurred in paradise by our first parents' eating, was done away with by the Lord's foregoing food in this world.

But the enemy, thus vanquished by the law, tried again to make an assault by quoting a commandment of the law himself. Taking him to the highest pinnacle of the temple, he said, "If you are the Son of God, throw yourself down; for it is written, 'He will command his angels concerning you,' and 'On their hands they will bear you up, so that you will not dash your foot against a stone'" [Matt 4:6, citing Ps 91:11–12]—thus trying to hide a falsehood under an appeal to Scripture, as all the heretics do. For it was indeed written that "He will command his angels concerning you," but Scripture never calls him to "cast yourself down"—that idea came from the devil. So the Lord answered him from the law, telling him, "Again it is written, 'Do not put the Lord your God to the test'" [Matt 4:7, citing Deut 6:16]. Thus he pointed out by the word contained in the law what the duty of a human being is, that he should not tempt God—and, in regard to himself (since he appeared in human form), that he would not tempt the LORD his God. The serpent's proud reason was thus nullified by the humility found in the man. Thus, the devil had been conquered from Scripture twice: he had been unmasked as advising things opposed to God's commandment, and he had been shown to be God's enemy by his thoughts.

So, roundly defeated so far, he concentrated his forces, as it were, pulling together the full panoply of his abilities for falsehood and "showed him all the kingdoms of the world and their splendor" [Matt 4:8], saying (as Luke relates), "To you I will give their glory and all this authority; for it has been given over to me, and I give it to anyone I please. If you, then, will worship me, it will all be yours" [Luke 4:6–7]. But the Lord exposed him in his true character when he responded, "Away with you, Satan! For it is written, 'Worship the Lord your God, and serve only him'" [Matt 4:10, citing Deut 6:13]. In this he both revealed him by this name and showed who he himself was, for the Hebrew word "Satan" signifies an apostate. Vanquishing him for the third time, he drove him away as having finally been conquered out of the law. He thus overcome the violation of God's commandment by Adam by holding steadfastly to the law, which the son of man observed, who did not transgress the commandment of God. (5:21,2)

Who, then, is this Lord God to whom Christ bears witness, whom no one is to tempt, whom all should worship, and alone serve? It is beyond all doubt the God who gave the law. . . . In the beginning Satan enticed humankind to transgress its maker's law, and in so doing obtained power over humanity. His power consists in transgression and apostasy, and with these he bound humanity. So it was necessary that through a human being Satan, when conquered, should be bound with the same chains with which he had bound humanity—so that humanity, being set free, might return to its Lord, leaving to Satan those bonds by which he himself had been fettered (that is, sin). For when Satan is bound, humankind is set free, since "no one can enter a strong man's house and plunder his property without first tying up the strong man" [Mark 3:27]. That is why the Lord shows that he [Satan] is speaking contrary to the Word of the God who made everything; he subdues him by way of the commandment.

The law is the commandment of God. The son of man shows Satan to be a fugitive from and a transgressor of the law, an apostate from God. Then the Word bound him securely as a fugitive from himself and spoiled his goods [Matt 12:29; Mark 3:27]—namely, those whom he held in bondage, whom he unjustly used for his own purposes. Justly is he led captive who had led humanity unjustly into bondage, while humankind, which had been led captive in times past, was rescued from the grasp of its possessor. This comes through the tender mercy of God the Father, who had compassion on his own handiwork and granted it salvation, restoring it by means of the Word—that is, by Christ—so that human beings might learn by actual proof that they receive incorruptibility not by their own efforts, but by the free gift of God. (5:21,3)

By his commandment he taught that when we who have been set free are hungry, we should accept whatever food is given by God. If we receive abundant grace, we should not be lifted up with pride because of special privilege or tempt God by relying on the righteousness we have done [Titus 3:5]. We should be humble in everything and keep in mind the prohibition, "Do not put the LORD your God to the test" [Deut 6:16]. The apostle also taught, "Do not be haughty, but associate with the lowly" [Rom 12:16], meaning that we should not be ensnared by riches, temporal glory, or present status. We must remember that we should "worship the LORD your God, and serve only him" [Matt 4:10], and not listen to the one who falsely promises things not his own, as when he said, "All these will I give you, if you will fall down and worship me" [Matt 4:9]. By what he says he acknowledges that to adore him and do his will is to fall from the glory of God. What can a person who has fallen enjoy that is either pleasant or good? What else can such a person hope for or expect but death? Death is next-door neighbor to one who has fallen. We should recognize that he will not give what he has promised. How can he make grants to the one who has fallen?

Moreover, since God rules over humankind and him, too, and without the will of our Father in heaven not even a sparrow falls to the ground [Matt 10:29], it follows that his declaration, "All this has been given over to me, and I give them to whomever I wish," flows out of his vaunted pride. The creation is not under his power, for he himself is one of the creatures. He cannot give away his rule over humankind to anyone, for everything and all human affairs are arranged according to God the Father's disposal. Besides, the Lord declares that "the devil . . . is a liar and the father of lies" [John 8:44]. So, if he is a liar and the truth is not in him, he certainly did not speak truth but a lie when he said, "All this has been given over to me, and I give it to anyone I please." (5:22,2)

He was already used to lying about God in order to lead people astray. At the beginning, God had given humankind a variety of things for food, while forbidding them to eat from only one tree. The Scripture tells us that God said to Adam, "You may freely eat of every tree of the garden; but of the tree of the knowledge of good and evil you shall not eat, for in the day that you eat of it you shall die" [Gen 2:16–17]. But the devil, lying against the Lord, tempted our first parents. The Scripture shows that the serpent asked the woman, "Did God say, 'You shall not eat from any tree in the garden'?" [Gen 3:1]. She exposed the falsehood and simply related God's command: "We may eat of the fruit of the trees in the garden; but God said, 'You shall not eat of the fruit of the tree that is in the middle of the garden, nor shall you touch it, or you shall die'" [Gen 3:2–3]. When he had heard the command of God from her, he brought his cunning into play and finally deceived her by a falsehood, saying, "You will not die; for God knows that when you eat of it your eyes will be opened, and you will be like God, knowing good and evil" [Gen 3:4–5]. He first of all disputed about God in the garden as if God were not there, for he was ignorant of the greatness of God. As well, after he had found out from the woman that God had said that they would die if they ate of that tree, he opened his mouth and uttered the third falsehood, "You will not die."

But that God was true and the serpent a liar was proved by the result, for death passed upon the ones who had eaten. By eating the fruit they fell under the power of death, since they ate in disobedience—and disobedience to God entails death. So at that very moment they became forfeit to death and were handed over to it. (5:23,1)

In the same day that they ate, they also died and became debtors to death. If anybody diligently tries to discover on what day out of the seven it was that Adam died, that person will find it by examining the dispensation of the Lord. In summing up in himself the whole human race from the beginning to the end, he also summed up its death. From this it seems clear that the Lord suffered death, in obedience to his Father, on the very day on which Adam died when he disobeyed God. He died on the same day in which he ate, for God had said, "In the day that you eat of it you shall die." The Lord, recapitulating this day in himself, underwent his sufferings on the day preceding the Sabbath—that is, the sixth day of the creation, the day on which humanity was created. He thus granted humankind a second creation through his passion, which is the creation out of death. . . . (5:23,2)

As the devil lied at the beginning, so he did also in the end when he said, "All these are given over to me, and I give them to anyone I please." He was not the one who has appointed the kingdoms of this world— God is, for "the king's heart is a stream of water in the hand of the Lord" [Prov 21:1]. The Word also says by Solomon, "By me kings reign, and rulers decree what is just; by me rulers rule" [Prov 8:15–16]. The apostle Paul also says upon this same subject, "Let every person be subject to the governing authorities; for there is no authority except from God, and those authorities that exist have been instituted by God" [Rom 13:1]. . . . (5:24,1)

In departing from God, human beings reached such a pitch of fury as even to look upon one's brother as an enemy and engage recklessly in all kinds of restless conduct, murder, and avarice. So God imposed on humankind the fear of human rulers, since they did not acknowledge the fear of God, so that by being subjected to the authority of other human beings and thus kept under restraint by their laws, they might attain to some degree of justice and show mutual forbearance through fear of the sword suspended full in their view, as the apostle says, "The authority does not bear the sword in vain! It is the servant of God to execute wrath on the wrongdoer" [Rom 13:4]. This is why magistrates, with laws

covering them like righteous garments when they act in a just and legitimate manner, are not to be called into question for their conduct or
be liable to punishment. But if they act in a way that subverts justice—
iniquitously, impiously, illegally, or tyrannically—then in these things
they also shall perish, for God's just judgment comes equally upon all
and is never defective. Earthly rule, thus, was appointed by God for the
benefit of nations, not by the devil.... (5:24,2)

... Since the devil is the apostate angel, he can only go as far as he
did at the beginning—namely, to deceive and lead astray human minds
disobeying God's commandments. He gradually darkens the hearts of
those in his bondage, so that they forget the true God and adore him as
God. (5:24,3)

This is as if some rebel, having hostilely seized another person's ter-
ritory, should harass its inhabitants, so that he might claim for himself
the glory of a king among those who did not know about his apostasy
and robbery. In the same way, the devil, as one of those angels who
are placed over the spirit of the air, as the apostle Paul declared in his
Letter to the Ephesians [Eph 2:2], having become envious of humankind
[Wis 2:24], became an apostate from the divine law—for envy is foreign to God. His apostasy was exposed by what he did with humankind,
and humanity ended up thus discovering his thoughts. He has gone this
same way with greater and greater determination, in opposition to human beings—envying their life, and wishing to involve them in his own
apostate power. However, the Word of God, the maker of all things, has
conquered him by human nature, shown him to be an apostate, and put
him under the power of humankind.... (5:24,4)

Not only what has happened since the beginning, but also what will
transpire in the time of Antichrist shows that he, always an apostate and
a robber, wants to be adored as God, and that, although a mere slave, he
wants to be proclaimed king. Endowed with all the power of the devil,
Antichrist will come, not as a righteous king or as a legitimate king subject to God, but as an impious, unjust, and lawless one—as an apostate,
full of iniquity, and a murderer. He will come as a robber, concentrating
satanic apostasy in himself. He will repudiate idols and attempt to per-
suade people that he is God. He will raise himself up as the only idol, in
whom will be concentrated all the multifarious errors of the other idols.
He will do this so that those who worship the devil in many different
abominable ways may serve himself by this one idol, about whom the

apostle speaks in the Second Letter to the Thessalonians: "The rebellion comes first and the lawless one is revealed, the one destined for destruction. He opposes and exalts himself above every so-called god or object of worship, so that he takes his seat in the temple of God, declaring himself to be God" [2 Thess 2:3–4]. The apostle thus clearly points out his apostasy, and that he is lifted up above all that is called God or that is worshipped—that is, above every idol, for that is what humans call them, even though they are not truly gods—and that he will tyrannically try to present himself as God. (5:25,1)

. . . When the apostles are speaking, they call no one "God" except him who truly is God, the Father of our Lord, by whose directions the temple at Jerusalem was constructed. . . . In that temple the enemy will sit, trying to show himself as the Christ, as the Lord declares: "When you see the desolating sacrilege standing in the holy place, as was spoken of by the prophet Daniel (let the reader understand), then those in Judea must flee to the mountains; the one on the housetop must not go down to take what is in the house. For at that time there will be great suffering, such as has not been from the beginning of the world until now, no, and never will be" [Matt 24:15–17, 21]. (5:25,2)

Daniel, looking forward to the end of the last kingdom (i.e., the ten last kings, amongst whom the kingdom of those men will be partitioned [Dan 7:23–24] and upon whom the son of perdition shall come), declares that ten horns shall spring from the beast, that another little horn shall arise in the midst of them, and that three of the former shall be rooted up before his face [Dan 7:8]. He says, "There were eyes like human eyes in this horn, and a mouth speaking arrogantly. . . . As I looked, this horn made war with the holy ones and was prevailing over them, until the Ancient One came; then judgment was given for the holy ones of the Most High, and the time arrived when the holy ones gained possession of the kingdom" [Dan 7:8, 21–22]. Further on, in the interpretation of the vision, he was told: "As for the fourth beast, there shall be a fourth kingdom on earth that shall be different from all the other kingdoms; it shall devour the whole earth, and trample it down, and break it to pieces. As for the ten horns, out of this kingdom ten kings shall arise, and another shall arise after them. This one shall be different from the former ones, and shall put down three kings. He shall speak words against the Most High, shall wear out the holy ones of the Most High, and shall attempt to change the sacred seasons and the law; and they shall be given into his power for a time, two times, and half a time" [Dan 7:23–25]—that is, for three years and six months, during which he will reign over the earth. Speaking about this one in his Second Letter to the Thessalonians, the apostle Paul tells why he comes: "And then the lawless one will be revealed, whom the Lord Jesus will destroy with the breath of his mouth, annihilating him by the manifestation of his coming. The coming of the lawless one is apparent in the working of Satan, who uses all power, signs, lying wonders, and every kind of wicked deception for those who are perishing, because they refused to love the truth and so be saved. For this reason God sends them a powerful delusion, leading them to believe what is false, so that all who have not believed the truth but took pleasure in unrighteousness will be condemned" [2 Thess 2:8–12]. (5:25,3)

The Lord also said to those who did not believe in him: "I have come in my Father's name, and you do not accept me; if another comes in his own name, you will accept him" [John 5:43], calling the Antichrist "another" because he is alienated from the Lord. . . . Daniel also says, "Because of wickedness, the host was given over to it together with the regular burnt offering; it cast truth to the ground, and kept prospering in what it did" [Dan 8:12]. In explaining the vision, the angel Gabriel states with regard to this person: "At the end of their rule, when the transgressions have reached their full measure, a king of bold countenance shall arise, skilled in intrigue. He shall grow strong in power, shall cause fearful destruction, and shall succeed in what he does. . . . By his cunning he shall make deceit prosper under his hand, and in his own mind he shall be great. Without warning he shall destroy many and shall even rise up against the Prince of princes" [Dan 8:23–25]. Then he points out how long this tyranny will last, during which the holy ones who offer pure sacrifice to God will be put to flight: "For half of the week he shall make sacrifice and offering cease; and in their place shall be an abomination that desolates, until the decreed end is poured out upon the desolator" [Dan 9:27]—three years and six months constitute the half-week. (5:25,4)

These passages reveal to us not only what the apostasy will be like and what he in whom every satanic error is concentrated will do but also that there is one and the same God the Father, who was declared by the prophets but made manifest by Christ. For if what Daniel prophesied concerning the end has been confirmed by the Lord when he said, "When you see the desolating sacrilege standing in the holy place, as was spoken of by the prophet Daniel" [Matt 24:15]—as the visions of Daniel were interpreted by the angel Gabriel, who is the archangel of the creator and the one who proclaimed to Mary the visible coming and incarnation of Christ—then one and the same God is most clearly pointed out, who sent the prophets, promised the Son, and called us into his knowledge. (5:25,5)

In a still clearer way, in the Apocalypse John indicated to the Lord's disciples what will happen in the last times regarding the ten kings who will arise then, among whom the empire which now rules the earth shall be partitioned. He teaches us what the ten horns which Daniel saw will be, telling us what he had been told: "And the ten horns that you saw are ten kings who have not yet received a kingdom, but they are to receive authority as kings for one hour, together with the beast. These are united in yielding their power and authority to the beast; they will make war on the Lamb, and the Lamb will conquer them, for he is Lord of lords and King of kings" [Rev 17:12–14]. It is clear, then, that he who is to come will kill three of these kings and subject the rest to his power, and that he himself will be the eighth among them. They will lay Babylon waste, burn her with fire, give their kingdoms to the beast, and put the Church to flight. After that they will be destroyed by the coming of our Lord.

That the kingdom must be divided and thus come to ruin is clear from what the Lord says, "Every kingdom divided against itself is laid waste, and no city or house divided against itself will stand" [Matt 12:25]. Consequently, it must happen that the kingdom, the city, and the house will be divided into ten—and that is why he foreshadowed the partition and division. Daniel says particularly that the end of the fourth kingdom consists in the toes of the image seen by Nebuchadnezzar, which was struck by the stone cut out without hands: "Its feet [were] partly of iron, and partly of clay. As you looked on, a stone was cut out, not by human hands, and it struck the statue on its feet of iron and clay and broke them in pieces" [Dan 2:33–34]. Afterwards, interpreting this, he said, "As you saw the feet and toes partly of potter's clay and partly of iron, it shall be a divided kingdom; but some of the strength of iron shall be in it, as you saw the iron mixed with the clay. As the toes of the feet were part iron and part clay" [Dan 2:41–42]. The ten toes are those ten kings, among whom the kingdom shall be partitioned; some of them will be strong and active, or energetic; the others, though, will be slow to act, weak, and will not agree. Daniel indicates this, too: "The kingdom shall be partly strong and partly brittle. As you saw the iron mixed with clay, so will they mix with one another in marriage, but they will not hold together, just as iron does not mix with clay" [Dan 2:42–43]. And since an end will come, he says, "And in the days of those kings the God of heaven will set up a kingdom that shall never be destroyed, nor shall this kingdom be left to another people. It shall crush all these kingdoms and bring them to an end, and it shall stand forever; just as you saw that a stone was cut from the mountain not by hands, and that it crushed the iron, the bronze, the clay, the silver, and the gold. The great God has informed the king what shall be hereafter. The dream is certain, and its interpretation trustworthy" [Dan 2:44–45]. (5:26,1)

Thus the great God showed future things by Daniel and confirmed them through his Son. Christ is the stone cut out without hands, who shall destroy temporal kingdoms and introduce an eternal one, which is the resurrection of the righteous. . . . So let all those persons who blaspheme the creator, whether by what they say openly (like the disciples of Marcion), or by perverting the sense of Scripture (like those of Valentinus and all the Gnostics falsely so called), be recognised as agents of Satan by all who worship God. By them Satan has recently been seen as speaking against God, who has prepared eternal fire for every kind of apostasy. Satan has not dared to blaspheme his Lord openly himself, just as in the beginning he led humanity astray by means of the serpent, concealing himself as it were from God.

Justin has rightly remarked[1] that before the Lord's appearance Satan never dared to blaspheme God, since he did not yet know his own sentence, which had been contained in parables and allegories, but that after the Lord's appearance, when he had clearly ascertained from the words of Christ and his apostles that eternal fire has been prepared for him for his freely chosen apostasy from God, and likewise for all who continue unrepentant in apostasy, through such people he now blasphemes the Lord who brings judgment upon him as one condemned. He imputes the guilt of his apostasy to his maker, not to his own free choice. That is the way it is with those who break the laws when punishment overtakes them: they throw the blame on those who framed the laws, not upon themselves. In the same way those heretics, filled with a satanic spirit, bring innumerable accusations against our creator, who has given us the

---

1. None of the extant works of Justin Martyr include the passage to which Irenaeus here refers; it must have been from one that has been lost.

spirit of life and established a law adapted for all, and they will not admit that the judgment of God is just. That is why they set about imagining some other father who neither cares about nor exercises providential concern for our affairs—one, even, who approves of all sins! (5:26,2)

If the Father does not exercise judgment, either judgment is not his or else he consents to whatever transpires. If he does not judge, all persons will be equal and accounted in the same condition. The advent of Christ would then have no purpose; indeed, it would be absurd, since he exercises no judicial power. But he says, "I have come to set a man against his father, and a daughter against her mother, and a daughter-in-law against her mother-in-law" [Matt 10:35]; and that when two are in one bed, he will take the one and leave the other, and while two women are grinding meal, he will take one and leave the other [Luke 17:34–35]; and that at the end of time he will tell the reapers, "Collect the weeds first and bind them in bundles to be burned, but gather the wheat into my barn" [Matt 13:30]; and that he will call the lambs into the kingdom prepared for them but will send the goats into everlasting fire, prepared by his Father for the devil and his angels [Matt 25:33, 34, 41]. And why is this? Has the Word come for the ruin and the resurrection of many? Unquestionably, he came for the ruin of those who do not believe him, to whom he has threatened a greater damnation in the day of judgment than what fell upon Sodom and Gomorrah [Luke 10:12], and for the resurrection of believers and those who do the will of his Father in heaven. If the advent of the Son comes alike to all but is for the purpose of judging and separating the believing from the unbelieving, since those who believe do his will freely, by their own choice, and since—also freely, by their own choice—the disobedient do not consent to his teaching, it is clear that his Father has put everyone in a similar condition, with each person having free choice and understanding, and that he oversees all things and exercises providence over all, "for he makes his sun rise on the evil and on the good, and sends rain on the righteous and on the unrighteous" [Matt 5:45]. (5:27,1)

To all who continue in their love towards God he grants communion with him. But communion with God is life and light, and the enjoyment of all the benefits which he has in store. But on all who by their own choice depart from God he inflicts that separation from himself which they have chosen of their own accord. Separation from God is death, separation from light is darkness, and separation from God includes the loss of all the benefits which he has in store. So those who by their apostasy cast away these things, being destitute of all good, experience every kind of punishment. However, God does not punish them immediately himself; punishment falls on them because they are destitute of all that is good. Since good things are eternal and without end with God, so the loss of these is also eternal and never-ending. In this matter it is like what happens in the case of overwhelming light: those who have blinded themselves or have been blinded by others are forever kept from enjoying light. The light has not inflicted the penalty of blindness on them; their blindness has brought this calamity upon them. That is why the Lord declared, "Those who believe in him are not condemned" [John 3:18]—that is, they are not separated from God, for they are united to God by faith. On the other hand, he says, "Those who do not believe are condemned already, because they have not believed in the name of the only Son of God" [John 3:18]—that is, they separated themselves from God of their own accord: "And this is the judgment, that the light has come into the world, and people loved darkness rather than light because their deeds were evil. For all who do evil hate the light and do not come to the light, so that their deeds may not be exposed. But those who do what is true come to the light, so that it may be clearly seen that their deeds have been done in God" [John 3:19–21]. (5:27,2)

Since, then, in this world some persons turn toward the light and unite themselves by faith with God, but others shun the light and separate themselves from God, the Word of God comes, preparing a fit habitation for both—for those who are in the light, that they may enjoy it and the good things that come with it, but for those in darkness, that they may endure its calamities. That is why he says that those on his right hand are called into the kingdom of heaven, but that those on his left he will send into eternal fire, for they have deprived themselves of all good. (5:28,1)

So also the apostle says, "Because they refused to love the truth and so be saved. For this reason God sends them a powerful delusion, leading them to believe what is false, so that all who have not believed the truth but took pleasure in unrighteousness will be condemned" [2 Thess 2:10–12]. For when Antichrist comes, he will be glad to concentrate the apostasy in himself and accomplish whatever he will do by his own will and choice, to the point of sitting in the temple of God so that his dupes may adore him as the Christ. He will deservedly be thrown into the lake of fire [Rev 19:20]. Foreseeing all this, at the right time God will send such a person "so that all who have not believed the truth but took pleasure in unrighteousness will be condemned" [2 Thess 2:12]. John has described his coming in the Apocalypse: "And the beast that I saw was like a leopard, its feet were like a bear's, and its mouth was like a lion's mouth. And the dragon gave it his power and his throne and great authority. One of its heads seemed to have received a death blow, but its mortal wound had been healed. In amazement the whole earth followed the beast. They worshiped the dragon, for he had given his authority to the beast, and they worshiped the beast, saying, 'Who is like the beast, and who can fight against it?' The beast was given a mouth uttering haughty and blasphemous words, and it was allowed to exercise authority for forty-two months. It opened its mouth to utter blasphemies against God, blaspheming his name and his dwelling, that is, those who dwell in heaven. Also it was allowed to make war on the saints and to conquer them. It was given authority over every tribe and people and language and nation, and all the inhabitants of the earth will worship it, everyone whose name has not been written from the foundation of the world in the book of life of the Lamb that was slaughtered. Let anyone who has an ear listen: If you are to be taken captive, into captivity you go; if you kill with the sword, with the sword you must be killed. Here is a call for the endurance and faith of the saints" [Rev 13:2–10].

After this he likewise describes his armor bearer, whom he also terms a false prophet: "It spoke like a dragon. It exercises all the authority of the first beast on its behalf, and it makes the earth and its inhabitants worship the first beast, whose mortal wound had been healed. It performs great signs, even making fire come down from heaven to earth in the sight of all; and by the signs that it is allowed to perform on behalf of the beast, it deceives the inhabitants of earth" [Rev 13:11–14]. Let no one imagine that he performs these wonders by divine power, but by magic. And we must not be surprised if, since the demons and apostate spirits are at his service, by their means he performs wonders, through which he leads the inhabitants of the earth astray.

John says further that he will order them to make "an image of the beast that had been wounded by the sword and yet lived; and it was allowed to give breath to the image of the beast so that the image of the beast could even speak and cause those who would not worship the image of the beast to be killed. Also it causes all, both small and great, both rich and poor, both free and slave, to be marked on the right hand or the forehead, so that no one can buy or sell who does not have the mark, that is, the name of the beast or the number of its name. This calls for wisdom: let anyone with understanding calculate the number of the beast, for it is the number of a person. Its number is 666" [Rev 13:14–18]—that is, six times a hundred, six times ten, and six units. This is the sum of the whole of that apostasy which has taken place during six thousand years. (5:28,2)

For in as many days as this world was made, in so many thousand years will it be concluded. Scripture says, "Thus the heavens and the earth were finished, and all their multitude. And on the seventh day God finished the work that he had done, and he rested on the seventh day from all the work that he had done" [Gen 2:1–2]. This is an account of the things originally created, but it is also a prophecy of what is to come, for one day with the Lord is as a thousand years [2 Pet 3:8]. Creation was all completed in six days; it is clear that they will come to an end at the six-thousandth year. (5:28,3)

In the previous books I have set forth the reasons why God permitted these things to be made and have pointed out that everything was created for the benefit of that human nature which is saved, ripening for immortality that which has its own free will and power, and preparing and adapting it better for everlasting subjection to God. So the creation was made for humankind; humanity was not made for the sake of creation, but creation for the sake of humankind. . . . (5:29,1)

When this beast comes, there will be a recapitulation of all kinds of iniquity and of every deceit, so that all apostate power, flowing into and being confined within him, may be sent into the furnace of fire. It is therefore fitting that his name possesses the number 666, since he sums up in his own person all the commixture of wickedness which took place before the flood, as brought on by the apostasy of the angels. For Noah was six hundred years old when the deluge came upon the earth, sweeping away the rebellious world because of that infamous generation in Noah's time. And Antichrist sums up all the errors of idolatry since the flood, together with the slaying of the prophets and the righteous. As well, the image set up by Nebuchadnezzar had a height of sixty cubits, while the breadth was six cubits. When Hananiah, Azariah, and Mishael refused to worship it, they were cast into a furnace of fire, thus pointing out prophetically, by what happened to them, the wrath against the righteous which shall arise at the end of time. That image, taken as a whole, prefigured the coming of this one, who will enact that he alone should be worshipped by all. Thus, the six hundred years of Noah, in whose time the flood occurred because of the apostasy, and the number of the cubits of the image for which these righteous men were sent into the fiery furnace, indicate the number of the name of that one in whom the whole apostasy of six thousand years, plus unrighteousness, wickedness, false prophecy, and deception will be concentrated—because of which a cataclysm of fire will also come upon the earth. (5:29,2)

So, this is the state of the case. This number is found in all the most approved and ancient copies of the Apocalypse, and those who saw John face to face bear their testimony to it. Reason also leads us to conclude that the number of the name of the beast, if reckoned by the Greek mode of calculating the numerical value of letters, will amount to 666. The number of tens is equal to that of the hundreds, and the number of hundreds equal to that of the units; the number six is found in each place, indicating the recapitulations of apostasy in its full extent, from the beginning, through the intermediate periods, and down to the end. I do not understand how some have erred following the ordinary manner of speech, and have changed the middle number in the name, deducting the amount of fifty from it, so that instead of six tens they assert that there is only one [so, 616]. Others have accepted this reading without examination—some simplistically, upon their own responsibility, have made use of this number expressing one ten; some, in their inexperience, have tried to discover a name which would contain the erroneous and spurious number.[2] As to those who have done this in simplicity, and without evil intent, we are free to assume that God will pardon them; but as for those who for pride's sake lay it down as a certainty that names counting up to the spurious number should be accepted, and who teach that this name, which they have hit upon by themselves, is the one of him who is to come—such persons shall suffer loss, since they have led both themselves and those who relied upon them into error. As to those in the first category, it is a loss if one wanders from the truth and takes something to be true when it is not; worse, such a person will certainly fall under the serious punishment which will be meted out to anyone who

---

2. In several of the cultures of the ancient world, letters of the alphabet received numerical values. Irenaeus is referring here to attempts by some Christians to use this practice to decode the number and thus identify the person who was (or would be) the Antichrist.

either adds to or subtracts anything from the Scripture [Rev 22:18–19]. As to those who falsely presume that they have figured out the name of the Antichrist, another daunting danger will overtake them: if they assume one number, when the Antichrist comes with another, they will be easily led away by him, since they will not recognize him as the expected one who must be guarded against. (5:30,1)

These people therefore ought to learn aright and go back to the true number of the name, so that they may not be numbered among false prophets. But knowing the sure number declared by Scripture—666—let them first await the division of the kingdom into ten; then, when these kings are reigning and beginning to set their affairs in order and advancing their kingdom, let them learn to acknowledge that the one who will come claiming the kingdom for himself, who will terrify those people about whom we have been speaking (since he will have a name containing the number noted above), is truly the desolating sacrilege. . . . (5:30,2)

It is therefore more certain and less dangerous to await the fulfilment of the prophecy than to make guesses and cast about for names that might present themselves, since many names can be found possessing the number mentioned. The question will, after all, remain unsolved. Since many names possess this number, it will be asked which of them the coming man will bear. I urge this, not because of a lack of names which amount to that number, but out of fear of God and zeal for the truth. . . .[3] We will not incur the risk of pronouncing positively as to the name of Antichrist; if it were necessary that his name should be distinctly revealed in this present time, it would have been announced by him who beheld the apocalyptic vision, for that was seen not so long ago, but almost in our day, towards the end of Domitian's reign. (5:30,3)

He sets forth the number of the name now, so that when this man comes we may avoid him, recognizing who he is. However, the name is suppressed because it is not worthy of being proclaimed by the Holy Spirit. For if it had been declared by him, the Antichrist might perhaps continue for a long period. He "was, and is not, and is about to ascend from the bottomless pit and go to destruction" [Rev 17:8], like one who has no existence; that is why his name has not been declared, for the name of that which does not exist is not proclaimed. But when this Antichrist

---

3. In the omitted section, Irenaeus goes on to suggest three names that would be the numerical equivalent of 666, to make his point.

will have devastated all things in this world, he will reign for three years and six months, and sit in the temple at Jerusalem; and then the Lord will come from heaven in the clouds, in the glory of the Father, sending this man and those who follow him into the lake of fire, but bringing in for the righteous the times of the kingdom—that is, the rest, the hallowed seventh day—and restoring to Abraham the promised inheritance, the kingdom in which the Lord declared that "many will come from east and west and will eat with Abraham and Isaac and Jacob in the kingdom of heaven" [Matt 8:11]. (5:30,4)

As well, some who are otherwise orthodox in faith depart from the pre-arranged plan for the exaltation of the righteous and do not recognize the ways they are disciplined ahead of time for incorruption. Because of this they entertain some heretical opinions.... If they do not believe in a resurrection for the entire person, but as far as they can cut it out of Christian teaching, can it be a surprise that they also know nothing about the plan of the resurrection? They choose not to understand that if these things are as they say, the Lord himself, in whom they profess to believe, did not rise again on the third day, but that immediately upon his expiring on the cross he undoubtedly departed into heaven, leaving his body to the earth. But for three days he dwelled in the place where the dead were.... The Lord himself said, "Just as Jonah was three days and three nights in the belly of the sea monster, so for three days and three nights the Son of Man will be in the heart of the earth" [Matt 12:40]. As well, the apostle wrote, "When it [Scripture] says, 'He ascended,' what does it mean but that he had also descended into the lower parts of the earth?" [Eph 4:9].... (5:31,1)

... As the Lord went away into "the valley of the shadow of death" [Ps 23:4], where the souls of the dead were, but afterwards arose in the body and after his resurrection ascended into heaven, it is clear that the souls of his disciples also, for whom the Lord did all this, will go away into the invisible place allotted to them by God, to remain there until the resurrection. They await that event when they will receive their bodies again and rise in their entirety—that is, bodily, just as the Lord arose. This is the way they will come into the presence of God.... Our master did not at once depart, taking flight into heaven; he awaited the time of his resurrection prescribed by the Father, which had been shown forth in Jonah, and rising again after three days, he was taken up into heaven. So we also will await the time of our resurrection determined by God and foretold by the prophets, and so, rising, all whom the Lord will account worthy will be taken up. (5:31,2)

Since, then, the views of certain orthodox persons are influenced by heretical discourses, they end up ignorant of God's plans, of the mystery of the resurrection of the righteous, and of the kingdom which will be the beginning of incorruption, that kingdom in which those who are accounted worthy will be gradually enabled to partake of the divine nature [2 Pet 1:4]. Consequently, it is necessary to tell them about those things, that it is proper for the righteous first to receive the inheritance which God promised to the fathers and to reign in it when they rise again to behold God in this renovated creation, and that the judgment will take place subsequently. It is appropriate that in the very creation in which they struggled and were afflicted, being tested in every way by suffering, they should receive the reward of their suffering; that in the creation in which they were slain because of their love to God they should be revived again; and that in the creation in which they endured servitude they should reign. For God is rich in all things, and all things are his. Therefore, it is fitting that the creation itself, being restored to its primeval condition, should be entirely under the dominion of the righteous. The apostle has made this plain in the Letter to the Romans when he said, "For the creation waits with eager longing for the revealing of the children of God; for the creation was subjected to futility, not of its own will but by the will of the one who subjected it, in hope that the creation itself will be set free from its bondage to decay and will obtain the freedom of the glory of the children of God" [Rom 8:19–21]. (5:32,1)

So the promise which God gave to Abraham remains steadfast: "Raise your eyes now, and look from the place where you are, northward and southward and eastward and westward; for all the land that you see I will give to you and to your offspring forever" [Gen 13:14–15]. And he went to on say, "Rise up, walk through the length and the breadth of the land, for I will give it to you" [Gen 13:17]. Yet Abraham did not receive an inheritance in it, not even a footstep, but was always a stranger and a pilgrim in it [Acts 7:5].... If, then, God promised him the land as his inheritance, but he did not receive it during all the time he was there, it must be that, together with his descendants—that is, those who fear God and believe in him—he will receive it at the resurrection of the righteous. For his seed is the Church, which has been adopted by God through the Lord, as John the Baptist said, "God is able from these stones to raise up children to Abraham" [Luke 3:8]. The apostle also says in the Letter to the Galatians, "Now you, my friends, are children of the promise, like Isaac" [Gal 4:28]; and again, in the same letter he plainly declares that those who have believed in Christ receive Christ, the promise to Abraham: "Now the promises were made to Abraham and to his offspring; it does not say, 'And to his offsprings,' as of many; but it says, 'And to your offspring,' that is, to one person, who is Christ" [Gal 3:16]. And again, confirming his former words, he says, "Just as Abraham 'believed God, and it was reckoned to him as righteousness,' so, you see, those who believe are the descendants of Abraham. And the scripture, foreseeing that God would justify the Gentiles by faith, declared the gospel beforehand to Abraham, saying, 'All the Gentiles shall be blessed in you.' For this reason, those who believe are blessed with Abraham who believed" [Gal 3:6–9]. So, then, those who believe will be blessed with faithful Abraham, and these are the children of Abraham. God promised the earth to Abraham and his seed, but neither Abraham nor his seed— that is, those who are justified by faith—receive any inheritance in it now; they will receive it at the resurrection of the righteous. God is true and faithful, and regarding all this he said, "Blessed are the meek, for they will inherit the earth" [Matt 5:5]. (5:32,2)

This is why, when he was about to undergo his sufferings, to declare to Abraham and those who were then with him the good news that the inheritance was being thrown open, after he had given thanks, while holding the cup and having drunk of it and given it to the disciples, he said to them: "Drink from it, all of you; for this is my blood of the covenant, which is poured out for many for the forgiveness of sins. I tell you, I will never again drink of this fruit of the vine until that day when I drink it new with you in my Father's kingdom" [Matt 26:27–29]. . . . He promised to drink of the fruit of the vine with his disciples, indicating by this both the inheritance of the earth in which the new fruit of the vine will be drunk and the resurrection of his disciples in the flesh. . . . (5:33,1)

. . . The blessing promised belongs unquestionably to the times of the kingdom, when the righteous will rule after their resurrection from the dead. Then the creation, having been renovated and set free, will be fruitful, abounding in all kinds of food from the dew of heaven and the fertility of the earth. The elders who saw John, the disciple of the Lord, related that they had heard from him how the Lord used to teach about these times and say, The days will come, in which vines will grow, each with ten thousand branches, and in each branch ten thousand twigs, and in each twig ten thousand shoots, and in each of the shoots ten thousand clusters, and on every cluster ten thousand grapes, and every grape when pressed will give twenty-five measures of wine. And when any of the saints will lay hold of a cluster, another will cry out, "I am a better cluster, take me; bless the Lord through me." In the same way, that a grain of wheat will produce ten thousand ears, and every ear will have ten thousand grains, and every grain will yield ten pounds of clear, pure, fine flour; and that all other fruit-bearing trees and seeds and grass will produce in similar proportions; and that all animals, feeding on what the earth produces, will become peaceful and harmonious among each other, and be completely subject to humankind. (5:33,3)

Papias, who heard John and was a companion of Polycarp, bears witness to these things in his fourth book (for he compiled five books). He says, "These things are credible to believers."[4] ... Prophesying of these times, Isaiah said, "The wolf shall live with the lamb, the leopard shall lie down with the kid, the calf and the lion and the fatling together, and a little child shall lead them. The cow and the bear shall graze, their young shall lie down together; and the lion shall eat straw like the ox. The nursing child shall play over the hole of the asp, and the weaned child shall put its hand on the adder's den. They will not hurt or destroy on all my holy mountain" [Isa 11:6–9]. I am quite aware that some persons try to refer these words to savage peoples of different nations and various habits who come to believe and, when they have believed, act in harmony with the righteous. But although this is true now with regard to some people coming from various nations to the harmony of the faith, nevertheless in the resurrection of the righteous the words will also apply to the animals mentioned. . . . (5:33,4)

According to God's will, the whole creation will enjoy a vast increase, so that it may bring forth and sustain such fruit, as Isaiah declares: "On every lofty mountain and every high hill there will be brooks running with water—on a day of the great slaughter, when the towers fall. Moreover the light of the moon will be like the light of the sun, and the light of the sun will be sevenfold, like the light of seven days, on the

---

4. Papias served as bishop of Hierapolis in Asia Minor. He authored a five-volume work known as *Expositions of the Sayings of the Lord*, which some early Christian leaders held in high esteem. However, only fragments of the work remain; they are available in *AposFrs* 562–95.

day when the LORD binds up the injuries of his people, and heals the wounds inflicted by his blow" [Isa 30:25–26]. Now "the wounds inflicted by his blow" refers to what was inflicted at the beginning upon disobedient humanity in Adam—that is, death—which the Lord will heal when he raises us from the dead. . . . (5:34,2)

If anyone tries to allegorize prophecies of this kind, they will not be found consistent with themselves in all points. . . . The resurrection of the righteous takes place after the coming of Antichrist and the destruction of all nations under his rule. In that resurrection the righteous will reign in the earth, growing stronger in the sight of the Lord. In him they will become accustomed to partake in the glory of God the Father, and in that kingdom they will enjoy interaction and communion with the holy angels (the spiritual beings), as well as with those whom the Lord will find in the flesh awaiting him from heaven, who have suffered tribulation and escaped the hands of the wicked one. . . . (5:35,1)

. . . In the Apocalypse John saw this new Jerusalem descending upon the new earth [Rev 21:2]. After the times of the kingdom, he says, "Then I saw a great white throne and the one who sat on it; the earth and the heaven fled from his presence, and no place was found for them" [Rev 20:11]. And he sets forth, too, the things connected with the general resurrection and the judgment, mentioning "the dead, great and small" [Rev 20:12]. He says, "the sea gave up the dead that were in it, Death and Hades gave up the dead that were in them, and all were judged according to what they had done, according to their works, as recorded in the books" [Rev 20:13, 12]. Moreover, "another book was opened, the book of life. And the dead were judged according to their works, as recorded in the books. Then Death and Hades were thrown into the lake of fire. This is the second death" [Rev 20:12,14]. This is what is called Gehenna, which the Lord called "eternal fire" [Matt 25:41]. "And anyone whose name was not found written in the book of life was thrown into the lake of fire" [Rev 20:15]. After this, he says, "Then I saw a new heaven and a new earth; for the first heaven and earth had passed away, and the sea was no more. And I saw the holy city, the new Jerusalem, coming down out of heaven from God, prepared as a bride adorned for her husband. And I heard a loud voice from the throne saying, 'See, the home of God is among mortals. He will dwell with them as their God; they will be his peoples, and God himself will be with them; he will wipe every tear from their eyes. Death will be no more; mourning and crying and pain will be no more, for the first things have passed away'" [Rev 21:1–4]. Isaiah declares the same: "For I am about to create new heavens and a new earth; the former things shall not be remembered or come to mind. Be glad and rejoice forever in what I am creating" [Isa 65:17–18]. This is also what the apostle said: "The present form of this world is passing away" [1 Cor 7:31]. To the same purpose the Lord also declared, "Heaven and earth will pass away" [Matt 24:35]. . . . (5:35,2)

. . . Neither the substance nor the essence of the creation will be annihilated, for the one who established it is faithful and true, but "the present form of this world is passing away" [1 Cor 7:31]—that is, all that in which transgression has occurred and humankind has aged. . . . But when this present fashion of things passes away, and humanity has been renewed and flourishes in an incorruptible state, which will preclude the possibility of becoming old, then the new heaven and the new earth will be, in which a new humanity will remain forever, always communing with God. . . . (5:36,1)

John distinctly foresaw the first "resurrection of the righteous" [Luke 14:14] and the inheritance in the kingdom of the earth; what the prophets have prophesied concerning it harmonizes with his vision. The Lord also taught this when he promised that he would drink the cup new with his disciples in the kingdom [Matt 26:29]. The apostle also has confessed that the creation will be free from the bondage of corruption and will pass into the liberty of the children of God [Rom 8:21].

In all these things, and by them all, the same God the Father is manifested, who fashioned humanity and promised the inheritance of the earth to the fathers, who will bring humankind forth at the resurrection of the righteous, and who fulfills the promises about the kingdom of his Son. He will in due course bestow in a paternal manner what "no eye has seen, nor ear heard, nor the human heart conceived" [1 Cor 2:9]. For there is one Son, who accomplished his Father's will; and one human race in which the mysteries of God are accomplished—"things into which the angels long to look" [1 Pet 1:12]. But they are not able to search out the wisdom of God, through which his handiwork, confirmed and incorporated with his Son, is brought to perfection—that his offspring, the first-begotten Word, should descend to the creature (that is, to what had been made) and should be contained in it; and, on the other hand, that the creature should contain the Word and ascend to him, passing beyond the angels, and be made after the image and likeness of God. (5:36,3)

Bibliography

Balthasar, Hans Urs von. *The Scandal of the Incarnation: Irenaeus Against the Heresies.* Translated by John Saward. San Francisco: Ignatius, 1990.

Beaven, James. *An Account of the Life and Writings of St. Irenaeus Bishop of Lyons and Martyr.* 1841. Reprint, Kessinger, 2004.

Behr, John. *Asceticism and Anthropology in Irenaeus and Clement.* Oxford Early Christian Studies. New York: Oxford University Press, 2000.

————, translator. *St. Irenaeus: On the Apostolic Preaching.* Crestwood, NY: St. Vladimir's Seminary Press, 1997.

Donovan, Mary Ann. *One Right Reading? A Guide to Irenaeus.* Collegeville, MN: Liturgical, 1997.

Ehrman, Bart D. *Lost Christianities: The Battles for Scripture and the Faiths We Never Knew.* New York: Oxford University Press, 2003.

Grant, Robert M. *Irenaeus of Lyons.* Early Church Fathers. New York: Routledge, 1997.

Hill, Charles. *From the Lost Teaching of Polycarp: Identifying Irenaeus' Apostolic Presbyter and the Author of Ad Diognetum.* Wissenschaftliche Untersuchungen zum Neuen Testament 186. Tübingen: Mohr/Siebeck, 2006.

Lawson, John. *The Biblical Theology of Saint Irenaeus.* 1948. Reprint, Eugene, OR: Wipf & Stock, 2006.

Nielsen, J. T. *Irenaeus of Lyons versus Contemporary Gnosticism: A Selection from Books I and II of Adversus Haereses.* Textus minores in usum academicum 48. Leiden: Brill, 1977.

Ochagavia, Juan. *Visibile Patris Filius: A Study of Irenaeus' Teaching on Revelation and Tradition.* Orientalia Christiana Analecta 171. Rome: Pontificium Institutum Orientalium Studiorum, 1964.

Osborn, Eric Francis. *Irenaeus of Lyons.* New York: Cambridge University Press, 2001.

Pagels, Elaine H. *The Gnostic Gospels.* New York: Vintage, 1981.

Payton, James R., Jr. "Condensing Irenaeus: A Review Article." *Calvin Theological Journal* 33 (1998) 175–85.

Smith, Joseph P., translator. *St. Irenaeus: Proof of the Apostolic Preaching.* Ancient Christian Writers 16. New York: Newman, 1952.

Stewart-Sykes, Alistair, translator. *Melito of Sardis: On Pascha, with the Fragments of Melito and Other Material Related to the Quartodecimans.* Popular Patristics. Crestwood, NY: St. Vladimir's Seminary Press, 2001.

Unger, Dominic J., translator. *St. Irenaeus of Lyons: Against the Heresies,* Vol. 1. Ancient Christian Writers 55. New York: Paulist, 1992.

Subject Index

Abraham
    on God, 90, 93–94
    God, promise from, 190–91
    prophet of faith, 119
Adam, 168–70, 169–70, 172–73
    death of, 177
    first, 18–19, 80–81, 169
    punishment of, 81
    repentance of, 82
    second, 78, 169
    spiritual vs. natural, 157
aeons, as Gnostic pattern, 7–8
Against Heresies
    assault on Gnosticism, 20–22
    as defense of Christian faith, 20
    significance of, 19–24
    structure of, 24–26
Anacletus, bishop of Rome, 3–4, 57
Antichrist, 71, 186, 188–89. *See also*
    devil; Satan
    resurrection and, 193
    Satan and, 178, 180
    satanic apostasy, 178
    satanic error, 180
Apocalypse, 181, 185–86, 193–94
apostate angel, devil as, 178
apostles
    doctrine of knowledge, 135
    gospels of, 65–66
    heretics and, 171–72
    on the Son of God, 67
    teachings of, 56, 69
    tradition of, 57–60

    on two testaments, 132
    as voice of the Church, 67–68
apostolic succession, Irenaeus on,
    14–15
apostolic tradition, 21
    Gnostic teaching and, 15–17
    Irenaeus on, 14
arche, 30
    Gnostic pattern, 7–8

baptism
    and being born again, 47–48,
    47n4
    heretics and, 35
    of Jesus Christ, 63, 69
    rule of truth received at, 15, 31
Basilides, 12, 13n34, 37
bishop of church in Smyrna,
    Polycarp as, 58–59
bishop of Rome
    Anacletus, 3–4, 57
    Clement, 57–58
    Eleutherus, 2
    Linus, 57
    Victor, 3
Bishop Pothinus, 2
blood, 166–67
blood and flesh, substance of,
    165–67
body, as God's temple, 160–63

carnal people, Gnosticism, category
    of, 6–7

Carpocrates, 12, 37–38

Cerinthus, 12, 38, 59

Christ. *See* Jesus Christ

Christian Faith
  apostles' teaching of, 55–84
  Christ, words spoken by, 85–154
  Christ and apostles' teachings,
    155–94

Christian faith, *Against Heresies* as
    defense of, 20

Christianity
  Gnostics and, 8–13, 11–12
  Irenaeus of Lyons, presentation
    by, 13–20
  normative, 22–23
  threat from Gnosticism, 4

Church
  apostles, voices of, 67–68
  on Christ, 32
  on miracles for humanity, 52–53
  on one God, 32
  pillars of, 65
  on points of doctrine, 32–33

church at Corinth, conflict within,
    58

church in Rome, letter to the
    Corinthians, 58

circumcision
  covenant of, 69
  as a sign of righteousness, 104–5

Clement, bishop of Rome, 57–58

Colossians, Letter to, 5, 166

commandments, 98–101

complete knowledge, 56

Corinthians, Letter to, 58

covenants, 66, 69, 73–74

creation, 42–43, 46, 186
  Gnostic teaching on, 10–11, 44
  order of, 170–71

crucifixion, of Jesus Christ, 78–81

Daniel, visions of, 179, 180–82

David
  on obedience, 109
  on the Word of God, 62–63

Demiurge, 7–8, 10–11

devil, 92, 153, 174–75, 183. *See also*
    Antichrist; Satan; serpent
  angels of, 152–53
  as apostate angel, 178
  as liar, 176, 177
  disobedience, 73–74, 79, 151, 169,
    171

Ebionites, 133–34

Eleutherus, bishop of Rome, 2

Ephesians, Letter to, 158, 161, 178

eternal life, 53

Eucharist, 111–12, 158

Eve, 19
  comparison to Mary, 80, 171
  punishment of, 81
  virginal disobedience of, 171

First Letter to the Thessalonians,
    160

flesh and blood, substance of,
    165–67

fleshly people, Gnosticism, category
    of, 6–7

furnace of fire, 152

Galatians, Letter to, 80, 163, 172–73,
    191

Gnosis, 56

Gnosticism, xiv
  categories of, 6–7
  fleshly people, category of, 6–7
  general pattern of, 6–8
  Against Heresies as assault on,
    20–22
  numbers and letters as knowl-
    edge, x, 7–8
  opposition to, 4–6
  threat to Christianity, 4

Gnostics. *See also* heretics; knowers
  apostolic tradition and, 15–17
  apostolic tradition of, 15–17
  on Christ, 11–13
  on Christianity, 11–12

Gnostics (cont.)
    Christianity of, 8–13
    on complete knowledge, 56
    on creation, 10–11, 44
    disunity among, 41–54
    on God of creation, 10–11
    on God of salvation, 11
    on God's power, 42–43
    heresy, views on exposing, 27–39
    letters fascination, 34
    manuscripts at Nag Hammadi, 6
    numbers fascination, 34
    as plagiarists, 45–45
    on prophecies, 53
    on redemption, 35
    on Scripture, 17
    as spiritual or intellectual, 7
    teacher of, 12–13
    teaching on creation, 44
    writings, 35, 35n6
God
    on Abraham, 90, 93–94
    benefits to humanity, 101–3
    communion with, 183–84
    comprehension of, 48–49,
        112–18
    in contrast to humans, 98–99
    of creation, Gnostics on, 10–11
    as *Demiurge,* 10–11
    heretics on, 87, 91, 159
    humanity, in contrast to, 98–99
    humanity, purpose of, 76–77
    humanity's relationship with,
        105–6
    humankind, work as, 167–68
    law as commandment of, 175
    plan for salvation, 76, 77, 79, 81,
        102–4, 110
    power in weakness, 159
    promise to Abraham, 190–91
    of salvation, Gnostics on, 11
    separation from, 183–84
God of the Jews
    Jesus and, 11, 36
    Saturninus on, 36

heresy, Gnostic views, exposing,
    27–39
heretics. *See also* Gnostics
    on animal people, 29
    apostles and, 171–72
    baptism and, 35
    beliefs of, 56
    on Christ, 29
    condemnation of, 34
    disagreements among, 142
    doctrine of, 70–71
    false teachings of, 70
    on formation of the universe, 28
    on God, 87, 91, 159
    incorruptibility and, 74, 158, 159
    Jerusalem and the Lord, on,
        87–88
    John on teachings, 64–65
    Pleroma, 28, 30
    on prophecy, 114–15
    on redemption, 35
    on rule of truth, 68
    salvation and, 74, 85–86, 134,
        157–58, 171–72
    Satan and, 35
    satanic spirit of, 182–83
    on the savior, 28
    Scriptures and, 56–57
    on spiritual people, 28–29, 30
    tradition of the apostles and, 57
    on types of people, 29–30
    universe, formation of, 28
    on Word of God, 65
    writings of, 35, 35n6
human being, definition of, 159–60
human will, independence of,
    146–47
humanity
    the Church on miracles for,
        52–53
    in contrast to God, 98–99
    enemy of, 73–74
    God's purpose of, 76–77
    goodness of, 147–49
    of Jesus Christ, 70–72, 74–77

humanity (cont.)
  relationship with God, 105–6
  on seeing God, 115–16
humankind
  covenants of, 66
  as God's work, 167–68
  human rules, in fear of, 177–78
  prophets on covenants with, 138,
    140–41
  temptation of, 174–75

immortality, 74, 150, 165
incorruption, 61, 71, 150, 151, 161
  as benefit of faith, 83, 91, 102,
    115, 123, 175
  as gift from the Lord, 76
  heretics and, 74, 158, 159
  passion of Jesus and, 47
  as salvation of the flesh, 164–65
Irenaeus of Lyons
  on apostolic succession, 14–15
  on apostolic tradition, 14
  on Aristotle's dialectic, 24–25
  Christianity, presentation of,
    13–20
  Against Heresies, ix–xiv
  life of, 1–4
  normative Christianity and,
    22–23
  One Lord, One Faith, One
    History, 17–18
  on oneness of God, 13
  Polycarp of Smyrna as mentor,
    1–2
  recapitulation, 18–19
  *A Refutation and Subversion
    of What Is Falsely Called
    Knowledge,* ixn2, 2–3
  on Scripture, 15
Isaac, 119–20

Jacob, 120–21
Jesus Christ
  baptism of, 63, 69

birth of, 63–64, 71–72
the Church on, 32
crucifixion of, 78–81
death of, 68, 72–73, 78–81, 126
Gnostics on, 11–13
God of the Jews and, 11, 36
heretics on, 29
as human, 91–93, 157–58,
  168–69
as incarnate, 13–14, 16, 18, 63,
  70–72, 74–77
Jews and, 67–69, 86, 90, 96–97,
  123, 128
John the Baptist on, 88
passion of, and incorruption, 47
Paul on, 68, 72–73
prophets on, 136–38
recapitulation in, 18–19
resurrection, 3–4, 89–90, 189–90
as salvation, 60, 61, 63–64, 68,
  70–72, 74, 96–97
salvation as recapitulation in,
  18–19
Jews, 120, 132–33
  God of, 11, 36, 37
  Jesus Christ and, 67–69, 86, 90,
    96–97, 123, 128
  laws of, 103
  oblations by, 110
  Paul on teaching, 122
John, 30
  on the Apocalypse, 185–86,
    193–94
  Cerinthus and, 59
  condemnation of heretics, 34
  on generation from the Father,
    65–66
  on heretical teachings, 64–65
  teachings of, 56
John the Baptist on Christ, 88, 93
Joseph, on Mary's pregnancy,
  121–22

knowers, 6, 8, 9–10. *See also*
    Gnostics
knowledge, 7–8
    as doctrine of the apostles, 135
    God, incomprehension of, 48,
        112–18
knowledge, doctrine of
    apostles, 135

law
    of bondage, 106
    as commandment of God, 175
    as course of discipline, 103
    of human liberty, 145–53
    Mosaic, 69, 88
Letter to the Colossians, 5, 166
Letter to the Corinthians, 58
Letter to the Ephesians, 158, 161,
    178
Letter to the Galatians, 80, 163,
    172–73, 191
Letter to the Philippians, 25, 59
Letter to the Romans, 80, 119–20,
    167, 190
Letter to the Thessalonians (first),
    160
Letter to the Thessalonians
    (second), 179
Linus, bishop of Rome, 57
Lot, 143–44
Luke
    on birth of Christ, 64
    gospels and, 69–70
    teachings of, 56
lust of the flesh, 161–64

Magus, Simon, 12, 35, 36n8, 39, 55
Marcion of Pontus, 38–39
    on the Lord, 133
    Polycarp and, 59
    on righteousness, 99–100
Mark, teachings of, 56, 66, 90
Martyr, Justin, 2, 18
Mary, 19

comparison to Eve, 80, 171
    pregnancy of, 121–22
    virgin birth, 78–79
    virginal obedience, 171
Matthew
    on birth of Christ, 63–64
    teachings of, 56
Melito of Sardis, 18
Mosaic law, 69, 88
Moses
    on humanity's relationship with
        God, 105–6
    on seeing God, 117–18
    writings of, 86

Nag Hammadi, 6, 9, 35n6
Noah, 143–44
nonbelievers, punishment of,
    128–30
normative Christianity, Ireneaus
    and, 22–23
Nous, 37, 45

obedience, 73–74, 106, 109, 169
oblations, 110–11. *See also* sacrifices

parables, interpretation of, 48–49
paradise, 83
Paul
    as apostle to the Gentiles,
        122–23
    condemnation of heretics, 34
    on Jesus' death, 68, 72–73
    Letter to the Colossians, 5, 166
    Letter to the Ephesians, 158, 161,
        178
    Letter to the Galatians, 80, 163,
        172–73, 191
    Letter to the Romans, 80, 167,
        190
    Letter to the Thessalonians
        (First), 160
    Letter to the Thessalonians
        (Second), 179

Paul (cont.)
    on salvation, 72
    on teaching the Jews, 122
    teachings of, 56
    on transgressors, 126–27
Peter, 13n34
    on God to Cornelius, 68
    teachings of, 56
Philip, the eunuch of the
        Ethiopians' queen, and, 122
Philippians, letter from Polycarp,
        25, 59
Photius, 3
Pleroma, 7–8, 30
Polycarp of Smyrna, 3–4
    as bishop of church in Smyrna,
        58–59
    Ireneaus and, 1–2
    letter to the Philippians, 25, 59,
        59n5
    Marcion and, 59
    teachings of, 58
presbyters, 124–25
prophecy
    heretics on, 114–15
prophets, 114–15
    on covenant with humankind,
        138, 140–41
    on the Lord, 136–38
    predictions of, 135–36
    on second coming, 136, 139–40
    on seeing God, 117–19
proto-orthodoxy, 22–23
Ptolemy, 12, 77–78

recapitulation in Christ, 18–19
redemption, 35
Rahab the harlot, 119
repentance, 75–76, 82
resurrection, 3–4, 89–90, 189–90,
        193
Romans, Letter to, 80, 119-120, 167,
        190
rule of truth, 15, 31, 35–36, 64, 68

Sabbath, 94–95, 104
sacrifices, 106–9, 107–12. *See also*
        oblations
salvation, 92–93, 109–10, 115
    Christ as, 60, 61, 63–64, 68,
        70–72, 74, 96–97
    God's plan for, 76, 77, 79, 81,
        102–4, 110
    heretics and, 74, 85–86, 134,
        157–58, 171–72
    human path to, 73, 83
    Isaiah on, 107
    Mary, as cause of, 80
    Paul on, 72
    as recapitulation in Christ, 18–19
    sin and, 160–61, 164, 165
    tradition and, 96–97
Satan, 37, 38, 182–83. *See also*
        Antichrist; devil
    agents of, 182
    Antichrist and, 178, 180
    heretics, satanic spirit of, 182–83
    heretics and, 35
    humankind, temptation of,
        174–75
Saturninus, 12, 36–37
Scripture
    Gnostics on, 17
    heretics and, 56–57
    Irenaeus on, 15
    translation of for Ptolemy, 77–78
Second Letter to the Thessalonians,
        179
serpent, 82, 172–73. *See also* devil
Severus, Septimius, 2
Simon of Cyrene, 37
sin, 160–64, 169–70. *See also*
        transgressors
    salvation and, 160–61, 164, 165
    Sodom and Gomorrah, 144
    worldly pleasures, warnings
        against, 86

666 number of the beast, 186, 187–88
Sodom and Gomorrah, 144
spiritual disciples, 132, 134

teleios, Gnostic pattern, 8
The Gospel of Truth, Valentinus followers, 66–67
The Word. *See* Jesus Christ
Thessalonians (first), Letter to, 160
Thessalonians (second), Letter to, 179
tradition of the apostles, 57–60
transgressors, 126–28, 170. *See also* sin

universe, formation of, heretics on, 28

Valentinus, 12, 13n34, 41, 60
disciples of, 27–28
followers of, 66–67, 133
teachings of, 55
Victor, bishop of Rome, 3
virgin birth, 78–79
virginal disobedience, 171
virginal obedience, 171

Word of God. *See* Jesus Christ
worldly pleasures, warnings against, 86

Scripture Index

OLD TESTAMENT

Genesis

1:1	42
1:3	132
1:26	36, 81, 112, 157
1:28	80
2:1–2	186
2:5	79
2:6	90
2:7	53, 113, 167
2:16–17	176
2:16	172
2:25	80
3:1	176
3:2–3	176
3:4–5	176
3:5	81
3:8	169
3:14	82
3:15	83, 152, 172
3:16	81
3:17	81
3:19	81
4:4–5	111
4:7	111
4:10	165
5:12	144
9:5–6	165
9:27	61
12:3	119
13:14–15	190
13:17	190
15:5	93
15:6	119
17:10–11	104
17:17	93
25:23	120
25:26	120
46:5–7	78

Exodus

3:8	62
3:14	62
3:19	129
3:21–22	129
17:11	133
25:17–22	65
25:40	103
31:13	104
33:20–24	117
33:20	115
34:6–7	117

Leviticus

19:18	99

Numbers

12:8	117
14:30	129
16:15	125
18:20	95
21:8	87
24:17	63

Deuteronomy

4:14	106
4:24	117
5:22	103, 105
5:24	115
6:5	99
6:13	174
6:16	174, 175
8:3	173
10:12	105
10:16	104
16:5–6	97
21:23	73
28:66	97, 170
30:19–20	105
32:6	97

1 Samuel

15:22	106
16:7	124

1 Kings

14:10	124
19:11–12	117

Psalms

2:8	120
3:5	138
19:6	138
22:7	137
22:15	137
22:18	137
23:4	189
24:1	144
24:7	138
32:1–2	170
33:6	35, 62
33:9	42, 153
34:12–14	109
34:13–14	143
38:11	137
40:6	106
45:2	136
45:7	136
45:11	151
49:12	89
50:9–12	107
50:14–15	107
51:12	71
51:16–17	107
51:19	107
69:21	75, 137
76:1	137
80:1	65
91:11–12	174
91:13	83
96:1	95
96:5	68
99:1	138
102:25–28	87
110:1	61, 136
115:3	62
118:22	133
148:5	62

Proverbs

8:15–16	177
9:10	82
19:17	112
21:1	177

Isaiah

1:11	107
1:16–18	107, 143
2:3–4	141
2:17	138
4:4	121
5:12	86
6:1	136
6:5	116
7:11	75
7:14	75, 76, 77, 136
8:3	136
9:6	75, 136
11:1–4	64
11:4	133
11:6–9	192
11:12	133

Isaiah (cont.)

25:9	96
26:19	137
27:6	88
29:13	99
30:25–26	193
35:3–4	77
35:3	137
35:5	137
35:6	137
40:12	112
41:4	89
42:10	95
42:3	118
42:5	164
43:10–12	89
43:10	62
43:18–21	138
43:23–24	108
48:22	34
50:6	137
50:8	138
50:9	138
51:6	87
53:2–3	75
53:3	75, 133, 137
53:4	137
53:7–8	122
53:7	133, 137
54:1	34
55:8	44
57:1	141
58:6–9	109
60:17	125
61:1	64, 73
61:2	47
65:2	137
65:17–18	194
66:2	108
66:3	111

Jeremiah

1:5	168
2:19	148
6:17–18	143
6:20	107
7:2–3	108
7:3	143
7:21–24	108
7:29–30	143
9:24	108
15:9	138
17:9	136
23:23	112
31:31–32	138
31:31	95
31:32	95

Ezekiel

20:12	104
36:26	138

Daniel

2:33–34	181
2:34	79
2:41–42	181
2:42–43	182
2:44–45	182
2:45	118
3:25	118
7:13	75, 133, 136
7:14	118
7:21–22	179
7:23–25	180
7:23–24	179
7:8	179
8:12	180
8:23–25	180
9:27	180
12:3	124

Hosea

1:2–3	118
1:6	119
1:9	119
2:7	33
6:6	109

Joel
2:28	71

Amos
8:9–10	137

Jonah
1:9	76
2:2	76
4:11	129

Micah
4:2–3	141

Habakkuk
2:4	140

Zechariah
12:10	136
7:9–10	109, 143
8:16–17	109
8:17	143
9:9	75, 133, 137

Malachi
1:2–3	120
2:10	113
4:1	88

APOCRYPHAL/ DEUTERON- CANONICAL BOOKS

2 Esdras
4:10–11	49

Judith
16:18	159

Wisdom of Solomon
2:24	152, 178

11:20	67, 88

Susanna
52–53	124
56	124

1 Enoch (Ethiopian canon)
6–7	105
12–13	105

NEW TESTAMENT

Matthew
1:1	66
1:10–11	110
1:18	66
1:20–21	121
1:22	121
2:2	63
2:13–15	78
3:9	93, 151
3:10	144
3:11–12	88
3:12	133, 136
3:16–17	63
4:3	92, 173
4:4	173
4:6	174
4:7	174
4:8	174
4:9	175
4:10	174, 175
5:5	191
5:8	96, 115
5:12	135
5:14	94
5:16	146
5:17–18	139
5:20	100
5:21–22	99
5:22	142
5:27–28	99
5:28	142

Matthew (cont.)

5:32	142
5:33	99
5:34	99, 142
5:35	87
5:37	99
5:39	141, 142
5:41	101
5:43–44	100
5:44	142
5:45	83, 101, 183
6:12	169
6:19	104
7:1–2	130
8:11	145, 189
8:13	147
9:17	139
9:29	147
10:6	86
10:8	28, 52
10:29	176
10:35	183
11:23–24	144
11:24	144
11:27	43, 90, 91, 93, 113
12:1–13	94
12:6	95
12:7	109
12:25	181
12:29	73, 175
12:36	106
13:17	97
13:25	152
13:30	183
13:38	123, 152, 153
13:42	127
13:44	123
13:52	95
15:14	172
17:3	117
18:8–9	127
19:7–8	103
19:21	100
20:1–16	145
21:4	75
21:5	75
21:19–20	144
21:31	119
22:20	145
22:29	89
22:31	89
22:37–40	99
23:24	134
23:27–28	111
23:37–38	147
23:37	145
24:15–17	179
24:15	181
24:21	138, 179
24:35	194
24:42	144
24:45–46	125
24:48–51	125, 146
25:19–27	126
25:33	183
25:34–36	112
25:41	82, 127, 128, 136, 153, 183, 193
26:26	109
26:27–29	191
26:29	194
26:41	162
27:48	75
28:19	71

Mark

1:1–2	66
1:20	90
1:24	92
2:5	169
3:27	175
7:13	99
9:23	147
12:1	142
12:2–9	143
12:26	51
12:27	51

Luke

1:2	85
1:3	33, 64
1:30	64
1:35	157
1:38	80
1:42	78
1:46–47	93
1:71	114
1:75	114
2:8–13	93
2:14	56, 64
2:29–32	93
3:2	28, 80
3:8	191
3:17	133
3:23	122
4:3	92
4:6–7	174
4:19	47
6:29–31	100
6:46	146
7:41–43	76
10:12	144, 183
10:16	55
10:22	90
11:21–22	134
11:50–51	166
12:35–37	146
12:35–36	143
12:47	146
12:48	126
14:14	194
15:11–32	66
15:22–23	103
16:9	131
16:16	88
16:19	86
16:31	86
17:26–30	144
17:34–35	183
18:8	136
18:27	115, 159
21:4	110

21:34–35	143
21:34	146
24:26	124
24:39	158
24:47	124
24:49	56

John

1:1–5	65
1:1	66, 72
1:3	30, 35, 42, 62, 66, 72, 79, 132
1:4	30
1:10	30
1:11	30, 170
1:12	62, 153, 170
1:14	31, 65, 114
1:18	30, 116
1:18a	118
1:18b	118
2:19	160
2:21	160
3:14	87
3:18	184
3:19–21	184
3:36	147
4:14	144
4:41	86
5:39–40	96
5:46–47	86
5:46	97
6:42	122
7:38–39	170
8:44	176
8:56	90, 93
9:3	167
9:6	168
9:7	168
10:7–8	59
11:25	90
13:5	121
13:23	56
14:6–7	94
14:6	60

John (cont.)

15:15	101
15:16	102
16:7	71
17:5	102
17:24	102
19:15	120
19:34	133
20:20	161

Acts

1:7	81
1:8	56
2:4–6	71
2:11	71
2:36	67
2:41	122
4:2	67
4:4	122
4:33	67
5:30–32	67
5:42	67
7:5	190
8:32–33	122
10:15	68
14:15	61
14:17	61
15:14	118

Romans

1:3–4	80
1:17	140
1:25	132
1:28	129
2:4	146
2:5	139, 146
2:7	146
2:27	99
3:3–4	159
3:8	38
3:21	140
3:23	126
3:30	121
4:3	90

5:19	74, 79
6:12–13	167
6:7	83
6:9	126
6:13	167
6:23	74
7:18	77
7:24	77
7:25	77
8:10–11	163
8:13–14	163
8:19–21	190
8:9	161, 163
8:11	161
8:13	163
8:15	96, 161
8:21	194
8:28	130
8:36	104
9:10–11	120
9:13	120
9:25–26	119
9:25	33
10:3–4	99
10:6–7	72
10:9	72
11:17	126
11:21	126
11:26	87
11:32	33
11:33	34
11:34	156
12:6–8	52
12:16	175
13:1	177
13:4	177
14:9	72
14:15	73

1 Corinthians

1:23	72
1:29	76
2:6	56
2:9	194

1 Corinthians (cont.)

2:14—3:1	162
2:15	132
3:16	160
5:6	127
5:11	127
6:9–11	164
6:9–10	127
6:11	127
6:13–14	161
6:15	160
7:1–6	103
7:14	118
7:31	87, 194
8:1	48
8:11	73
10:1–12	127
10:16	72, 158
10:19–20	68
12:7	52
12:10	52
12:28	125
13:9–10	96
13:12	51
13:13	50, 135
14:20	129
14:33	88
15:3–4	73
15:10	122
15:12	73
15:20–22	80
15:21	73
15:22	157, 164
15:49	162
15:50	162
15:53	33, 74, 150, 158, 163

2 Corinthians

2:15–16	128
4:4	129
5:4	161
6:14	60
12:9	75, 159

Galatians

1:15–16	168
3:5–9	119
3:6–9	191
3:7	94
3:13	73
3:16	191
3:19	173
3:24	87
3:29	94
4:4–7	94, 173
4:4	70, 80
4:5	74
4:27	34
4:28	191
5:19–21	163
5:21	29
5:22–23	163

Ephesians

1:7	167
1:10	32
1:13–14	161
1:21	112, 123
2:2	178
2:7	89
2:13	73, 167
2:17	61
2:19	33
3:3	68
4:4	113
4:6	113, 132, 170
4:9	62, 189
4:10	31, 62
5:4	128
5:30	158
6:12	32

Philippians

2:8	68, 72, 123, 169
2:10–11	32
2:15	90
3:12	96
3:20–21	165
4:23	130

Colossians

1:14	158
1:15–20	70
1:18	114
1:21–22	166
1:22	166
2:11	104
2:14	170
2:19	132, 167
3:5	164

1 Thessalonians

5:23	160

2 Thessalonians

1:6–8	136
1:9–10	136
2:3–4	179
2:8–12	180
2:10–12	184
2:11–12	129

1 Timothy

1:4	27
1:19	105
2:5	74, 169
3:15	56, 65
4:3	37
4:7	34
6:20	36

2 Timothy

2:23	85
3:7	172
4:21	57

Titus

3:5	35, 175
3:10	34, 59
3:11	34

Hebrews

1:1	33

1:2	142
6:46	126

James

2:23	101, 104

1 Peter

1:8	96
1:12	139, 194
2:9	61, 94
2:16	106
2:22	114
3:19–20	125, 133
4:14	135

2 Peter

1:4	128, 190
3:8	186

1 John

4:1–3	71
5:6	83

2 John

7–8	71
11	34

Jude

7	144

Revelation

1:5	80
1:20	172
3:7	113
4:7	65
5:3–6	113
5:8	110
6:2	120
13:2–10	185
13:11–14	185
13:14–18	186
15–16	131
17:8	188

Revelation (cont.)

17:12–14	181
19:20	184
20:11	193
20:12	193
20:13	193
20:14	193
20:15	193
21:1–4	194
21:2	193
22:17	59
22:18–19	188